TC

2nd edition

Jennifer McMorran
Alain Rondeau
Jill Borra

ULYSSES
TRAVEL PUBLICATIONS
Travel better... enjoy more

Research and Composition Jennifer McMorran Alain Rondeau	**Production Director** Pascale Couture	**Series Director** Claude Morneau
Updating Jill Borra	**Layout** Stephanie Heidenreich Tara Salman	**Illustrations** Lorette Pierson
English Editing Stephanie Heidenreich Tara Salman	**Cartography** Patrick Thivierge Yanik Landreville	**Photography** *Cover Photo* Grant V. Faint (Union Station) *Inside Photos* T. Philiptchenko
Collaboration Pascale Couture Claude Morneau Benoit Prieur François Remillard	**Graphics** André Duchesne *Assistant* Stéphanie Routhier **Design** Patrick Farei (Atoll Dir.)	G. Jones P. Quittemelle W. Bibikow N. Valois M. Grahame

DISTRIBUTORS

AUSTRALIA: Little Hills Press, 11/37-43 Alexander St., Crows Nest NSW 2065, ☎ (612) 437-6995, Fax: (612) 438-5762

BELGIUM AND LUXEMBOURG: Vander, Vrijwilligerlaan 321, B-1150 Brussel, ☎ (02) 762 98 04, Fax: (02) 762 06 62

CANADA: Ulysses Books & Maps, 4176 Saint-Denis, Montréal, Québec, H2W 2M5, ☎ (514) 843-9882, ext.2232, 800-748-9171, Fax: 514-843-9448, www.ulysses.ca

GERMANY AND AUSTRIA: Brettschneider, Fernreisebedarf, Feldfirchner Strasse 2, D-85551 Heimstetten, München, ☎ 89-99 02 03 30, Fax: 89-99 02 03 31, E-mail: Brettschneider_Fernreisebedarf@t-online.de

GREAT BRITAIN AND IRELAND: World Leisure Marketing, Unit 11, Newmarket Court, Newmarket Drive, Derby DE24 8NW, ☎ 1 332 57 37 37, Fax: 1 332 57 33 99, E-mail: office@wlmsales.co.uk

ITALY: Centro Cartografico del Riccio, Via di Soffiano 164/A, 50143 Firenze, ☎ (055) 71 33 33, Fax: (055) 71 63 50

NETHERLANDS: Nilsson & Lamm, Pampuslaan 212-214, 1380 AD Weesp (NL), ☎ 0294-494949, Fax: 0294-494455, E-mail: nilam@euronet.nl

PORTUGAL: Dinapress, Lg. Dr. Antonio de Sousa de Macedo, 2, Lisboa 1200, ☎ (1) 395 52 70, Fax: (1) 395 03 90

SCANDINAVIA: Scanvik, Esplanaden 8B, 1263 Copenhagen K, DK, ☎ (45) 33.12.77.66, Fax: (45) 33.91.28.82

SPAIN: Altaïr, Balmes 69, E-08007 Barcelona, ☎ 454 29 66, Fax: 451 25 59, altair@globalcom.es

SWITZERLAND: OLF, P.O. Box 1061, CH-1701 Fribourg, ☎ (026) 467.51.11, Fax: (026) 467.54.66

U.S.A.: The Globe Pequot Press, 6 Business Park Road, P.O. Box 833, Old Saybrook, CT 06475, ☎ 1-800-243-0495, Fax: 800-820-2329, sales@globe-pequot.com

Other countries, contact Ulysses Books & Maps (Montréal), Fax: (514) 843-9448

No part of this publication may be reproduced in any form or by any means, including photocopying, without the written permission of the publisher.

© July 1999, Ulysses Travel Publications.
ISBN 2-89464-121-4   All rights reserved.   Printed in Canada.

"I just want people to understand Toronto for what it is –
a world-class city with small-town civility."

– Art Eggleton
former Toronto Mayor

TABLE OF CONTENTS

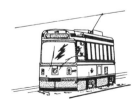

WRITE TO US

The information contained in this guide was correct at press time.
However, mistakes can slip in, omissions are always possible, places
can disappear, etc. The authors and publisher hereby disclaim any
liability for loss or damage resulting from omissions or errors.

We value your comments, corrections and suggestions, as they allow
us to keep each guide up to date. The best contributions will be
rewarded with a free book from Ulysses Travel Publications. All you
have to do is write us at the following address and indicate which title
you would be interested in receiving (see the list at the end of guide).

Ulysses Travel Publications
4176 Rue Saint-Denis
Montréal, Québec
Canada H2W 2M5
www.ulysses.ca
E-mail: guiduly@ulysses.ca

CATALOGUING

McMorran, Jennifer, 1971-

Toronto

2nd ed.
(Ulysses travel guide)
Includes index.

ISBN 2-89464-121-4

1. Toronto (Ont.) - Guidebooks. 2. Toronto (Ont.) - Tours.
I. Title. II. Series

FC3097.18.M348 1999   917.13'541044   C98-941543-0
F1059.5.T683M348 1999

"We acknowledge the financial support of the Government of
Canada through the Book Publishing Industry Development
Program (BPIDP) for our publishing activities".

Canadä

LIST OF MAPS

MAP SYMBOLS

Tourist Information   Airport   Church

Beach   Passenger Ferry

SYMBOLS

🌴	Ulysses' favourite
☎	Telephone number
≠	Fax number
≡	Air conditioning
≈	Pool
ℜ	Restaurant
⊕	Whirlpool
ℝ	Refrigerator
K	Kitchenette
P	Free parking
△	Sauna
⊙	Exercise room
tv	Television
pb	Private bathroom
sb	Shared bathroom
bkfst	Breakfast

ATTRACTION CLASSIFICATION

★	Interesting
★★	Worth a visit
★★★	Not to be missed

HOTEL CLASSIFICATION

Prices in the guide are for one room, double occupancy in high season, not including taxes.

$	$50 and less
$$	$50 to $75
$$$	$75 to $125
$$$$	$125 to $175
$$$$$	$175 and more

RESTAURANT CLASSIFICATION

$	$10 or less
$$	$10 to $20
$$$	$20 to $30
$$$$	$30 and more

Prices in the guide are for a meal for one person, including taxes, but not drinks and tip.

All prices in this guide are in Canadian dollars.

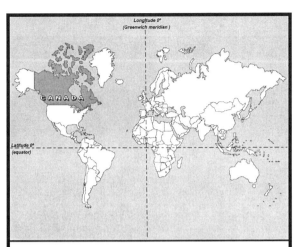

 Where is Toronto?

© ULYSSES

ONTARIO
Capital: Toronto
Population: 10,753,573 inhab.
Area: 1,068,630 km²
Currency: Canadian dollar
TORONTO
Population: 4,600,000 inhab.

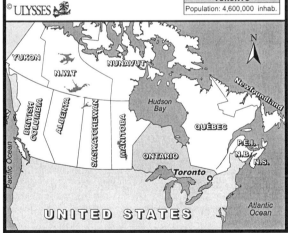

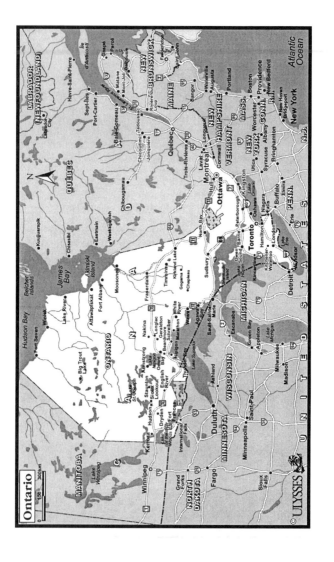

PORTRAIT

For all too many people, Toronto still evokes the image of a lifeless, nondescript city. For much of this century the words that came most readily to mind in describing the Queen City included "virtuous", "monotonous", "conservative" or, a common moniker, "Toronto the Good". Fortunately, the city has gone through a series of transformations that, slowly but surely, have opened it to the world. It is only in fairly recent times that Torontonians have come truly to possess and to inhabit their city. This revitalization started around the time the new city hall was built, giving Torontonians their first public space with real character and personality, and providing citizens with somewhere new to create links with one another. The character of Canada's biggest city has been enlivened by the desire of its many ethnic communities to bring a reflection of their countries of origin to their adopted city, creating a myriad of different neighbourhoods with special colour, taste and charm.

The "Toronto the Good" label dates back to the time when nearly all work and leisure were prohibited on Sundays under the Lord's Day Act, which banned all money-making activity and virtually all social or cultural activities, except of course for religious worship. Toronto was also a business-minded and work-oriented place where outdoor cafés were forbidden and most available entertainment was offered in private clubs. This state of affairs, which made Toronto simply too dreary in the eyes of many inhabitants, led much of the cultural community to abandon the city. For example, the Group of Seven, a famous group of painters started in the 1920s, showed little interest in the city and concentrated mostly on painting wild landscapes in northern Ontario. Literature was produced only on a small scale. It was a dull, lifeless place, a prisoner unto itself. This reputation continues to cling to the city even today to a certain extent, despite many efforts to get rid of it. Toronto thrives as Canada's most important financial and industrial centre, with Montreal in second place. Its traditional Anglo-Saxon majority slowly yielded to the transformations brought about by massive immigration from continental Europe after the Second World War, but it was immigration from Asia and the West Indies that really changed the cultural face of Canada's biggest city.

The city of Toronto encompasses the six former municipalities of Toronto, North York, Scarborough, York, Etobicoke and East York, which now form one city. The Greater Toronto Area also includes a wide swath of suburbia beyond the metropolitan boundary. The region's economic and financial might makes it one of the most attractive places in North America for immigrants to settle. Toronto is home to Canada's biggest Italian community and to North America's second biggest Chinese community, after San Francisco. It also has substantial Jewish, Portuguese, Ukrainian, Jamaican and Greek communities. This massive influx of immigrants over the last half-century has transformed Toronto's visage, making it not only the largest but also the most culturally diverse city in Canada. You can live this multicultural experience by exploring different areas of the city, where you will discover countless restaurants, cafés and shops. Despite all the changes it has gone through, though, Toronto has kept much of its Anglo-Saxon heritage, a clear reminder of its past.

HISTORY

When Europeans discovered the new world, a mosaic of indigenous peoples had already occupied this vast continent for thousands of years. Ancestors of these native peoples had crossed the Bering Strait toward the end of the last Ice Age more than 12,000 years ago, slowly taking control of the whole continent. During the following millenia, as the glaciers retreated, some of them began migrating to the northern reaches of eastern Canada. At the time of the first intensive European forays into North America, several nations forming part of the Iroquoian and Algonkian language families shared the territory on the northern shore of Lake Ontario, the future site of Toronto.

The city, with its fine Great Lakes location, appeared on maps for the first time under the name Tarantou, an Amerindian word with several possible meanings, the likeliest of which is "meeting place". This seemed appropriate for the simple trading post located at the beginning of a trail favoured by natives headed from Lake Ontario to Lake Huron. This trail was part of an efficient, centuries-old communications and trading network. With their tradition as traders, natives in southern Ontario received fur from Iroquois tribes in exchange for produce from their gardens. Canoes proved to be a suitable form of transport on the lakes and rivers that lay at the heart of this network.

Canoe

The Meeting of Two Civilizations

During the decades that followed the European discovery of America, the growing fashion in Europe for fur hats and clothing, meant that enormous profits could be expected from the fur trade, rekindling official French interest in North America. The fur trade required constant links with local suppliers, namely the indigenous peoples, and thus a permanent presence was necessary.

Located deep inside the continent, far from both the Atlantic coast and the easily navigable portion of the St. Lawrence River, Toronto was never favoured by the French authorities as a suitable spot for settlement but was seen rather as a simple trading post. Ontario was nonetheless crisscrossed early on by French explorers. Starting in 1610, only two years after Québec City was founded, the explorer Étienne Brûlé set out for the interior of the continent. Like several of his predecessors, Brûlé was looking for a land route that could lead him to the fabulous riches of the Orient. After setting out alone, he became the first European to reach Lake Ontario and Lake Huron.

To do this, he followed a route heavily used by natives and fur traders. Toward the end of the 17th century, the village of Teiaigon, inhabited by Mississauga Indians, was located at the beginning of this route and formed an important meeting place in the fur trade. Noting the importance of this region, French merchants set up a trading post here around 1720, followed in 1750 by a fortified trading site called Fort Rouillé (pronounced rwee-YAY).

The French and the Huron Indians who populated the region reached a deal under which the Hurons agreed to trade exclusively with the French, who in return offered to protect them against their Iroquois enemies living further south. The conflict between Hurons and Iroquois was part of a vast military campaign launched by the powerful Iroquois Five Nations confederacy, which wiped out all its rivals between 1645 and 1655. The Hurons, the Petuns, the Eries and the Neutrals, nations each comprising at least 10,000 people, nearly disappeared in the space of a decade.

These Iroquoian-speaking nations of southern Ontario were victims of a war for the fur trade monopoly being waged by the European powers through native surrogates. The Iroquois Five Nations confederacy, allied with the English, had traditionally lived in areas further south, in what is now the United States, and they sought to appropriate this lucrative trade for themselves. Meanwhile, France was conquered in Europe, a defeat that would prove costly in the Americas. Under the 1713 Treaty of Utrecht, France officially yielded control of Hudson Bay, Newfoundland and Acadia to England. This treaty caused New France to lose strategic military positions, weakening it considerably.

In the following years, the noose tightened around the French possessions in North America. When the Seven Years' War (1756-63) broke out in Europe, the American colonies soon figured among the major stakes. In what is now Ontario, French troops managed in the early years to contain the British thrust and to remain in control of navigation on the Great Lakes. The French forces were not very numerous, but they operated from several strategic positions, including Fort Frontenac, at the mouth of Lake Ontario; Niagara, the land link between Lake Ontario and Lake Erie; Detroit, at the tip of Lake Erie; Michilimackinac, where Lake Michigan and Lake Huron meet; and Fort Rouillé, built at the excellent port at what is now Toronto. Fort Rouillé was destroyed by its commander, Captain Alexander Douville, in 1759, soon after British troops captured another French stronghold, Fort Niagara. One after another, each of these fortifications fell to the British.

British North America

In the years immediately following the British conquest of Canada, little changed in Ontario, which remained a vast and largely unoccupied territory, apart from native bands and fur traders. The British Crown did not decree any colonization or development plans during this period apart from the fur trade. Ironically, it was the American War of Independence (1775-83) that would give birth to Ontario, radically changing the history of Canada.

In the early years of the conflict that pitted England against insurgents in its 13 southern colonies, British forces established strategic positions in Ontario, from which they launched attacks against the American rebels. Overall, however, the war went against the British troops and their allies, and they finally had to concede defeat. The American Revolution, at least in the beginning, had been a genuine civil war between two factions: the supporters of independence and the Loyalists who wished to maintain colonial ties with the British. More than 350,000 of these Loyalists played an active part, fighting on the British side.

The signing of the Treaty of Versailles (1783), which recognized the British defeat at the hands of the American Revolutionaries, pushed tens of thousands of these Loyalists to seek refuge in Canada. Between 5,000 and 6,000 of them settled on the virgin western lands of what is now Ontario and developed the first permanent colonies in this territory. The majority, however, settled along the St. Lawrence River and Lake Ontario, mainly in the vicinities of Kingston and Niagara, the two biggest towns at that time. This led to the division of Canada in 1791, creating the provinces of Upper Canada (now Ontario) and Lower Canada (now Québec).

The background of the vast majority of the Canadian population remained French and Catholic. In response to the rise of pro-independence sentiment in the 13 southern colonies, the British Crown gave these former subjects of the King of France the right to maintain their religion and customs to ensure their loyalty. To keep the Loyalists from being a minority, while at the same time upholding the rights of French Catholics, London promulgated the Constitutional Act of 1791, dividing Canada into two provinces, Lower Canada and Upper Canada. Lower Canada, with its large French majority, remained subject to French civil law, while Upper Canada, located west of the Ottawa River, was inhabited mostly by Loyalists of British stock and was subject to English common law. The Constitutional Act also introduced to Canada the beginnings of a parliamentary system, with the creation of a House of Assembly in each province. Upper Canada at first chose Newark (Niagara) as its capital. This did not last long, however, for the site was poorly protected and could easily fall if the Americans decided to invade Canada.

It was thus in August 1793 that the attention of John Graves Simcoe, the lieutenant-governor of Upper Canada, was drawn to the impressive naval and military possibilities offered by the bay facing Toronto. Accordingly, he decided to build a city near the site of the former Fort Rouillé, at the edge of the Don River, on land that the British had bought from natives for the sum of 1,700 pounds sterling. Simcoe undertook the construction of York, which was later renamed Toronto. Because of the vulnerability of Newark (now Niagara-on-the-Lake) to American attack, Simcoe decided it would be wise to move the capital to York. The site was ideal from a strategic standpoint, but "Muddy York", as it was called because of its location on a muddy plain that descended gradually to the shores of Lake Ontario, was not very hospitable. Furthermore, it was still very sparsely populated. The capital of Upper Canada still had only 700 inhabitants in 1812 and filled a purely administrative role. The main centre of economic activity was Kingston, a dismal little village that grew quickly following the building of the Rideau Canal. Kingston remained the biggest town in Upper Canada until 1820, but the governor's decision to move the capital to York led the colonial administrators and the small group of intellectuals to head gradually to the new capital which soon dominated.

The Upper Canadian settlers certainly had reason to mistrust their southern neighbours, who soon justified these fears. In 1812, allegedly fed up with excessive British control over the Great Lakes, the Americans declared war on Britain and, thus, on Canada. Loyalists and their descendants still formed the majority of Upper Canada's population, lending a rather emotional aspect to this conflict. Britain, tied down in Europe by the Napoleonic Wars, could not provide significant aid to its colony.

The strategic location of the new town of York was put to the test by this war. Fort York, located at the entrance to the bay, formed the main defence of Upper Canada against American attacks. At the end of April 1813, an American invasion force landed near the present site of Sunnyside Beach. After a brief skirmish, British troops quickly retreated inside Fort York, but they could not resist the American assault. Before leaving the fort, the British exploded their arms depot at the very moment the Americans captured it, killing General Zebulon M. Pike of the American army. In reprisal, the Yankee troops set fire to the fort and to the parliament at York, located at the foot of Parliament Street, and then sacked the town. This pillaging left Upper Canada's pro-British population with deeply anti-American sentiments, which to a small extent have lasted up to this day. York's Loyalist character was clearly revealed by the choice of street names of the period, including King, Queen, Duke, Duchess, Frederick and Princess. Despite York's overthrow, colonists elsewhere in Upper Canada managed to repulse American attacks and inflicted the United States of America's first military defeat in its young history.

In 1814, the Treaty of Ghent ended the hostilities and re-established the pre-war boundaries between Canada and the United States. With the threat of war set aside, York and the rest of Upper Canada underwent a substantial wave of British immigration. The Loyalists who had made Upper Canada their home since 1783 were joined by large numbers of immigrants, mostly from the British Isles, who were seeking to escape the recession and unemployment that spread in Britain after the Napoleonic wars. Upper Canada continued to settle its fine agricultural lands. This ever-growing flux of immigrants moving on to nearby lands caused the population of the little town of York to grow considerably. With the development of the hinterland, the town became a centre of economic activity and an important meeting place where area farmers could sell their cattle, poultry, grains and other products at the Weekly Public Open Market, which later became the St. Lawrence Market. Trade developed little by little, and York also became the centre for Upper Canada's banking activities. In 1834, York became the municipality of Toronto, and in less than seven years its population grew from 1,800 to 9,000. When Toronto was created, it was divided into five wards: St. Andrews, St. David, St. George, St. Lawrence and St. Patrick.

The development of new communications links with the outside world in the middle of the 19th century also played an important role in Toronto's economic growth. With the massive arrival of colonists, who cleared and cultivated land in the valley surrounding the town, the fur trade gave way to a new economy based on staples such as wood and grains. Part of this production was exported to Europe in exchange for manufactured goods from Britain, such as farming equipment and clothing. Upper Canada thus needed a way to export its goods quickly and easily. The province's and Toronto's geographic isolation had been made obvious by the War of 1812. Quite apart from rendering the colony vulnerable in wartime, the various sets of rapids that blocked navigation along the St. Lawrence River limited commercial trade with the colony even in peacetime. To open the route to Upper Canada, canals were built in several places, notably at Lachine (1814), at Fort Erie (1825) and at Welland (1824). Once the new canals were open, traffic could move freely between Lake Erie and the Welland River, between the Niagara River and Lake Ontario, and also between Toronto and the Atlantic Ocean.

PORTRAIT

The Family Compact

These major changes had an understandably profound effect on the social structures of Toronto and the rest of Canada. The British government came to the conclusion that the loss of 13 of its colonies (creating the United States) had been caused by the excessive freedom they had enjoyed. Governor Simcoe himself intended to reproduce the British class system in Toronto so as to avoid a second American Revolution. The Constitutional Act of 1791 aimed to restrict the powers of the legislative assemblies elected by the people. Under the terms of this act, the executive functions of government were carried out by a governor appointed by the British government, who in turn would name the members of the Executive Council who were to assist him. The legislature took the form of an elected Legislative Assembly holding very little real power and subject to vetos by the governor and the Executive Council.

The governor surrounded himself with some of the colony's most powerful and influential men. Together they ruled, taking little account of the wishes of the people's elected representatives. This oligarchy became known in Upper Canada as the Family Compact (its Lower Canada equivalent was called the *Clique du Château*). The Grange, a Georgian-style mansion built by the Boulton family on lot number 13 (see p 129) at the beginning of the 19th century , quickly became a symbol of the power of the Family Compact and of the superiority of the British aristocracy. Despite the rebellions of 1837, The Grange remained a seat of political power and a sign of the Toronto elite's deep conviction that everything good in Canada must be British.

Disagreements between the Executive Council and the Legislative Assembly were substantial, and political quarrels became inevitable. The farming and working classes became convinced that the Family Compact was using its political monopoly to assure its economic monopoly. Two political parties emerged, the Conservatives, also known as Tories, who wanted to maintain the status quo, and the Reformists, whose aim was to make the government more democratic. In Upper Canada as in Lower Canada, reform movements developed. In largely French-speaking Lower Canada, the movement was intensified by the racial element, with parts of the English-speaking minority allied to the ruling class and a French-speaking majority made up largely of farmers and low-paid workers. French-Canadians chose Louis-Joseph Papineau as spokesman. He took charge of the reform movement and went as far as declaring that authority in Lower Canada should return to the French-Canadian majority.

Similar events were taking place in Upper Canada, despite the absence of intense cultural conflicts. The reformist leader was William Lyon Mackenzie, a Torontonian of Scottish descent who launched his first attacks against the government and the Family Compact in his newspaper, *The Colonial Advocate*. He was later elected to the Legislative Assembly, where he immediately attacked government finances. As time went on, Mackenzie's remarks became ever harsher regarding the protectionism and abusive powers of the Family Compact, which expelled him from the Assembly for defamation. In 1835, he was elected the first mayor of Toronto, but his increasingly extreme views worried some of his more moderate supporters, who ended up rejecting his program completely. The ideas put forth by Mackenzie were shared by a great number of those who expressed their discontent with the Family Compact, but many were unwilling to break ties with Britain.

With the arrival of a new governor, Sir Francis Bond Head, who had the Assembly completely under his thumb, Mackenzie's more radical supporters lost all hope of achieving change through constitutional means. When Mackenzie learned of this, he decided to launch his revolutionary forces. Unfortunately, despite its leader's enthusiasm, this movement of workers and small farmers was very poorly organized, and its attempt to capture Toronto was put down quickly, with little violence. A vanquished Mackenzie would follow Papineau into exile in the United States, where they would try in vain to reassemble their troops and to win American support.

If the period preceding the Act of Union (1851) was characterized by great canal-building projects and the establishment of various infrastructures destined to bring Toronto into the industrial age (gas, water, electricity, etc.), it was the construction of the railways that took precedent as of the 1850s. The establishment of the railway network was seen then as the solution to Canada's communications problems. The many Irish immigrants who had come to live in Canada toward the 1850s to escape the famine and poverty that raged in their homeland became the biggest foreign group in Toronto by 1851. Many of them took part in the major construction projects that were undertaken then, including the building of the Grand Trunk Railway, which would link many of the bigger towns in Canada. Although a great many of these Irish immigrants were Ulster Protestants, a certain number were Catholic; ultimately some of the old battles between Catholics and Anglicans were revived. Irish Catholics were not always made to feel welcome, and rising tensions eventually led to violence. The Orange Lodges, created by Ulster-born Irish, came to the defence of the old Anglo-Protestant social order, joining it in dominating municipal politics up to the end of the 19th century.

Thanks to its exceptional geographic location, Toronto became an important hub of the Canadian railway network. Several other lines linked the American railway network to the major Canadian cities, opening the door to the enormous American market. The building of this complex network of communications links was joined by increased exploitation of Canadian mines and forests, transforming Toronto and helping develop industries such as steel foundries, rolling mills and locomotive factories. The coming of the railway not only ended the isolation of distant regions but also produced an enormous economic entity in North America, while also creating new markets and new needs.

These enormous infrastructure projects were laying a heavy burden on the public treasury, however. At the same time, the Canadian economy was hard hit by the British decision to abandon its mercantilist policies, ending the preferential tariff for its colonies. To lessen the impact of this change in British colonial policy, Canada signed a treaty in 1854 allowing free entry of certain goods to the United States, in particular its two most important exports, wood and wheat. But the Canadian economy had barely recovered when the treaty was renounced in 1866 under pressure from American business interests. The loss, first of the colonial preference and then of the reciprocity treaty, left the Canadian economy in bad shape. This gloomy economic climate was both a backdrop to and a major impetus for the birth of the Canadian Confederation.

Confederation

Upper Canada was reshaped under the 1867 Confederation, adopting the name Province of Ontario from an Iroquoian word probably meaning beautiful lakes or beautiful waters, an obvious reference to the province's hydrographic wealth. Three other provinces, Québec (formerly Lower Canada), New Brunswick and Nova Scotia joined this pact, which was soon to unite a vast territory reaching from the Atlantic to the Pacific. The confederation pact established a division of powers between two levels of government, the federal government, based in Ottawa, and the provincial governments, with Ontario choosing Toronto as its capital. This capital of the former Upper Canada had become an important commercial city over the decades and the province's biggest population centre, with about 45,000 inhabitants. From a political standpoint, the establishment of the federal system turned to Ontario's advantage. In the new Parliament in Ottawa, the number of members representing each province was proportionate to its population. Ontario, the most populous of the Canadian provinces, had much to gain from the parliamentary stipulation of representation by population, while Toronto took control of the natural riches of the province (lumber, minerals). As of the 1860s, Toronto became a powerful economic centre linking north, south, east and west, and through which grain, lumber and minerals for exportation were transported.

From an economic standpoint, Confederation failed initially to provide the expected results. It was not until three decades had passed, characterized by sharp fluctuations, that Ontario really experienced its first great period of rapid economic growth. The foundations for this growth were laid several years after Confederation by Sir John A. Macdonald, the federal Conservative Prime Minister re-elected in 1878 after five years out of office. His electoral campaign had centred around his National Policy, a series of measures aimed at protecting and promoting Canada's nascent industries by means of protective tariffs, the creation of a big internal market unified by a transcontinental railway, and the growth of this internal market by a policy of populating the Prairies through massive immigration. At the same time, the arrival in Canada of the industrial revolution and the use of steam as a power source brought about enormous changes that enabled the city to become the main centre for the manufacture of farm equipment and heavy machinery.

Growth and Internationalization

The beginning of the 20th century coincided with the start of a prodigious era of economic growth, helped by an abundance of raw materials and cheap energy. Substantial mineral deposits, in particular cobalt, nickel, silver, iron and zinc, were discovered in the northern part of the province. These discoveries, together with the development of the railway network, led to the settlement of northern Ontario and contributed markedly to Toronto's prosperity during much of the century, as the north furnished raw materials for the city's growing industries. Of course, this industrialization affected the farming sector, which became more mechanized and forced a portion of the province's rural population to seek work in the city. These discoveries also contributed to the development of heavy industry, which would become the backbone of the entire province's industrial infrastructure.

Thanks to Toronto's geographic location, local industry was able to benefit from the relative proximity of booming new markets in Western Canada, whose development and intense settlement activities created a strong demand for equipment and manufactured goods which were being produced in Canada instead of being imported from Britain. Western development also contributed to the establishment of department stores such as Eaton's in 1869 and Simpson's in 1872. These companies would grow quickly, holding an important place in Toronto but also across Canada thanks to their catalogues and extensive mail order businesses. The national policy of settling Western Canada helped create a new wave of industrialization in Toronto, part of a gradual North American movement favouring the Great Lakes basin, both in Canada and the United States, over the older industrial centres further east.

These transformations led to strong growth in the city's population, largely of British descent. In 1871, Toronto had only 56,000 inhabitants, but a mere 20 years later it had grown to 181,000. This growth was caused by a massive rural exodus and also by the arrival of Irish immigrants who continued to flee famine in their homeland.

This unprecedented economic growth did not favour everyone equally, of course. Industrialization led to the rapid development of sometimes insalubrious neighbourhoods such as Cabbagetown and the Ward, which became home to large groups of poorly paid workers. Meanwhile, fine mansions were built near the city centre, and wealthy families moved to prime areas of the city. The concentration of industry around the railway lines and port installations would also lead to a radical transformation of the urban landscape. The area just beyond the factories and warehouses that lined the port was soon filled with inexpensive housing built for the numerous workers.

Almost everywhere in the city, red- and yellow-brick houses, gradually replaced old wooden firetraps. As early as 1834, the City of Toronto forbade the use of wood as a structural material, but this did not prevent two devastating fires, the first in 1849, which destroyed St. James Cathedral (see p 117) and the second in 1904. During the 1890s, Toronto became illuminated by electricity. The telephone appeared, and the famous streetcar network, still in use today, was already spreading across the city.

Starting around that time, the City of Toronto began taking over neighbouring villages. The coming of the streetcars gave people greater mobility and enabled them to live away from the city centre. The annexation of surrounding municipalities began with Yorkville in 1883. By 1912, Toronto and many of its suburbs had merged.

"Toronto the Good"

Toronto was achieving a special place among Canadian cities, of which it was then the second biggest. It obtained its famous moniker "Toronto the Good" because of its attachment to the British Empire and its austere values. Even some Torontonians at that time had little admiration for their city, which they themselves often saw as quite dull. This attribute was reinforced by a 1906 law forbidding any sort of work or entertainment on the Lord's Day, scrupulously respected by many inhabitants. Torontonians had to wait until 1950 before they could attend sporting events such as hockey or baseball games on a Sunday. It was also in true British spirit that affluent members of Toronto society formed numerous private clubs and organizations, such as the Albany Club, the National Club, the Royal Yacht Club and the Toronto Cricket Club. All of this proper British living actually held back the Toronto arts scene. Painters and writers did not choose to live in Toronto, nor did they use it in their material. Even if the city has changed enormously since then, Toronto has trouble to this day shaking off its reputation as a dull, puritanical city.

During the years before the First World War, immigration to Toronto got a second wind. This time, it was Italians, Jews and Ukrainians who accounted for many of the new arrivals, eventually constituting nearly 13 per cent of the total population. Drawn by the city's flourishing economy, these immigrants established the first ethnic neighbourhoods and slowly transformed Toronto's cultural character.

In 1914, on the eve of the First World War, Montréal was the biggest city in Canada, with Toronto still playing a second-string role in banking and some aspects of industry. Toronto grew in importance during the war, which had substantial repercussions on the city's social and economic life. The city used its industrial might to play a major role in the war, with the establishment of munitions factories and meat-packing plants. Due to a serious shortage of male labour, factories turned to female workers, giving women in Canada a social role they had never held before. Even though most of these women returned to traditional roles after the war, their expectations were higher than they had been before. In 1917, even before the war ended, the Canadian and Ontario governments had resolved to give women the right to vote, a longtime demand that had been turned down earlier. As well, the prohibition on the sale and consumption of alcohol in Ontario, a measure that had been intended only for the duration of the war, seemed to have many supporters among the people even afterward. Even as Ontarians prepared to enjoy the exhilarating postwar years, the majority of voters in a 1919 referendum decided to maintain the prohibition on alcohol.

Ontario's economy emerged strengthened from the First World War, and the following decade was marked by steady economic growth that was slowed only by the Stock Market Crash of 1929 in the United States. During the period between 1920 and 1930, Toronto continued to grow, with new municipalities popping up in the suburbs. The total population was about half a million by then. As elsewhere in North America, Toronto saw the growth of hostility toward immigrants during the 1920s and 1930s. In the postwar years, especially with the effects of the Great Depression, immigrants were less welcome in a place that no longer felt it really needed them. The Canadian Government tightened its borders and set in place a selective immigration process that favoured Americans and British subjects over Jews, blacks, southern Europeans and eastern Europeans. It even went as far as imposing a tax on all Chinese immigrants to reduce their numbers. When this policy achieved only mixed success, Chinese immigration was simply halted between 1923 and 1947. This wave of xenophobia swept through Toronto along with the rest of Canada, but it seemed to vary according to economic conditions. When things were going well, non-Anglo-Saxon immigrants seemed to be tolerated as long as they were not too visible.

During the period following the 1929 Stock Market Crash, Canada as a whole felt the consequences. Toronto, however, seemed to be less hard hit by the Depression than most other Canadian cities. The wealth and diversity of natural resources available from Ontario's hinterland enabled it to absorb the effects of the American crisis and to maintain a stronger economy, while the rest of the Canadian economy, more highly dependent on export markets, collapsed with the decline in international trade. To deal with the misery afflicting much of the population, the government decided that certain private businesses should set up a scheme to help those who were in the most desperate straits. This slow turn to the left would gradually convert Canada to the welfare state that emerged after the Second World War.

The Postwar Years

Following ten years of economic crisis, the Second World War revived the Canadian economy and revitalized Toronto with the arrival of new technologies such as electronics and avionics. In terms of natural resources, one of the world's richest uranium deposits was discovered in the 1950s near Elliot Lake. These developments were topped off by the 1959 opening of the St. Lawrence Seaway, which greatly helped in exporting products from Toronto bound for new markets, and this despite the fact that Toronto's port freezes over in the winter. Toronto would soon increase its control over Canada's service and financial sectors, reducing the gap that separated it from Montréal and taking the lead among Canadian cities. Even though the farming and manufacturing sectors declined in relative importance as production moved toward Asia with its lower costs, any slack was quickly absorbed by the finance, retail, urban development and telecommunications sectors. The provincial and federal governments became more involved in the economy and in social programs, creating a new welfare state. Besides its role as a leading centre of manufacturing and finance, Toronto also housed the national headquarters of many trade unions. The city had been at the centre of trade union development in Canada ever since the beginning of the industrial era, but the years following the Second World War saw unionized labour become a significant economic force.

After 1945, Toronto's population rose again as a new wave of immigrants settled in the city. The end of the war brought optimism and prosperity, while the racism that had marked the 1920s and 1930s disappeared and the country opened its doors once again to immigration. People from Britain and then large numbers of Italians in the 1960s were followed by streams of Germans, Poles and other Slavs, Hungarians, Greeks and Portuguese.

Metropolitan Toronto and the Contemporary Era

In 1951, the greater Toronto area found itself short of revenues. This was felt especially in the suburbs, where the need for services was simply not being met. In response to this situation, Canada's first metropolitan government was created in 1953, the Municipality of Metropolitan Toronto. Made up of people from Toronto and 12 surrounding municipalities, this new council would become responsible for areas such as education, finance, public transit, water management and police services. From the start, it fell under the domination of one Frederick Gardiner, a lawyer turned politician known for his aggressive and imposing personality. Upon his arrival at the municipal council, Gardiner had to answer the needs of the whole area surrounding the City of Toronto, plagued by problems relating to sewage and water supplies. He also had to look to the problems of Toronto itself, including its serious downtown traffic congestion. This period coincided with a massive move to the suburbs.

One step in the right direction was accomplished with the opening in 1954 of the first phase of Toronto's subway system, the first such system in Canada. But the real solution to the problems faced by many motorists lay not in public transit but rather in the improvement and expansion of the road network. Toronto already had a port and a well established railway network, but it needed new road links to the rest of Ontario. A project to build an expressway crossing the city along Lake Ontario was adopted by the Metropolitan Toronto council just a few months after its creation in 1953. The building of this expressway began in 1954 and continued until 1966. An expressway across the heart of the city did not please everyone, of course, but there was widespread agreement on the need to improve vehicular flow in the city centre. Despite all the opposition to the Gardiner Expressway, only a citizens' coalition formed to protect the Fort York historic site succeeded in having the expressway's route modified. With the refusal of the coalition to have the fort moved to the very shores of Lake Ontario, the metropolitan council resigned itself to building the highway around the fort. Today, the Gardiner Expressway is in poor shape, with its metal supporting structure rusting away quickly because of the salt used in the winter to melt snow and ice on the roadway. Metal wrapped in epoxy resin is now used to prevent premature rust attacks, but that does not prevent many Torontonians from loathing this expressway, which blocks access to Lake Ontario; it remains a necessary evil, it seems.

Starting in the early postwar years, the halo surrounding "Toronto the Good" had begun to tarnish. In 1947, the first cocktail bars began to appear across the city, raising the ire of many citizens. Of far greater importance was the massive influx of immigrants from all over Europe, which accentuated the city's multi-ethnic character. In 1960 Toronto moved a step closer to modern life and greater freedom with the lifting of the

Yonge Street

According to the Guinness Book of World Records, Toronto has the longest street in the world. Yonge Street (pronounced "young"), which marked its bicentennial in 1996, stretches 1,897 kilometres (1,178.3 mi) from the shores of Lake Ontario to the town of Rainy River, in northwestern Ontario. Originally a trail used by the Hurons and then by the French explorer Étienne Brûlé, this road was started in the 1790s under orders from Governor John Graves Simcoe to improve links between the new town of York (now Toronto) and Georgian Bay in case of armed conflict with the Americans. Once the risk of war with the neighbours to the south was eliminated during the 19th century, Yonge Street became a busier artery than before, but was still somewhat muddy. Today it is full of activity and lined with all sorts of shops.

Sunday prohibition on activities such as movies, plays and other cultural events. But it was the building of the new city hall, completed in September 1965, that really signalled the winds of change that were blowing over the city. The building, designed by Finnish architect Viljo Revell, broke the conservative shell that had stifled the city. It showed the benefits of modern architecture, perhaps with a little too much enthusiasm. During the following years, a number of historic buildings were demolished, in the name of progress and modernism, to make way for new buildings. Fortunately, some of the developers found themselves facing fierce opposition from citizens who were determined to save these reminders of a not very distant past. Some of the buildings that escaped the wrecker's ball are among the city's finest attractions today; these include Union Station, Old City Hall and Holy Trinity Church. It is ironic to note that Torontonians finally became aware of the architectural value of these old buildings, which add so much to the charm of many urban neighbourhoods, only when faced directly with their demolition. A certain balance between 19th-century conservatism and an enthusiasm for everything new in the 1950s and 1960s was achieved with the election of David Crombie as mayor. He would lead the city toward a more harmonious development, setting height limits on new buildings and encouraging the revitalization of many older neighbourhoods through the restoration of old buildings.

Ontario's domination over the Canadian economy became unquestionable in the mid-1970s when Toronto overtook Montréal, its longtime rival, to become the biggest city in Canada. The remarkable performance of the Ontario and Toronto economies depended in large measure on the proximity of the United States. This enormous market absorbed three-quarters of all Canadian exports, and more importantly the majority of Canadian subsidiaries of big American companies were established in and around Metropolitan Toronto.

Following its role as a major transport and industrial centre, Toronto turned toward a service economy that grew with the computer age, while its financial power continued to reign as the greatest in Canada. Tourism also began to account for an appreciable portion of the city's economy.

POPULATION

During the 1960s, the central area of Toronto began to attract residents back from the suburbs. People moved downtown and restored entire neighbourhoods, some of them endowed with a great many Victorian-style buildings. A good example of this sort of neighbourhood is Yorkville, which briefly was the centre of the local hippie movement before taking on more bourgeois tones.

The prosperity Canada enjoyed up to the 1980s brought in its wake a renewed immigration following the interruption of the Depression and the war years. In the quarter-century after the Second World War, nearly two million immigrants came to live in Ontario, accounting for nearly two-thirds of the Canadian total. Most of these new arrivals chose Toronto. No longer did a majority of them come from the British Isles, as had been the case before. Now many of them were people from southern and eastern Europe who headed into exile because of the difficult living conditions following the war in Europe, as well as communism. In just a few decades Toronto's cultural face became radically transformed by the various ethnic neighbourhoods that contributed to making this city one of

Canada's most cosmopolitan. During the 1970s and 1980s many immigrants from Asia and the Caribbean chose Toronto as their new home.

Chinese immigration was no longer prohibited, as it had been between 1923 and 1947 by Canadian Government decree, and it bounced back. The influx of this so-called visible minority would change the face of Toronto completely. The city now has seven Chinatowns, which together form North America's second biggest Chinese community after San Francisco's. Along Dundas Street, between Spadina and Bay, lies a city within a city where one can easily live without speaking a single word of English. Later in the 1970s many immigrants from the Caribbean and southern Asia added to the mix. Once again, immigration would transform Toronto's image in the space of a decade, giving the city the international flavour of a true metropolis. Even today, however, the city is run to a large extent by people of British descent, some of whom continue to form the elite of local society and who fill most key posts in the city's main financial institutions.

The profound changes in Québec that began in the 1960s and gathered steam in the 1970s also contributed to Toronto's changing face. As the French-speaking majority gradually took control of the Québec economy, and as the Québec Government passed laws to protect and promote the French language, some big firms that had traditionally operated in English found it too difficult and costly to adjust to some of the changes and chose to move to Toronto. This exodus benefited the Toronto economy and greatly strengthened the financial sector.

The Greater Toronto area now has a population of about 4.6 million, making it the biggest city in Canada and the fifth largest in North America.

Toronto: City of Neighbourhoods

Toronto is one of North America's most successfully multi-cultural cities, with immigrants from every corner of the globe managing to blend into its society, while still maintaining their own cultural identity and traditions. It is this harmonious coming together of cultures that makes Canada, and Toronto as its largest, most diverse city, a cultural mosaic, as opposed to the melting pot which characterizes our neighbours south of the border. As sprawling as it may seem, Toronto is really a city of neighbourhoods. From Rosedale to Cabbagetown, from the Beaches to Little Italy, from one Chinatown to the next, Toronto's neighbourhoods each have their own character. While some areas are defined by their architectural eccentricities, the most interesting ones are defined by the people that live in them. Toronto's ethnic diversity is dizzying, with over 70 nationalities speaking more than 100 languages living side by side — and restaurant-goers are the happier for it!

Chinatown

Toronto's best-known ethnic neighbourhood is Chinatown (see p 126). There are actually seven Chinatowns in greater Toronto, but the most exciting and vibrant is probably the one bound by University, Spadina, Queen and College. During the day, fresh vegetables line the sidewalks around the intersection of Spadina and Dundas, the area's core, while at night, the bright yellow and red lights are reminiscent of Hong Kong. Picturesque, adjacent **Kensington Market** is often associated with Chinatown. The vintage clothing stores and specialty food shops from Europe, the Caribbean, the Middle East and Asia are veritable must-sees.

Little Italy

Italians make up the city's largest ethnic group, and their spiritual home is Little Italy, located on College Street west of Bathurst, where *trattorias* and boutiques add a bit of Mediterranean flavour to Toronto's scene. In recent years, the area has been redefined by a younger crowd who've marked it as a hip place to be, causing a number of trendy bars and restaurants (not all Italian) to spring up. The result is a vibrant mix of traditional shops and Italian eateries side-by-side with chic pool halls and cozy wine bars. It's a marvellous spot to sip a cappuccino or try an Italian *gelato*. In the summertime, Little Italy is one of the liveliest night spots in the city, its streets crowded with animated outdoor patios which are busy into the early hours of the morning.

Greektown

Greektown is also known as the Danforth, after the road that runs through it. The area, which runs between Broadview and Coxwell (near Chester subway stop), is peppered with Greek pie shops (where you'll find the best spinach and feta pie in town), boutiques and *tavernas*. Even the street signs are written in both English and Greek. Some of the smaller, locally-owned restaurants are closed in the summer as their owners return to the Greece during those months. In addition to the smaller, traditional places, there are a number of trendy Greek restaurants perfect for a lively dinner out. The Danforth, one of the city's most interesting dining hot spots, has everything from Cuban tapas to Sushi, but the Greeks still dominate when it comes to restaurants, and Greektown, with its late-night fruit markets, specialty food shops, taverns and summer cafés, is a real culinary experience.

Little Poland

Between the Lakeshore and Dundas Street West, Roncesvalles Avenue is known as Little Poland, a pleasant area of grand trees and stately Victorians. This is where you can catch an Eastern European film or savour traditional home-made cabbage rolls and pirogies at one of its many cafés.

Portugal Village

The traditional *azulejos* (ceramic tiles) and a glass of port will make you think you are in Portugal when you visit the area around Dundas Street West, Ossington Avenue, Augusta Avenue and College Street, an area known as Portugal Village. The bakeries here sell some of the best bread in town, while cheese stores, fish markets and lace and crochet shops occupy every other corner.

Little India

Little India, which runs along Gerrard Street between Greenwood and Coxwell has all the character (if less of the chaos) of New Delhi. Strings of coloured lights are draped on

PORTRAIT

restaurant facades, lighting up the street as if every night was a festival. Sari palaces abound, their windows showcasing glittery garments, and supermarkets spill onto the street with baskets full of mustard seeds, pappadams, coconuts and stalks of sugar cane. Everywhere the sound of modern Indian music plunks from scratchy speakers. Unless you're looking for a souvenir gold-coloured Buddha, the main reason for visiting Little India (besides soaking up the atmosphere) is for the food. Every second shop, it seems, is a restaurant, each specializing in a different type of Indian cuisine and most of them offering an all-you-can-eat buffet for around $8.

Caribbean Village

The area around Bathurst Street north of Bloor Street is the commercial district known as the Caribbean Community. Great food shops sell delicious treats, including the savoury patties (pastry turnovers with a spicy meat filling) and *roti* (flat bread with meat, fish or vegetable filling).

The Gay Village

Toronto has the largest population of gays and lesbians in Canada, and is very supportive and accepting of the city's gay community. The Gay Village (affectionately known as the "Ghetto") runs along Church Street between Carlton and Bloor streets. Rainbow flags hang from its lamp posts and gay couples stroll hand in hand. During Toronto's Gay Pride parade and festival at the end of June, the streets of the Village are blocked off for three days and filled with beer tents, vendors and the 700,000 people (both gay and straight) who show up every year. It is definitely one of the city's best parties. Church is lively and bustling, especially in summer, with bars, cafés, restaurants, shops and lots of outdoor patios. Hanlan's Point on the Toronto Islands is also a popular gay summertime hangout, and in May, 1999 was officially designated as a nude beach.

Rosedale

Both of Toronto's most distinguished and affluent neighbourhoods lie just north of the downtown area. Rosedale is bound by Yonge Street to the west, the Don Valley Parkway to the east, Bloor Street to the south and St. Clair Avenue to the north. Rosedale began as the estate of Sheriff William Jarvis, and was so named by his wife Mary after the wild roses that once abounded here. The wild roses and the original house overlooking the ravine are now gone, replaced by a collection of curved streets lined with exquisite residences representing quite a variety of architectural styles. See also p 158.

PORTRAIT

Forest Hill

North of St. Clair Avenue, the posh area known as Forest Hill begins, extending north to Eglinton Avenue, east to Avenue Road and west to Bathurst Street. Perhaps in keeping with its name, one of Forest Hill's first bylaws back in the 1920s was that a tree be planted on every lot. This haven of greenery is home to some of the city's finest dwellings; many of the loveliest grace Old Forest Hill Road. The community is also home to one of the country's most prestigious private schools, Upper Canada College. See also p 162.

Cabbagetown

Cabbagetown was once described as the "biggest Anglo-Saxon Slum" and was for many years an area to be avoided. The area has been transformed in recent years, however, and is now the epitome of gentrification in Toronto. Its name originated with Irish immigrants who arrived here in the mid-19th century and grew cabbages right on their front lawns. It contains grand trees and quaint small-scale Victorian homes, many of which have historic markers. Winchester, Carlton, Spruce and Metcalfe Streets are all lined with true gems. See also p 145.

The Annex

Extending north and west of the intersection of Bloor Street and Avenue Road to Dupont and Bathurst streets is an area which was annexed by the city of Toronto in 1887, and is now appropriately called The Annex. As this was a planned suburb, a certain architectural homogeneity prevails; even the unique gables, turrets and cornices are all lined up an equal distance from the street. It is now home to university professors and students, journalists and people from all walks of life. The Annex is another of Toronto's restaurant- and shop-lined corridors, perfect for shopping, eating or just strolling along to soak up a bit of the city's atmosphere. See also p 152.

The Beaches

Last but not least, there are The Beaches (Toronto really does have everything!). Known to locals only as the Beach, this is one of Toronto's most charming neighbourhoods, for obvious reasons — sun, sand, a beach-side boardwalk, classic clapboard and shingle cottages and the open water all lie just a streetcar ride (along Queen Street) away from the hectic pace of downtown. Bounded by Kingston Road, Woodbine Road, Victoria Park Avenue and Lake Ontario, the Beach is more than just a neighbourhood, it's a way of life. Along the main stretch of Queen Street, there are countless restaurants, cafés and boutiques, with everything from designer children's shops to designer pet shops. The sidewalks, boardwalk and beach-side bike path are more crowded with in-line skaters, cyclists and dog walkers than the streets are with cars. Travellers will revel in the chance to sunbathe on the hot sand, take a quick dip in the refreshing water or, as the sun sets, do some window shopping and lounge about on a pretty patio. See also p 166.

POLITICS

In 1953, Toronto and 12 surrounding municipalities formed the Municipality of Metropolitan Toronto, Canada's first metropolitan government. When Toronto amalgamated its six former municipalities in 1998 to form a singular City of Toronto, a new City Council was created, with two councillors per ward, for a total of 58 councillors plus the mayor of Toronto. The ward boundaries will be reconfigured in 2000. The City of Toronto is in charge of most services, but consolidation is still ongoing. The former city councils of the six municipalities still exist as "Community Councils".

Some years ago, serious frictions arose between the municipal government and residents of the Toronto Islands. The islands belong to the city, which rents out parcels of land to the people living there. When the council decided to take back the land and expel residents to make way for a park, residents fought back and eventually won.

Municipal politics in Toronto do not run along party lines, but the city's large population exerts considerable influence on the provincial and federal political scenes, as it accounts for a substantial part of the electorate. Toronto has been the capital of Ontario since before Canadian Confederation in 1867. To fight a huge provincial deficit, the Ontario premier since 1995, Conservative leader Mike Harris, has enacted drastic spending cuts, especially in the areas of education, health and social services.

PORTRAIT

THE ECONOMY

Since the mid-1970s, Toronto has been Canada's biggest city, and it exerts a strong degree of control over the national economy. Although the manufacturing sector has lost some ground in recent years, Toronto has maintained a preponderant role due largely to its powerful financial sector. The five biggest Canadian banks have consolidated most of their head-office operations in Toronto, and most of the big securities firms and insurance companies have their headquarters in the city. The Toronto Stock Exchange plays an important role on North American markets; only the New York Stock Exchange is bigger.

In the manufacturing sector, the automobile industry plays a vital role in Toronto's economy, followed by heavy equipment, iron and steel, chemical products and the dynamic electronics field. Most of the bigger factories are concentrated in the area along Lake Ontario, from Toronto to Hamilton, in what is commonly called the "Golden Horseshoe", Canada's most heavily industrialized area. This area benefits from easy access to the St. Lawrence Seaway and is served by an extensive railway network, as well as by the fast highways that crisscross Ontario. The tourism industry is also playing a growing role in this future-oriented city.

THE ARTS

Whether in painting, literature, music or film, Ontario artists have sought over the years to create Canadian-accented works and have managed to differentiate themselves from the undeniably influential English and American artistic movements. This quest has not been easy, although it has been helped by government bodies such as the Canada Council and the Ontario Arts Council, whose role is to subsidize the artistic endeavours of Canadian artists.

Painting

It was not until the 19th century that it became possible to speak of Toronto's art movements. Starting in the early days of settlement, talented painters emerged and found a source of inspiration in the European masters. Their main clients at first were the Church and the bourgeoisie, who encouraged them to produce religious works such as altars and silver carvings or to paint family portraits.

In the early years of the 20th century, some of the great Ontario landscape painters became known for creating genuinely Canadian art. Tom Thomson, whose paintings provide a distinctive portrayal of landscapes unique to the Canadian Shield, was an originator of this movement. He died prematurely in 1917 at the age of 40. Nevertheless, his work had an indisputable effect on one of the most notable groups of painters in Ontario, the Group of Seven, whose first exhibition was held in Toronto in 1920. These artists, Franklin Carmichael, Lawren S. Harris, Frank H. Johnson, Arthur Lismer, J.E.H. MacDonald, Alexander Young Jackson and Frederick Varley, were all landscape painters. Although they worked together closely, each developed his own pictorial language. They were distinguished by their use of bright colours in their portrayal of typical Canadian landscapes. Their influence over Ontario painting is substantial, and only a handful of other artists of the same period distinguished themselves from the movement, which modern-day artists view as too conformist.

One artist who has had a great impact on the arts in Toronto is not even Canadian. Scottish sculptor Henry Moore's *The Archer*, dominating Nathan Philips Square, is an early example of public art in Toronto and helped transform the city. Moore has donated his complete works to the Art Gallery of Ontario, whose entrance is marked by his curious *Form*.

PORTRAIT

Literature

As the largest city in the country, it is no wonder that Toronto is the publishing mecca of English Canada. As home to many of the major publishing companies in the country, and as the forum for the International Festival of Authors, Toronto has a rich literary history.

Toronto's first settlers considered themselves British subjects. These Loyalists had decidedly British concerns and sought to champion them in the literature of their new homeland. The break with the crown and with tradition would have come of its own accord, but the presence of the newly independent Americans south of the border helped things along. In the United States, many authors had established themselves not merely as writers of English, but as American writers. This emancipation drew envy from Toronto writers, and English-Canadian writers in general.

Though Toronto writer Mazo de la Roche is well remembered as an excellent Canadian writer, she nevertheless still called for solid links with the British Empire. Her *Jalna* (1927-1960) novels described life on the outskirts of Toronto.

Toronto writer and journalist Morley Callaghan is known for his novel *That Summer in Paris* (1963) which relates the summer of 1929, which he spent with Ernest Hemingway and other members of the Lost Generation (expatriates in Paris). As a contributor to *The New Yorker* and winner of the Governor General's Award in 1951 for *The Loved and the Lost*, Callaghan often chose to obscure his environment in his fiction, and his work is therefore an exception to the norm of Canadian literature, which is forever striving to establish a Canadian identity. His fiction often depicts the hard anonymous life of city-dwellers in an effort to promote a stronger social engagement.

The 1970s saw the appearance of modern movements such as Open Letter in Toronto, seeking to bring new contributions to old ideas.

The city figures prominently as the setting for many works by two of Canada's most eminent writers. The first is Robertson Davies, a novelist and playwright, among other things. His *Deptford Trilogy* and *Cornish Trilogy*, both set in Toronto, are analytical and thoughtful looks at the growth of the city from provincialism to sophistication. *The Cunning Man*, the last novel in the latter trilogy, is particularly noteworthy.

The second writer is Margaret Atwood, a feminist, satirist, nationalist, poet and novelist who carried modernism into the seventies. Her literary and critical writings have contributed immensely to attempts at defining Canadian culture and literature. Atwood is considered one of the greatest Canadian writers in this country's literary cannon. Her most recent success was *Alias Grace* (1996).

Toronto is the multicultural capital of English Canada. It is only fitting therefore that many immigrant writers have chosen the city as their home. Sri-Lankan-born writer Michael Ondaatje now resides here and his novel *In the Skin of the Lion* (1987) is set in the city. The construction of the Bloor Street viaduct and the Harris Filtration Plant both figure in the novel, making for an interesting read. Ondaatje's latest novel, *The English Patient*, which won the Booker Prize in 1993, is a sequel of sorts to *In the Skin of a Lion*, and was the basis for the 1996 Oscar-winning movie of the same name. Austin Clark is also a resident of Toronto. His novel *The Meeting Point* describes Caribbean life in the city.

Theatre

Toronto is the theatre capital of Canada and the third largest centre of English-speaking theatre production in the world, behind only London and New York. Everything goes, from the great classics to experimental works. During much of the

PORTRAIT

20th century, Toronto offered a rather limited theatrical scene. In 1960, the city had only two professional theatre companies; now there are more than 200 professional theatre or dance companies. Together they put on more than 10,000 performances a year. More than seven million tickets are sold each year to different shows, running the gamut from musicals to dramas to comedies. There is something for everyone. It was not surprising when UNESCO named Toronto the world's most culturally diverse city in 1993.

Toronto has numerous theatres, some dating from early in the century. The Royal Alexandra Theatre is a fine example. Saved from demolition by Ed Mirvish, the bargain store king, the theatre was renovated at great expense and brought back to its former splendour. Several former factories and firehalls have also been converted to theatres, with seating at the various venues now totalling 43,000. Numerous festivals, among them the Fringe of Toronto Festival, the Fringe Festival of Independent Dance Artists, Summer Works and the du Maurier World Stage Festival, showcase new local talents as well as many visiting artists.

A great Canadian cultural centre, Toronto is home to most of Canada's English-language book and magazine publishers and to numerous broadcasters.

Film

Throughout the first half of the 20th century, Canadian film-making, with a few exceptions, was almost nonexistent. For many Canadians, it seemed futile and almost useless to go up against American films, the most popular and successful in the world. Starting in the 1950s, however, Canadian cinema began to develop and to acquire a certain identity. But it was not until 1963, with the film *Nobody Waved Goodbye*, that Toronto really found a cinematographic identity, at the same time opening the way to a Canadian film-making culture. Figures like Norman Jewison, best known for having produced films such as *Moonstruck* and *Fiddler on the Roof*, came onto the scene and had an important influence on the Toronto film industry. Canadian cinema is still quite marginal compared to the American monster. Even today, the proportion of Canadian films showing in Canadian movie theatres is only about 2.5 percent of the total. It is thus not surprising to see Toronto creators such as Rick Moranis and David Cronenberg drawn to the huge American film industry.

All the same, Toronto is a very active city in the film area. Nicknamed Hollywood North, Toronto is sought after by many producers for its diversity, the quality of its production centres and the broad local talent. Among North American venues, only Hollywood and New York account for more film production. Because of the number and variety of its neighbourhoods, Toronto is able to offer a variety of sites that can stand in for cities such as Boston, New York, Tokyo, Philadelphia and even Vienna. Many American producers have chosen to use Toronto for their film shoots because of the financial savings available, since Toronto is a far cheaper place to film in than the United States. The film industry provides Toronto with annual revenues of about $684 million and creates about 30,000 jobs. In 1998, there were 177 film and television productions in Toronto. Advertising shoots alone bring in $135 million a year. It goes without saying that Toronto's International Film Festival, which takes place each September, draws countless film-goers. Not only is it a forum for the world film industry, including of course the American colossus, but its Perspective Canada program also showcases new Canadian film talents.

Music

Many musical artists from Ontario have become known on the international scene. Here is a brief retrospective of some of the better known ones.

Born in Toronto on September 25, 1932, **Glen Gould** was raised in musical surroundings from a very early age. His mother, who was related to Norwegian composer Edvard Grieg, taught him the basics of piano and organ until the age of 10. The young Glen Gould stood out very quickly as an exceptionally gifted pupil who learned musical composition starting at age five. His virtuosity was recognized unanimously during his first public concert, in 1945. Scarcely a year later, he set out as a soloist in a concert at the Royal Academy in London, where he interpreted Beethoven's fourth piano concerto, and he joined the Toronto Symphony at age 14.

Working with the greatest musicians, including Herbert von Karajan, musical director of the Berlin Philharmonic Orchestra, and Leonard Bernstein of the New York Philharmonic Orchestra, Gould stood out on the world scene as one of the most talented musicians of his period. Drawn more by composition and studio recording than by public concerts, Gould decided prematurely to leave the stage after a recital in Los Angeles on April 10, 1964. He devoted the rest of his career to composition and to the recording of numerous works. He died in Toronto on October 4, 1982.

Neil Young was born in Toronto on November 12, 1945. He spent only part of his youth there before moving with his mother to Winnipeg, Manitoba, where he began his career as a musician, eventually moving to California. At first he was a member of various groups, including The Squires, Buffalo Springfield and, most notably, Crosby, Stills, Nash and Young. He began his solo career in 1969, and in 1972 he recorded *Harvest*, his most popular and best-known album.

Toronto's Yorkville Avenue spawned some major talent in the 1960s. Crooner **Gordon Lightfoot** and folk sensations **Ian and Sylvia** are among those who got their start in the clubs and cafés of trendy Yorkville.

The Band is another famous name in the history of rock and roll. Originally from Toronto, they rose to popularity in the late 1960s after achieving considerable success on the Toronto music scene. Following successes like the song *The Weight* and the film *The Last Waltz*, The Band split up, though one member, Robbie Robertson has gone on to a successful solo career, which includes the hit albums *Robbie Robertson* (1987) and *Storyville* (1991).

More recently, the **Barenaked Ladies** have made quite a splash, with their music that blends rock, jazz and folk. The **Cowboy Junkies** foursome, who also come from Toronto, had great success with their *The Trinity Session* album, recorded inside Holy Trinity Church just a few steps from the Eaton Centre.

PORTRAIT

ARCHITECTURE

The impetus for Toronto's (then York's) founding in 1793 was military. A 10-square-block grid of streets centred around King and Sherbourne Streets was quickly laid out east of Fort York and the harbour, thus "Muddy York" was born. York was nevertheless the capital of Upper Canada, and therefore an air of civility was needed. The hastily built wooden structures that lined its streets were just as quickly replaced with refined Georgian edifices. A courthouse, jail, church, post office and harbour yard were among the permanent fixtures that established their place in this compact new town. The English gentlemen who arrived in this military outpost thus succeeded in turning it into an orderly reflection of the British Empire.

Beyond the compact streets of the town, essentially to the north of today's Queen Street, the governor parcelled off long, narrow park lots to encourage the aristocracy to settle in the colonies. The Georgian period was just ending and the Georgian style, with its formal solidity, was the first architectural style of the new city. It was used for churches and public and commercial buildings; however, one of the most poignant Georgian legacies in the city today was a private residence, the Grange (see p 129) built in 1817, on park lot 13. The wealthy classes of the Victorian era went on to use Gothic, Italianate, Romanesque and Queen Anne styles to show their importance.

The use of brick was the first law passed by the new city of Toronto in 1834. Not only did it lend the city a look of permanence, which in turn inspired confidence in the newly-arriving aristocracy, but it was also a cautionary measure. The prevention of fire was a major concern for the new city-fathers. To this day, the majority of Toronto's older buildings are all made of brick. Nearby claypits meant that there was an unlimited supply or both red and yellow bricks, the latter being something of a trademark in Toronto architecture. Called "white" in the 19th century, they were an inexpensive alternative to granite and limestone, which had to be imported.

Toronto was busy annexing neighbouring villages in the late 19th century. An action that greatly increased the city's population and also introduced new elements to Toronto

CN Tower

architecture. The addition of Yorkville, Brockton, Riverdale, The Annex, Seaton Village and Parkdale very quickly gave Toronto a large residential area. These areas were characterized by classic, orderly single-detached or semi-detached row houses, often employing Queen Anne and Richardsonian Romanesque styles.

The heavy and bulky lines of Richardsonian Romanesque were popular in the last years of the 19th century. Toronto architect E.J. Lennox used this style, created by American Henry Hobson Richardson, on many of his and the city's most famous buildings, notably the Parliament Building and Old City Hall.

As the 20th century dawned, Toronto City Council chose not to put a height limit on buildings in its downtown area as was the case in London and Paris. A series of buildings constructed after the 1905 decision were the tallest in the British Commonwealth, the last being the Canadian Bank of Commerce (see p 107) built in 1929 and 34 stories tall.

The most significant developments in Toronto's architecture in the last half of the 20th century were felt in the city's core. Here the International Style was in sharp contrast to the picturesque Victorian city that had remained for the most part intact since its creation. "Form follows function", "less is more" and an emphasis on purism characterize this by-product of the Modern Movement, spearheaded in North America by Ludwig Mies van der Rohe. The Toronto-Dominion Centre (see p 105) is Toronto's "boring box", a stunning building that became a model for glass towers all over the world. It heralded a transformation of Toronto's financial district that was ultimately criticized for its isolation of people from the space that surrounds them. The trend these days has shifted away from these impersonal mega-towers. Since the emergence of post-modernism, there has been a shift back to the lavish forms of the past. So much so, that not only do new buildings borrow from the past, but often the old buildings are rehabilitated instead of being replaced.

The post-war era was also characterized by a general shift away from the city to newly developed suburbs, where rows of identical houses and trees spelled Utopia. Toronto has its fair share of these, most located quite a fair distance from downtown. Thankfully the city's original residential areas, somewhere between the new and the old, were starting to lose favour, and provided inexpensive housing for Toronto's growing immigrant communities. These areas have a real sense of character and an address here is almost as coveted as a Rosedale or Forest Hill address.

Recent masterpieces like the CN Tower, Skydome, the Royal Bank Plaza and the Toronto-Dominion Centre make Toronto's skyline truly unique. Yet it is perhaps the scattered nature of the city's architectural history, with the new embracing the old, that distinguishes this Canadian metropolis. A stroll through Cabbagetown, The Annex, Rosedale and the financial district proves this.

PRACTICAL INFORMATION

The information in this section will help visitors from English-speaking countries better plan their trip to Toronto.

ENTRANCE FORMALITIES

Passport

A valid passport is usually sufficient for most visitors planning to stay less than three months; visas are not required. A three-month extension is possible, but a return ticket and proof of sufficient funds to cover this extension may be required.

Caution: some countries do not have an agreement with Canada concerning health and accident insurance, so it is advisable to have the appropriate coverage. For more information, see the section entitled "Health" (see p 73).

European citizens who want to enter the United States will need a visa. It is best to apply for this visa from your home country, although it is obtainable abroad, usually without problems.

Extended Visits

Visitors must submit their request **in writing** and **before** the expiration of their visa (the date is usually written in your passport) to an Immigration Canada office. To make a request, you must have a valid passport, a return ticket, proof of sufficient funds to cover the stay, as well as the $50 non-refundable filing fee. In some cases (work, study), however, the request must be made **before** arriving in Canada. Contact Immigration Canada at ☎973-4444 or www.cicnet.ci.gc.ca.

EMBASSIES AND CONSULATES

Canadian Embassies and Consulates Abroad

Australia
Canadian Consulate General
Level 5, Quay West Building
111 Harrington Road
Sydney, N.S.W. 2000
☎(612) 9364-3050
⊷(612) 9364-3099

Belgium
Canadian Embassy
2 Avenue de Tervueren
1040 Brussels
☎(32-2) 741-0611
⊷(32-2) 741-0643

Denmark
Canadian Embassy
Kr. Bernikowsgade 1,
1105 Copenhagen K,
☎(45) 33 48 32 00
⊷(45) 33 48 32 20

Finland
Canadian Embassy
Pohjos Esplanadi 25 B,
00101 Helsinki
☎(358-9) 17 11 41
⊷(358-9) 60 10 60

Germany
Canadian Embassy
Godesberger Allee 119
D53175 Bonn
☎(49-228) 968-3410
⊷(49-228) 968-3458

Great Britain
Canadian High Commission
38 Grosvenor Street
London W1X 0AA
☎(44-171) 258-6600
⊷(44-171) 258-6506

Toronto's Waterfront has a distinctive maritime atmosphere.
– *Walter Bibikow*

One of the three bridges linking the pod structures of Ontario Place.
– *Walter Bibikow*

The modern palm-tree design of the atrium in BCE Place.
– *T. Philiptchenko*

Netherlands
Canadian Embassy
Sophialaan 7, 2500 GV
The Hague
Postal Address:
P.O. Box 30820
The Hague, The Netherlands
☎31 (70) 311-1600
✻31 (70) 311-1620

Norway
Canadian Embassy
Wergelandsveien 7
0244 Oslo
☎47 22 99 53 00
✻47 22 99 53 01

Sweden
Canadian Embassy
Tegelbacken 4, 7th floor,
Stockholm
Postal Address:
P.O. Box 16129
S-10323 Stockholm, Sweden
☎(46) 8-453-3000
✻(46) 8-24-2491

Switzerland
Canadian Embassy
Kirchenfeldstrasse 88
3005 Berne
Postal Address:
P.O. Box 234
Berne 6, Switzerland
☎41 (31) 357-3200
✻41(31) 357-3210

United States
Canadian Embassy
501 Pennsylvania Ave. N.W.
Washington, DC
20001 U.S.A.
☎(202) 682-1740
✻(202) 682-7726

Consulate General of Canada
1175 Peachtree Street N.E.
100 Colony Square,
Suite 1700
Atlanta, Georgia
30361-6205 U.S.A.
☎(404) 532-2000
✻(404) 532-2050

Canadian Consulate General
Three Copley Place
Suite 400
Boston, Massachusetts
02116 U.S.A.
☎(617) 262-3760
✻(617) 262-3415

Canadian Consulate General
Two Prudential Plaza
180 N. Stetson Avenue,
Suite 2400,
Chicago, Illinois
60601 U.S.A.
☎(312) 616-1860
✻(312) 616-1877

Canadian Consulate General
St. Paul Place, Suite 1700
750 N. St. Paul Street
Dallas, Texas
75201 U.S.A.
☎(214) 922-9806
✻(214) 922-9815

PRACTICAL INFORMATION

Canadian Consulate General
600 Renaissance Center
Suite 1100
Detroit, Michigan
48243-1798 U.S.A.
☎(313) 567-2085
⊷(313) 567-2164

Canadian Consulate General
1251 Avenue of the Americas
Concourse Level
New York, New York
10020-1175 U.S.A.
☎(212) 596-1600
⊷(212) 596-1793

Consulate General of Canada
550 South Hope Street,
9th floor
Los Angeles, California
90071-2627 USA
☎(213) 346-2700
⊷(213) 620-8827

Canadian Consulate General
One Marine Midland Center
Suite 3000
Buffalo, New York
14203-2884 U.S.A.
☎(716) 858-9500
⊷(716) 852-4340

Canadian Consulate General
701 Fourth Avenue South
Suite 900
Minneapolis, Minnesota
55415-1899 U.S.A.
☎(612) 333-4641
⊷(612) 332-4061

Canadian Consulate General
412 Plaza 600
Sixth and Stewart Streets
Seattle, Washington
98101-1286 U.S.A.
☎(206) 443-1777
⊷(206) 443-9662

Foreign Embassies and Consulates in Toronto

United States
Consulate General
360 University Avenue
Toronto, Ont.
M5G 1S4
☎(416) 595-1700
⊷(416) 595-0051 or
595-5419

Belgium
Consulate
2 Bloor Street West
Suite 2006
Toronto, Ontario
M4W 3E2
☎(416) 944-1422
⊷(416) 944-1421

Australia
Consulate General
175 Bloor Street East #316
Toronto, Ont.
M4W 3R8
☎(416) 323-1155
⊷(416) 323-3910

Great Britain
Consulate General
777 Bay Street
Suite 2800
Toronto, Ont.
M5G 2G2
☎(416) 593-1290
⇤(416) 593-1229

Holland
Consulate of the Netherlands
1 Dundas Street West
Suite 2106
Toronto, Ont.
M5G 1Z3
☎(416) 598-2520
⇤(416) 598-8064

Germany
Consulate General
77 Admiral Road
Toronto, Ont.
M5R 2L4
☎(416) 925-2813
⇤(416) 925-2818

Switzerland
Consulate General
154 University Avenue
Suite 601
Toronto, Ontario
M5H 3Y9
☎(416) 593-5371
⇤(416) 593-5083

PRACTICAL
INFORMATION

TOURIST INFORMATION

The main offices of **Tourism Toronto** are at Queen's Quay Terminal *(207 Queen's Quay W., Suite 590, M5J 1A7, ☎203-2500 or 800-363-1990, www.torontotourism.com)* but this location is just that, offices. The staff are very friendly, and all sorts of pamphlets are available, but a much more complete tourist office, run by Ontario Travel, is located on the lower level of the Eaton Centre at Queen and Yonge Streets; the **Visitor Information Centre** *(☎800-668-2746, www.travelinx.com)* is open year-round, Monday to Friday 10am to 9pm, Saturday 9:30am to 6pm and Sunday noon to 5pm.

The **Traveller's Aid Society** *(in Union Station, on the arrivals level, ☎366-7788; at Pearson International Airport, Terminal 1 ☎905-676-2868, Terminal 2 ☎905-676-2869, Terminal 3 ☎905-612-5890)* is a volunteer organization that can provide information about hotels, restaurants, sights and transportation.

Travel Agencies

The Flight Centre

Despite its name, this company is a full-service travel agency which specializes in discount flights and guarantees the lowest airfare. Many of their locations are open on Sundays.

Queen St. West: ☎595-1449
Yonge St. at King: ☎304-6170
The Annex: ☎934-0670
Bay St. at Adelaide: ☎363-9004

Travel Cuts

Specializes in student fares and travel.

313 Queen St. W., ☎977-6272
187 College St., ☎979-2406
49 Front St. E., ☎365-0545

American Express Travel Service

50 Bloor St. W., ☎967-3411
Royal York Hotel: 100 Front St. W., ☎363-3883

Thomas Cook Travel

Toronto Eaton Centre: 290 Yonge St., ☎593-1303

GETTING TO TORONTO

By Car

Most people arriving by car from the east or the west will enter Toronto on Highway 401, which crosses the northern part of the city. If you're coming from the west, take Highway 427

Table of distances (km/mi)
Via the shortest route

© ULYSSES

Example : The distance between Montréal and Toronto is 547km.

1 mile = 1.62 kilometres
1 kilometre = 0.62 miles

	Chicago (Il.)	Hamilton	Kingston	Kitchener-Waterloo	London	Montréal (Qué.)	New York (N.Y.)	Niagara Falls	Ottawa	Sault Ste. Marie	Sudbury	Toronto	Thunder Bay
Hamilton	788												
Kingston	1100	338											
Kitchener-Waterloo	767	69	369										
London	661	140	451	110									
Montréal (Qué.)	1383	621	299	650	738								
New York (N.Y.)	1294	765	583	838	911	618							
Niagara Falls	896	77	408	156	227	689	690						
Ottawa	1242	480	203	511	600	202	719	544					
Sault Ste. Marie	780	748	894	777	699	1003	1498	814	806				
Sudbury	1079	460	609	490	572	700	1212	529	508	302			
Toronto	855	75	263	123	198	547	829	144	410	696	411		
Thunder Bay	1058	1469	1623	1496	1414	1638	2212	1534	1516	723	1019	1421	
Windsor/Detroit (Mi.)	460	318	626	306	191	912	1018	413	773	584	751	386	1310

south to the Queen Elizabeth Way (QEW) Eastbound. Continue along the QEW (which eventually turns into the Gardiner Expressway), and exit at either York, Bay or Yonge street for downtown. If you're coming along the 401 from the east, take the Don Valley Parkway south to the Gardiner Expressway, then take the Gardiner Expressway west to either the York, Bay or Yonge street exits. Those coming from the United States will travel east along the QEW, following the shores of Lake Ontario until the QEW turns into the Gardiner Expressway, where either the York, Bay or Yonge street exit can be taken. Rush-hour traffic can be very heavy on all of Toronto's highways.

By Plane

Toronto's Lester B. Pearson International Airport

Information

Lester B. Pearson International Airport *(General Information:* ☎*247-7678)* welcomes international flights from Europe, the United States and Asia, as well national flights from the other Canadian provinces. It is the biggest and busiest airport in Canada. There are three terminals at the airport, which is served by over 50 airline companies. Each terminal has a variety of services, including Canadian Immigration offices, lost and found, Canada Customs offices, currency exchange offices, bank machines that exchange money, gift shops, duty-free shops and offices of the Traveller's Aid Society.

Delta Airlines and Northwest Airlines are among the major airlines at **Terminal 1** *(information:* ☎*905-676-3506)*.

Air Canada, United and Lufthansa are among the major airlines at **Terminal 2** *(information:* ☎*905-676-3506)*.

Finally, Canadian Airlines, American Airlines, USAir, Air France, British Airways and KLM are among the major airlines at **Terminal 3** *(information:* ☎*905-612-5100)*.

Location

The airport lies 27 km from downtown Toronto, in the town of Malton. To get downtown from the airport by car, take Highway 427 south to Queen Elizabeth Way (QEW), and follow the latter east until it joins the Gardiner Expressway. Take the York, Yonge or Bay exit for downtown.

City Bus

If you are not renting a car, expect to pay about $40 for a taxi. You can also take advantage of a shuttle bus service called the **Pacific Western Airport Express** *($12.50 one way, $21.50 return;* ☎*905-564-6333 or 800-387-6787)*, which links the airport with various points throughout downtown, including some of the major hotels. This is an economical way to get into town, and you do not have to be staying at one of the hotels on its route to take the bus. There are daily departures every 40 minutes from the airport starting at 6:05am and ending at 12:55am; from downtown Toronto from various hotels such as the Delta, Chelsea, Sheraton Centre, Royal York, and from the Bus Terminal, there are daily departures every 20 minutes starting at 4:45am and ending at 11:20pm. The buses have the added advantage of being equipped for handicapped travellers: there is room for two wheelchairs, and braille signage and a visual signboard announce stops.

Limousine Service

Finally, travellers also have the option of taking a limousine to and from the airport: **Official Airport Limousine** *(information:* ☎*905-624-2424)*.

Toronto City Centre Airport

Location

This local airport is located on Hanlan's Point on the Toronto Islands. It is reached by a special ferry at the foot of Bathurst Street.

PRACTICAL INFORMATION

Information

For information call ☎203-6945.

This airport is served by private flights and by planes from Newark, Montréal, Ottawa and London, Ontario.

By Bus

Bus service in and out of Toronto is provided by Greyhound Lines of Canada. There is frequent service to cities both near and far. This is an affordable and convenient way of getting to Toronto if you haven't got a car. Note that travel times can be long, however. For example, it takes 6 hrs and 45 min to reach Toronto from Montreal, 5 hrs and 30 min from Ottawa, and 5 hrs and 15 min from Detroit.

The bus station in Toronto is located right downtown at 610 Bay Street; for information call Greyhound Lines of Canada at ☎367-8747.

For information in other cities:

Montreal ☎(514) 842-2281
Ottawa ☎(613) 238-5900
Vancouver ☎(604) 662-7575

By Train

All VIA trains arrive at Union Station at the corner of Front and Bay Streets. For information on VIA trains call ☎366-8411; 800-561-8630 from elsewhere in Ontario or 888-842-7245 from the United States.

GETTING AROUND TORONTO

The City of Toronto consists of six former municipalities which now form one city; the City of Toronto, the Borough of East York and the Cities of York, North York, Scarborough and Etobicoke. The Greater Toronto Area also encompasses

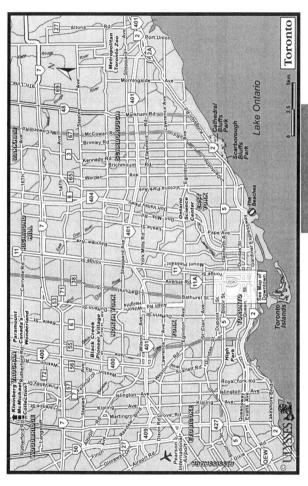

Toronto

municipalities outside Metro Toronto, such as Mississauga and Markham. Toronto is Canada's largest city: the City of Toronto has 2.4 million inhabitants and Greater Toronto has 4.6 million.

The city lies 174 metres above sea level and covers an area of 624 square kilometres.

Toronto's grid system of streets makes it easy to get around. Yonge (pronounced *young*) Street is the main north-south artery and divides the city between east and west. At 1,896 kilometres, it is also the world's longest street, running from the shores of Lake Ontario to Rainy River, Ontario.

Street addresses in the city that have the suffix "East" (E.) or "West" (W.) lie east or west respectively of Yonge; 299 Queen St. W. is therefore a few blocks west of Yonge. Toronto's downtown is generally considered to be the area south of Bloor, between Spadina and Jarvis.

By Public Transportation

Toronto's public transportation system is run by the **Toronto Transit Commission**, the **TTC**; it includes a subway, buses and streetcars. There are three subway lines: the yellow, Yonge–University line is U-shaped and runs north-south, with the bottom of the U at Union Station; the green, Bloor–Danforth line runs east-west along Bloor and Danforth from Kennedy Road to Kipling Road; the blue, Scarborough RT line runs north and east up to Ellesmere Road. There is also the Harbourfront LRT, which runs from Union Station along Queen's Quay to Spadina. The commuter train to the eastern and western suburbs is called the GO. It can be accessed from Union Station, at Bay and Front streets. These trains are all safe and clean. Buses and streetcars run along the city's major arteries. You can transfer between buses, streetcars and the subway without paying another fare, but you will need a transfer, so always take one just in case. Pick up a copy of the TTC's *Ride Guide* for a map of the system. It shows most of the major attractions and how to reach them by public transportation.

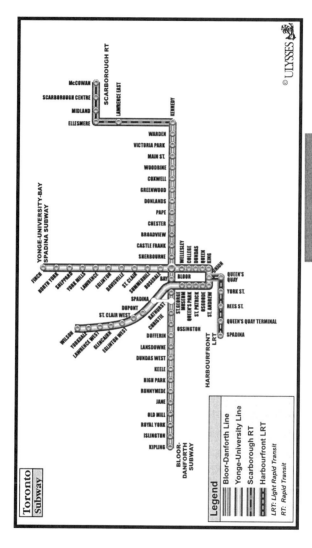

PRACTICAL INFORMATION

Toronto Subway

SCARBOROUGH RT

McCOWAN
SCARBOROUGH CENTRE
MIDLAND
ELLESMERE
LAWRENCE EAST
KENNEDY

WARDEN
VICTORIA PARK
MAIN ST.
WOODBINE
COXWELL
GREENWOOD
DONLANDS
PAPE
CHESTER
BROADVIEW
CASTLE FRANK
SHERBOURNE

YONGE-UNIVERSITY-BAY SPADINA SUBWAY

WELLESLEY
COLLEGE
DUNDAS
QUEEN
KING

FINCH
NORTH YORK
SHEPPARD
YORK MILLS
LAWRENCE
EGLINTON
DAVISVILLE
ST. CLAIR
SUMMERHILL
ROSEDALE
BAY
BLOOR
UNION

ST. GEORGE
MUSEUM
QUEEN'S PARK
ST. PATRICK
OSGOODE
ST. ANDREW

SPADINA
DUPONT
ST. CLAIR WEST
BATHURST
CHRISTIE

QUEEN'S QUAY
YORK ST.
REES ST.
QUEEN'S QUAY TERMINAL
SPADINA

WILSON
YORKDALE
LAWRENCE WEST
GLENCAIRN
EGLINTON WEST
OSSINGTON
DUFFERIN
LANSDOWNE
DUNDAS WEST
KEELE
HIGH PARK
RUNNYMEDE
JANE
OLD MILL
ROYAL YORK
ISLINGTON
KIPLING

BLOOR-DANFORTH SUBWAY

HARBOURFRONT LRT

Legend

Bloor-Danforth Line
Yonge-University Line
Scarborough RT
Harbourfront LRT

LRT: Light Rapid Transit
RT: Rapid Transit

© ULYSSES

Streetcar

The TTC also runs a wheelchair user's service called Wheel-Trans. It costs the same as regular public transit and service is door-to-door. Transportation must be booked one day in advance by calling ☎393-4222.

A single **fare** is $2 for adults, $1.40 for students (you must have a TTC student card) and seniors and 50¢ for children under 12. Five adult tickets or tokens cost $8.50, 8 student or senior tokens cost $9, and 10 child tickets or tokens cost $4. If you plan on taking several trips in one day, buy a Day Pass for $7, which entitles you to unlimited travel on that day. Sundays are really economical, since one Day Pass can be used by two adults, or by a family (two adults and four children, or one adult and five children). A monthly pass costs $88.50 for adults and $75 for students and seniors.

Bus and streetcar drivers do not give change; you can purchase tickets at subway booths and in certain stores (Shopper's Drug Mart in most malls).

For route and schedule information call ☎393-4636; for fare and general information call ☎393-TONE(8663).

By Car

Toronto is well served by public transportation and taxis, so having a car is not essential to visiting the city, especially since most of the sights are located relatively close to one another, and all of the suggested tours can be done on foot, except the tours of the north, the east and Niagara Falls. Nevertheless, it is quite easy to get around by car. Parking lots, though quite expensive, are numerous in the downtown area. Parking on the street is possible, but be sure to read the signs carefully. Ticketing of illegally parked cars is strict and can be expensive.

Things to Consider

Driver's License: As a general rule, foreign driver's licenses are valid for six months from the date of arrival in Canada.

Winter Driving: Although roads are generally in good condition, the dangers brought on by changing climatic conditions must be taken into consideration.

Driving and the Highway Code: Signs marked "Stop" in white against a red background must always be respected. Come to a complete stop even if there is no apparent danger.

Traffic Lights: Turning right on a red light after a full stop is permitted unless otherwise indicated; traffic lights are often located on the opposite side of the intersection, so be careful to stop at the stop line, a white line on the pavement before the intersection; a flashing green light is an advance light for left turners.

Streetcars travel in the centre lanes, where they have right of way. When they stop to let off passengers, you must stop as well.

When a **school bus** (usually yellow) has stopped and has its signals flashing, you must come to a complete stop, no matter what direction you are travelling in. Failing to stop at the flashing signals is considered a serious offense, and carries a heavy penalty.

Seatbelts must be worn in both the front and back seats at all times.

PRACTICAL INFORMATION

There are no tolls on Ontario highways, and the speed limit on highways is 100 km/h. The speed limit is usually 90 km/h on secondary highways and 50 km/h in urban areas.

Gas Stations: Because Canada produces its own crude oil, gasoline prices are less expensive than in Europe. However, due to hidden taxes, gas prices are higher than those in the United States and in Western Canada. Some gas stations (especially in the downtown area) might ask for payment in advance as a security measure, especially after 11pm.

Renting a Car

Vacation packages that include flight, hotel and car, or simply hotel and car, are generally less expensive than car rentals on the spot. Many travel agencies have agreements with the major car-rental companies (Avis, Budget, Hertz, etc.) and offer good deals; contracts often include added bonuses (reduced show ticket prices, for example). Package deals usually prove to be a good deal.

When renting a car, find out if:

- the contract includes unlimited kilometres or not;

- the insurance offered provides full coverage (accident, property damage, hospital costs for you and passengers, theft).

Remember:

- To rent a car in Ontario, you must be at least 21 years of age and have had a driver's license for **at least** one year. If you are between 21 and 25, certain companies (for example Avis, Thrifty, Budget) will ask for a $500 deposit, and in some cases they will also charge an extra sum for each day you rent the car. These conditions do not apply for those over 25 years of age.

- A credit card is extremely useful for the deposit to avoid tying up large sums of money, and can in some cases (gold cards) cover the insurance.

• Most rental cars have an automatic transmission, but you can request a car with a manual shift.

• Child safety seats cost extra.

Car Rental Agencies

Avis
800-TRY-AVIS
Pearson International Airport ☎(905) 676-1100
BCE Place ☎777-AVIS (2847)
Hudson Bay Centre at Yonge and Bloor ☎964-2051

Budget
Pearson International Airport T1 ☎(905) 676-0311; T2 ☎(905) 676-1500; T3 ☎(905) 676-0522
141 Bay St. ☎364-7104
1319 Bay St. ☎961-3932
150 Cumberland St. ☎927-8300

Hertz
Pearson International Airport ☎(905) 676-3241
128 Richmond St. E. ☎363-9022
Hudson Bay Centre at Yonge and Bloor ☎961-3320

Thrifty
Pearson International Airport ☎(905) 673-9308
134 Jarvis St. (at Queen) ☎868-0350
Sheraton Centre Hotel ☎862-7262
7 Erskine Ave. ☎482-1400

National Car Rental
Pearson International Airport T1 ☎(905) 676-2647; T2 ☎(905) 676-2648; T3 ☎(905) 676-4000
65 Front St. ☎364-4192
Union Station ☎364-4191

Accidents and Emergencies

In case of serious accident, fire or other emergency, dial ☎**911.**

PRACTICAL INFORMATION

If an accident occurs, always fill out an accident report. In case of a disagreement as to who is at fault, ask a police officer for assistance. Be sure to alert the car rental agency as soon as possible.

If you are planning a long trip and have decided to buy a car, it is a good idea to become a member of the Canadian Automobile Association, or CAA, which offers assistance throughout Ontario and Canada. If you are a member of an equivalent association in your home country (American Automobile Association, Automobile Club de Suisse, etc.), you can benefit from some of the services offered. For more information, contact your association or the CAA in Toronto (☎221-4300 or 222-5222).

By Taxi

Co-op Cabs: ☎504-2667

Royal Taxi: ☎785-3322

Metro/Yellow Cab Co.: ☎504-4141

On Foot

Toronto's underground city, called the **PATH**, is the largest in the country. It weaves its way under the streets from Union Station on Front Street all the way to the Atrium on Bay at Dundas Street. The perfect escape for those cold winter days, it provides access to shops, restaurants, hotels and the subway (see map).

By Bicycle

One of the most enjoyable ways to get around in the summer is by bicycle. Bike paths have been laid out to allow cyclists to explore various neighbourhoods in the city. One of the most interesting paths is the Martin Goodman Trail, which runs along the shores of Lake Ontario from High Park to the Beaches.

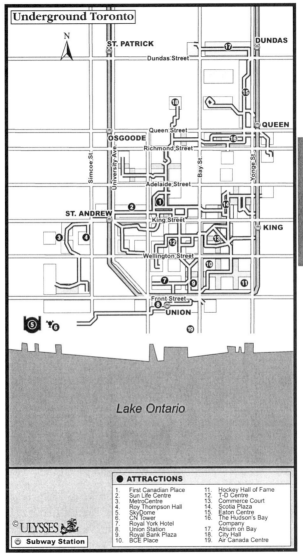

Underground Toronto

N

ST. PATRICK

DUNDAS

Dundas Street

QUEEN

Queen Street

OSGOODE

Richmond Street

Adelaide Street

ST. ANDREW

King Street

KING

Wellington Street

Front Street

UNION

Simcoe St.

University Ave.

Bay St.

Yonge St.

Lake Ontario

● **ATTRACTIONS**

1. First Canadian Place
2. Sun Life Centre
3. MetroCentre
4. Roy Thompson Hall
5. SkyDome
6. CN Tower
7. Royal York Hotel
8. Union Station
9. Royal Bank Plaza
10. BCE Place
11. Hockey Hall of Fame
12. T-D Centre
13. Commerce Court
14. Scotia Plaza
15. Eaton Centre
16. The Hudson's Bay Company
17. Atrium on Bay
18. City Hall
19. Air Canada Centre

© ULYSSES

Ⓞ **Subway Station**

PRACTICAL INFORMATION

There are two free maps of Toronto's bike paths. One is published by the Sports Swap store and is available at the store at 2045 Yonge Street *(☎481-0249)* and at the information desks at Toronto City Hall or Metro Hall. The other map is published by Metro Parks and Culture and is available at City Hall and Metro Hall *(for information: ☎392-8186)*.

Since drivers are not always attentive, cyclists should be alert, respect road signs (as is required by law) and be careful at intersections. Bicycle helmets are mandatory in Toronto. Refer to the Outdoors chapter for rental locations p 182.

In-line Skating

The growing popularity of in-line skating is particularly evident in Toronto. Unfortunately, according to the driving code, in-line skating on the streets of Canadian cities is officially prohibited. It is nevertheless tolerated on the city's bicycle paths. In-line skating fans can also flock to the Toronto Islands, where the wide bicycle paths allow for worry-free gliding. The craze over this new activity and mode of transport has lead to the opening of several specialized boutiques which sell and rent skates and all the necessary equipment that goes with them; some even offer lessons. Refer to the Outdoors chapter for rental locations, p 182.

GUIDED TOURS

Various companies organize tours of Toronto, offering visitors interesting ways to explore the city. Walking tours lead to an intimate discovery of the city's neighbourhoods, while bus tours provide a perspective of the city as a whole. Boat cruises highlight another facet of the city, this time in relation to the lake. Though the options are countless, the following companies are worth mentioning.

Tours on Foot or by Bicycle

A Taste of the World - Neighbourhood Bicycle Tours & Walks
☎923-6813
Tours of Chinatown, Cabbagetown and the Beaches are offered by Shirley Lum, an energetic Torontonian who will let you in on some little-known secrets of the city's neighbourhoods. The Chinatown tour with dim sum is a favourite.

Royal Ontario Museum
100 Queen's Park
☎586-5797
The ROM offers historic walking tours of the city.

Toronto Historical Board
205 Yonge St.
☎392-6827
These walking tours are ideal for history buffs, as visitors are lead to some of the city's most intriguing historic sites.

Ghostwalks
☎690-2825
Two night-time tours, one of the area around the University of Toronto and the other around Old City Hall, highlight more than 200 years of hauntings and folklore. In the spring and summer the tour is on foot, while in the fall and winter it is by bus!

PRACTICAL INFORMATION

Tours By Bus

Gray Line
☎594-3310
Gray Line offers several tours of the city (from 2 to 3.5 hours) as well as an excursion to Niagara Falls. The tour picks up passengers at various downtown points prior to the start of the tour, which officially begins at the bus terminal at Bay and Dundas streets.

Olde Town Toronto Tours
☎36-TOURS (368-6877)

Visitors can hop on and off this trolley at any of 15 stops along the way. The tours start every day at 8:30am in the summertime and tickets can be purchased when boarding.

Tours by Boat

Mariposa Cruise Line
207 Queen's Quay W.
☎203-0178
Daily cruises of the harbour offer another perspective of this bustling metropolis. Lunch and dinner cruises are also available.

Great Lakes Schooner Company
☎260-6355
This company offers a variety of tours in and around Toronto. You can take an extended cruise on Lake Ontario, or a tour of the harbour aboard a real tall ship.

MONEY AND BANKING

Currency Exchange

Several banks in the downtown area readily exchange foreign currency, but almost all charge a commission unless you're changing cash. There are exchange offices, on the other hand, that do not charge commission, but their rates are sometimes less competitive. It is a good idea to shop around. All banks change American money, and most of them change English money as well.

Thomas Cook Foreign Exchange
9 Bloor St. W. (at Yonge Street), ☎923-6549
218 Yonge St. (in the Eaton Centre), ☎979-1590

American Express
50 Bloor St. W. (Concourse Level), ☎967-3411
100 Front St. W. (lower level of the Royal York Hotel), ☎363-3883

Exchange Rates

$1 US	=	$1.45 CAN	$1 CAN	=	$0.68 US
1 Euro	=	$1.50 CAN	$1 CAN	=	0.66 Euro
1 £	=	$2.31 CAN	$1 CAN	=	£0.43
$1 AU	=	$0.95 CAN	$1 CAN	=	$1.04 AU
$1 NZ	=	$0.78 CAN	$1 CAN	=	$1.29 NZ
1 fl	=	$0.68 CAN	$1 CAN	=	1.46 fl
1 SF	=	$0.94 CAN	$1 CAN	=	1.06 SF
10 BF	=	$0.37 CAN	$1 CAN	=	26.83 BF
1 DM	=	$0.76 CAN	$1 CAN	=	1.30 DM
100 PTA	=	$0.90 CAN	$1 CAN	=	110 PTA
1000 lire	=	$0.78 CAN	$1 CAN	=	1,286 lire

Automatic teller machines that exchange currency have been installed at the airport. They are open every day from 6am to 2am and change various foreign currencies into Canadian money. Canadian money can also be changed into American, English and French money.

PRACTICAL INFORMATION

Traveller's Cheques

Remember that Canadian dollars are different from American dollars. If you do not plan on travelling to the United States on the same trip, it is best to get your traveller's cheques in Canadian dollars. Traveller's cheques are accepted in most large stores and hotels; however, it is cheaper and to your advantage to change your cheques at an exchange office. Traveller's cheques in American and Canadian dollars can be purchased at most banks in Toronto.

Credit Cards

Most credit cards are accepted at stores, restaurants and hotels. While the main advantage of credit cards is that they allow visitors to avoid carrying large sums of money, using a credit card also makes leaving a deposit for car rental much easier and some cards, gold cards for example, automatically insure you when you rent a car. In addition, the exchange rate with a credit card is generally better. The most commonly accepted credit cards are Visa, MasterCard, and American Express.

For lost or stolen credit cards or traveller's cheques:
American Express ☎800-221-7282
MasterCard ☎232-8020 or 800-8361-3361
Visa ☎982-5042 or 800-336-8472
Diners Club ☎800-363-3333

Banks

Banks can be found almost everywhere, and most offer the standard services to tourists. Visitors who choose to stay in Ontario for a long period of time should note that **non-residents** cannot open bank accounts. If this is the case, the best way to have ready money is to use traveller's cheques. Withdrawing money from foreign accounts is expensive. Visitors who have attained resident status, permanent or not (immigrants, students), can open a bank account. A passport and proof of resident status are required.

Money withdrawals from automatic teller machines are possible across Canada, thanks to the Interac network. Most machines are open at all times. Many machines accept foreign bank cards, so that you can withdraw directly from your account (check before to make sure you have access). Cash advances on your credit card are another option, although interest charges are higher. Money orders are a final alternative for which no commission is charged. This option does, however, take more time.

Banks are open Monday to Friday, from 10am to 3pm. Many are also open Thursdays and Fridays until 6pm, and sometimes until 8pm.

Currency

The monetary unit is the dollar ($), which is divided into cents. One dollar = 100 cents (¢).

Bills come in 5, 10, 20 and 50 and 100 dollar denominations, and coins come in 1, 5, 10 and 25 cent coins, and in 1 and 2 dollar coins.

Europeans may be surprised to hear "pennies" (1¢), "nickels" (5¢), "dimes" (10¢), "quarters" (25¢), "loonies" ($1), and sometimes even "twoonies" ($2).

MAIL AND TELECOMMUNICATIONS

PRACTICAL INFORMATION

Mail

Canada Post provides efficient mail service (depending on who you speak to) across the country. At press time, it cost 46¢ to send a letter elsewhere in Canada, 55¢ to the United States and 95¢ overseas.

There are post offices throughout the city. Stamps can be purchased at post offices and from postal counters located in some drug stores and department stores.

General Information
☎979-8822

Post Office Locations
36 Adelaide St. E.
595 Bay St.

Telephone

There are two area codes for the Greater Toronto Area. Downtown Toronto and most of the metropolitan area uses the ☎416 area code, while surrounding cities like Ajax, Kleinberg, Malton, Mississauga and Oakville use ☎905. For the most part, however, there are no long distance charges to these cities. Check in the beginning of a phone book (located in phone booths) for more precise information.

The area code for telephone numbers in this guide is 416, unless otherwise indicated.

Much cheaper than in Europe, but more expensive than in the U.S., pay phones can be found everywhere, often in the entrances of some of the larger department stores, and in restaurants. They are easy to use and some even accept credit cards. In Toronto and the surrounding area, a call costs 25¢ for unlimited time. Have a lot quarters on hand if you are making a long distance call. Calling direct from a private phone is less expensive.

Telegrams

These are sent by private companies, so it is a good idea to consult the *Yellow Pages* under the heading "telegrams". Listed below are two companies:

American Telegram
☎(800) 343-7363

AT&T Canada
☎(888) 353-4726

BUSINESS HOURS AND PUBLIC HOLIDAYS

Business Hours

Stores

The law respecting business hours allows stores to be open the following hours; it wasn't always this way, however. Toronto used to have a law, The Lord's Day Act, which forbade any businesses from opening on a Sunday!

● Monday to Wednesday from 8am to 9pm, though most stores open at 10am and close at 6pm;

● Thursday and Friday from 8am to 9pm, though most open at 10am;

● Saturday from 8am to 6pm, though most open at 10am.;

● Sunday from 8am to 5pm, most open at noon, but not all stores are open Sundays.

Public Holidays

The following is a list of public holidays in Ontario. Most administrative offices and banks are closed on these days.

January 1 and 2
Easter Monday and/or Good Friday (dates vary)
Victoria Day (the 3rd Monday in May)
Canada Day (July 1)
Civic Holiday (1st Monday in August)
Labour Day (1st Monday in September)
Thanksgiving (2nd Monday in October)
Remembrance Day (November 11; only banks and federal government services are closed)
December 25 and 26

CLIMATE

Toronto enjoys a relatively mild climate, at least compared to the rest of Canada. In the summer, temperatures can climb to above 30°C, though the average is 23°C (73°F). In the winter the temperature can drop down around -10 or -15°C, though the average temperature is -6°C; the city is usually hit with two or three big snowstorms per winter.

Weather information is available by calling the following number: ☎661-0123

Visiting Ontario during the two "main" seasons (summer and winter) is like visiting two totally different countries, with the seasons influencing not only the scenery, but also the lifestyles and behaviour of the local population.

HEALTH

Vaccinations are not necessary for the majority of visitors. On the other hand, it is strongly suggested, particularly for medium

Emergencies

- For police, ambulance and fire dial ☎**911**
- 24-hour medical emergency ☎926-7037
- Dental emergency ☎485-7121
- Hospital for Sick Children, 555 University, ☎813-1500
- Rape Crisis Hotline ☎597-8808
- Toronto Hospital emergency entrance,
    150 Gerrard St. W., ☎340-3944

or long-term stays, that visitors take out health and accident insurance. There are different types, so it is best to shop around. Bring along all medication, especially prescription medicine. Unless otherwise stated, the water is drinkable throughout Ontario.

Canadians from outside Ontario should take note that in general your province's health care system will only reimburse you for the cost of any hospital fees and procedures at the going rate in your province. For this reason, it is a good idea to get extra private insurance. In case of accident or illness, be sure to keep your receipts in order to be reimbursed.

INSURANCE

Cancellation Insurance

Your travel agent will usually offer you cancellation insurance when you buy your airline ticket or vacation package. This insurance allows you to be reimbursed for the ticket or package deal if your trip must be cancelled due to serious illness or death. Healthy people are unlikely to need this protection, which is therefore only of relative use.

Theft Insurance

Most residential insurance policies protect some of your goods from theft, even if the theft occurs in a foreign country. To make a claim, you must fill out a police report. It may not be necessary to take out further insurance, depending on the amount covered by your current home policy. As policies vary considerably, you are advised to check with your insurance company. European visitors should take out baggage insurance.

Life Insurance

Several airline companies offer a life insurance plan included in the price of the airplane ticket. However, many travellers already have this type of insurance and do not require additional coverage.

Health Insurance

This is the most useful kind of insurance for travellers, and should be purchased before your departure. Your insurance plan should be as complete as possible because health care costs add up quickly. When buying insurance, make sure it covers all types of medical costs, such as hospitalization, nursing services and doctor's fees. Make sure your limit is high enough, as these expenses can be costly. A repatriation clause is also vital in case the required care is not available on site. Furthermore, since you may have to pay immediately, check your policy to see what provisions it includes for such situations. To avoid any problems during your vacation, always keep proof of your insurance policy on your person.

ACCOMMODATIONS

A wide choice of accommodations, including 32,500 hotel rooms to fit every budget, is available in Toronto. Costs vary depending on the season. Summer is the high season, however, since Toronto is an important city for conventions it is best to book ahead of time no matter when you plan on visiting. The weekends of the Caribana Festival and the Film Festival are particularly busy as are Canadian and American holiday weekends. Prices are generally lower on weekends than during the week.

PRACTICAL INFORMATION

Depending on your mode of travel, the choice is extensive. Most places are very comfortable and offer a number of extra services. Prices vary according to the type of accommodation and the quality-to-price ratio is generally good, but remember to add the 7% G.S.T (federal Goods and Services Tax) and the provincial sales tax of 8%. The Goods and Services Tax is refundable for non-residents in certain cases (see p 80). A credit card will make reserving a room much easier, since in many cases payment for the first night is required.

Accommodation prices listed in this guide are for one night's lodging, double occupancy during the high season. The actual cost to guests is often less as many hotels and inns offer considerable discounts to employees of corporations or members of automobile clubs (CAA, AAA). Be sure to ask about corporate and other discounts as they are often very easy to obtain.

There is a reservation service at the Tourism Office in the Eaton Centre; you can also reserve accommodations by calling Tourism Ontario at ☎800-ONTARIO or Tourism Toronto at ☎800-363-1990. Packages that combine accommodations with show tickets are often available when you reserve this way.

Hotels

Hotels rooms abound, ranging from modest to luxurious. Most come equipped with a private bathroom.

Bed and Breakfasts

Unlike hotels, rooms in private homes are not always equipped with a private bathroom. There are several bed and breakfasts in Toronto. Take note that credit cards are not always accepted in bed and breakfasts. The following associations can reserve bed and breakfast accommodations in the city, whatever your needs.

Bed & Breakfast Associations

Bed & Breakfast Homes of Toronto
P.O. Box 46093
College Park Post Office
Toronto, Ontario
M5B 2L8
☎363-6362

Toronto Bed & Breakfast Inc.
P.O. Box 269
253 College Street
Toronto, Ontario
M5T 1R5
☎588-8800, ⊨927-0838

Abodes of Choice Bed & Breakfast Association of Toronto
P.O. Box 73546
509 St. Clair Avenue West
Toronto, Ontario
M6C 1C0
☎537-7629, ⊨537-0747

**Downtown Toronto Association of
Bed & Breakfast Guest Houses**
P.O. Box 190, Station B
Toronto, Ontario
M5T 2W1
☎368-1420, ⊨368-1653

Metropolitan Bed & Breakfast Registry of Toronto
650 Dupont St., Suite 113
Toronto, Ontario
M6G 4B1
☎964-2566, ⊨960-9529

PRACTICAL
INFORMATION

Motels

There are many motels, but they are usually located in the
suburbs. Though less expensive, they often lack atmosphere;
they are particularly useful when pressed for time, or when
driving into the city.

University Residences

Due to certain restrictions, this can be a complicated alternative. Residences are only available during the summer (mid-May to mid-August) and making reservations in advance is strongly recommended; these can usually be made by paying the first night with a credit card.

This type of accommodation, however, is less costly than the "traditional" alternatives, making the effort to reserve early worthwhile. Visitors with valid student cards can expect to pay approximately $20 plus tax, while non-students can expect to pay around $33. Bedding is included in the price, and there is usually a cafeteria in the building (meals are not included in the price). See the "Accommodations" section on p 75 for more detailed information.

RESTAURANTS AND BARS

Restaurants

Toronto has a cornucopia of unique restaurants to choose from. The burgeoning of the city's ethnic communities, which have managed to maintain their own cultures and niches within the city, has led to a vibrant restaurant scene with cuisines from cultures the world over. Toronto's dining scene is not only one of the finest in the country, but has a myriad of unique gems for every budget. The choices are nearly endless, with dining spots specializing not only in Japanese, Vietnamese, Italian, Greek and Indian, but in cuisines such as Ethiopian, Mauritian and Sri Lankan, as well.

Cafés

In recent years, Toronto has experienced an explosion in café culture, and has embraced the coffee phenomenon whole-heartedly. Everywhere in the city, but particularly in the trendy parts of town, there are cafés serving rich, fresh brews and special coffees from café au lait to iced mocaccino. In addition to the ubiquitous java giants such as Seattle-based Starbucks and the home-grown Second Cup, dozens of independent cafés dot the city streets, and it is here that you will find the heart of every neighbourhood. On Queen West, artists, actors and writers linger on sidewalk cafés, and even in the downtown business core office workers spend their lunch hours sipping designer brews. Many cafés serve fresh salads and gourmet sandwiches, although some have only cookies and muffins.

Bars and Nightclubs

PRACTICAL INFORMATION

Toronto has always had a vibrant underground live music scene that has only become stronger in recent years. On any night of the week there are bands from big names to local acts playing live at one of the city's many notorious watering holes. The club scene has burgeoned of late as well, and in "clubland", downtown clubs with sleek, industrial-looking exteriors and beefy bouncers outside are all the rage. Most bars do not have a cover charge unless a band is playing, but most of the clubs charge $5 to $10 for entry.

Happy Hour (two-for-one)

Bars in the downtown often offer two for one specials during "Happy Hour" (usually from 5pm to 7pm). During these hours you can buy two beers for the price of one, and drinks are offered at a reduced price. Some snack bars and dessert places offer the same discounts.

TAXES AND TIPPING

Taxes

The ticket price on items usually **does not include tax**. There are two taxes, the GST (federal Goods and Services Tax) of 7% and the PST (Provincial Sales Tax), which is 8%. They are cumulative, and apply to most items and to restaurant and hotel bills.

There are some exceptions to this taxation system, such as books, which are only taxed at 7%.

Tax Refunds for Non-Residents

Non-residents can be refunded for taxes paid on purchases made while in Ontario. To obtain a refund, it is important to keep your receipts. A separate form for each tax (federal and provincial) must be filled out to obtain a refund. The conditions under which refunds are awarded are different for the GST and the PST.

In Toronto:

- Forms are available at customs (at the airport) and certain department stores.

- For further information, call ☎800-66-VISIT (800-668-4748).

Tipping

In general, tipping applies to all table service in restaurants and to both table and bar service in bars and nightclubs (no tipping in fast-food restaurants). Tipping is also standard in taxis and hair salons.

The tip is usually about 15% of the bill before taxes, but varies, of course, depending on the quality of service.

WINE, BEER AND ALCOHOL

The legal drinking age in Ontario is 19. Beer can only be purchased at the provincially-run "Beer Store", and wine and liquor purchased at the "Liquor Store". Ontario wines can also be purchased at the Wine Rack, a chain of shops that can be found downtown and in some supermarkets. Different locations will have different hours, but on weekdays and Saturdays most beer stores are open until 9pm or 11pm, most liquor stores until

9pm or 10pm, and all Wine Rack outlets until 9pm. All three are open from 11am to 6pm on Sundays.

Beer

Ontario has a thriving micro-brewing industry that produces some fine beers. Among these, be sure to try Sleemans, Upper Canada Brewing Company, Creemore and Amsterdam.

Wine

Ontario wine has developed quite a good reputation in recent years. Most of it is produced at wineries in the Niagara region. Probably the most well-known Ontario vintage is the curious sweet dessert wine called Ice Wine. Keep an eye out for it; it makes a wonderful souvenir.

ADVICE FOR SMOKERS

As in the United States, cigarette smoking is considered taboo in Toronto and is being prohibited in more and more public places. It is illegal to smoke in an office building or in the city's transit system. A by-law was passed in Toronto in 1996 prohibiting smoking in all public places, including bars. The public outcry was so persuasive that just weeks after the by-law was passed it was repealed. Many cafés and smaller restaurants do prohibit smoking except on outdoor patios; however the majority of restaurants have both smoking and non-smoking sections and bars are as smoky as they ever have been. The issue is still on the table at City Hall, however, and was still being debated in the summer of 1999. The currently proposed changes would make all restaurants and bars 75 per cent smoke-free by 2000 and 100 per cent smoke-free by 2001, so be sure to check before lighting up!

Many public places (restaurants, tearooms) have smoking and non-smoking sections. Cigarettes are sold in bars, grocery stores and newspaper and magazine shops.

SAFETY

Violence is far less prevalent in Toronto than in most American cities. In fact, the crime rate here is lower than in any other major North American city. This doesn't mean, however, that people should not take the necessary precautions.

If trouble should arise, remember to call ☎911.

GAY AND LESBIAN LIFE

Toronto is a big city and by consequence there are countless bars, restaurants, bookstores and organizations serving the gay and lesbian community. These are mostly concentrated in the part of town known as **The Village**, located along Church Street, north and south of Wellesley Street.

There are two free newspapers that provide information about activities in and around the city. These are distributed throughout downtown in bars and restaurants. The most popular is *XTRA!*, which is published every two weeks; the other is *Fab*.

As far as general information is concerned, the people at *XTRA!* *(☎925-6665)* are very friendly and will answer any questions you might have. If they can't, they will direct you to someone who can.

Finally, there are two directories of businesses that serve the community. The first one, the *Rainbow Book*, is published by the **519 Community Centre** *(519 Church St., ☎392-6874)*, which organizes various activities and events. The second one, *The Pink Pages*, is available in bookstores and bars or by calling ☎972-7418.

Lesbian and Gay Pride Day at the end of June is a huge affair. There are a host of activities during Pride Week, culminating in Pride weekend, when the streets of the Village are blocked off for three days and filled with beer tents, stages for music and comedy performances, vendors and the 700,000 people (both gay and straight) that show up every year for the festivities and the massive Sunday parade. It is one of the city's biggest parades and one of the largest Gay Pride days in North America, rivalled only by New York's and San Francisco's.

Toronto also puts on an impressive, comprehensive **gay and lesbian film festival** called **Inside Out** annually at the end of May. For more information on Inside Out, call XTRA! (☎925-6665).

DISABLED TRAVELLERS

Tourism Toronto (☎800-363-1990) has prepared a brief information pamphlet on getting around for the wheelchair-using tourist. It is available at their information offices at Queen's Quay (see p 51).

There is another booklet called *Toronto With Ease*, which is available through the **March of Dimes** (10 Overlea Blvd., M4H 1A4, ☎425-3463, ⊷425-1920). This last organization can also provide information on services for handicapped individuals in the city.

Toronto Transit operates a wheelchair accessible bus (see p 60), and the Airport Express bus from Pearson International Airport is equipped for handicapped individuals (see p 55).

Finally, for general information, contact the **Centre for Independent Living in Toronto** at ☎599-CILT (2458).

TRAVELLING WITH CHILDREN

Children in Ontario are treated like royalty, and the wealth of activities for children in Toronto is impressive. There is plenty to keep the young busy. See the list of the top Toronto attractions for children on p 176. Facilities are available almost everywhere, whether it be transportation or leisure activities. Generally, children under five travel for free, and those under 12 are eligible for fare reductions. The same rules apply for various activities and shows. Find out before you purchase tickets. High chairs and children's menus are available in most restaurants, and a few of the larger stores provide a babysitting

PRACTICAL INFORMATION

service while parents shop; otherwise, you can contact the Daycare and Babysitting Info Line at ☎416-392-0505.

TRAVELLING WITH PETS

Dogs on a leash are permitted in most public parks in the city. Small pets are allowed on the public transportation system, as long as they are in a cage or well controlled by the owner. Pets are generally not allowed in stores, especially not food stores; however, many residents tie their pets up near the entrance while they run in. Pets are not allowed in restaurants.

MISCELLANEOUS

Time Zone

Most of Ontario, including Toronto, is in the Eastern Standard Time Zone, as is most of the Eastern United States. It is three hours ahead of the west coast of the continent. There is a six-hour time difference between Toronto and most continental European countries and five hours between Toronto and the United Kingdom. Daylight savings time goes into effect in Ontario on the first Sunday in April and ends on the last Sunday in October. All of Ontario (except the extreme western part) is on the same time.

Drugs

Non-prescription drugs are illegal and not tolerated (even "soft" drugs). Anyone caught with drugs in his or her possession risks severe consequences.

Electricity

Voltage is 110 volts throughout Canada, the same as in the United States. Electricity plugs have two parallel, flat pins (sometimes there is a third round pin, which is the ground).

Adaptors are available here in most hardware stores or Radio Shack stores, found in malls.

Language

Though English clearly predominates in Toronto, more than 100 languages are spoken in the city.

Laundromats

Laundromats are found almost everywhere in urban areas. In most cases, detergent is sold on site. Although change machines are sometimes provided, it is best to bring plenty of quarters (25¢) with you.

Movie Theatres

There are no ushers and therefore no tips. Movie listings can be found in major newspapers and free weekly papers, such as "Now" and "eye", found on street corners downtown. Ticket prices are reduced on Tuesdays.

Museums

Most museums charge admission; however, permanent exhibits at certain museums are free on Wednesday evenings between 6pm and 9pm. Special rates are offered for temporary exhibits during the same period. Reduced prices are available at any time for seniors, children and students. Call ahead to check.

Hairdressers

A tip of 15% before taxes is standard, as in restaurants.

PRACTICAL INFORMATION

Newspapers

International newspapers can easily be found in Toronto on newsstands, at Chapters and Indigo bookstores or magazine shops such as The Great Canadian News Company and La Maison de la Presse Internationale. Toronto has three major daily newspapers: *The Toronto Star*, the *Toronto Sun*, the *Globe and Mail* and the *National Post*. The latter two are national papers, with Toronto as their biggest market. There are two free weekly arts and entertainment newspapers, *Now* and *eye*, which can be picked up in restaurants and cafés or from street corner stands all over the city.

Pharmacies

Apart from the smaller drug stores, there are large pharmacy chains that sell everything from chocolate to laundry detergent, as well as the more traditional items, such as cough drops and headache medications.

Religion

Almost all religions are represented in Toronto.

Weights and Measures

Although the metric system has been in use in Canada for more than 20 years, some people continue to use the Imperial system in casual conversation. Here are some equivalents:

1 pound (lb) = 454 grams (g)
1 kilogram (kg) = 2.2 pounds (lbs)
1 inch = 2.54 centimetres (cm)
1 foot (ft) = 30 centimetres (cm)
1 mile = 1.6 kilometres (km)
1 kilometre (km) = 0.63 miles
1 metre (m) = 39.37 inches

EXPLORING

We have outlined 10 walking tours as well as two driving tours to the surrounding areas in this chapter to lead travellers on a discovery of Toronto and the neighbouring municipalities. The chapter is wrapped up with a driving tour to magnificent Niagara Falls.

TOUR A: THE WATERFRONT ★★★

Being near a major body of water often determines the location of a city, and Toronto is no exception. For many years, however, the city of Toronto neglected its waterfront. The Gardiner Expressway, the old railway lines and the numerous warehouses that disfigured the shore of Lake Ontario offered few attractions in the eyes of residents. Fortunately, large sums of money were spent to return this area to life, and it is now home to a luxury hotel, many shops and numerous cafés bustling with constant activity.

The tour makes its way from east to west along Toronto's waterfront, from the factory yards to the mega-development project of Ontario Place. Start at the corner of Queen's Quay East and Cooper Street, at the Redpath Sugar Museum.

Redpath Sugar Museum *(free admission; call for hours, ☎366-3561)* The arduous history of this staple crop is related in this small museum buried within the Redpath Refinery. You'll learn about how sugar was one of the first industries that brought African slaves to the Americas, as well as production and harvesting methods. Just about everything related to sugar and the Redpath family is presented in this fascinating museum. There are even samples!

A few blocks away at the foot of Bay Street, a ferry can take you to the Toronto Islands. The dock is just behind the Harbour Castle Westin Hotel. The Toronto Islands are the ideal spot to relax, take a little sun, go for a bike ride, take a stroll, or go for a swim. A walking tour of the islands is outlined on p 95.

● **ATTRACTIONS**

1. Redpath Sugar Museum
2. Queen's Quay Terminal
3. The Pier: Toronto's Waterfront Museum
4. Harbourfront Centre
5. Power Plant Contemporary Art Gallery
6. Du Maurier Theatre Centre
7. York Quay Centre
8. Harbourfront Antique Market
9. SkyDome
10. Air Canada Centre
11. CN Tower
12. Fort York
13. Ontario Place
14. Cinesphere / IMAX cinema
15. *HMCS Haida,*

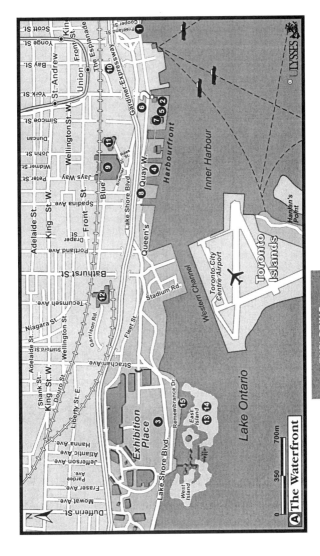

A The Waterfront

A few steps away, at the foot of York Street, is **Queen's Quay Terminal** ★★★ *(207 Queen's Quay W.)*, where boats leave for trips around the bay and the Toronto Islands (the ferries depart from the foot of Bay Street). Queen's Quay is a former warehouse that has been completely renovated and modified to house a theatre devoted exclusively to dance, as well as about 100 restaurants and shops. Among these is Tilley Endurables, founded by Alex Tilley of Toronto, designer of the famous Tilley Hat, a highly resistant piece of headgear much appreciated by lovers of the outdoors.

The Pier: Toronto's Waterfront Museum *($8.50; every day 10am to 6pm; 245 Queen's Quay W., ☎338-PIER/7437)* is the city's newest cultural heritage attraction. Located in a restored 1930 shipping warehouse, The Pier replaces and far supercedes the old Marine Museum. Young visitors will find steam whistles to pull, along with the Discovery Gallery set up inside the hull of a ship. Other fascinating displays include those on Toronto's changing shoreline and harbour, Lake Ontario shipwrecks and historic battles and simulated race against famous oarsman Ned Hanlan. Visitors can also watch artisans constructing traditional wooden boats, and even sign up for a course. Finally, you can take one of these boats out for a tour of the harbour. The short waterfront walking tours offered in summer are also interesting.

Harbourfront Centre ★ *(free admission, Queen's Quay W.; ☎973-4000 or 973-3000 for information on special events, www.harbourfront.on.ca)* is a good example of the changes on Toronto's waterfront. It is easily reached by the new Union Station trolley running west toward Spadina Avenue. Since the federal government purchased 40 hectares (100 acres) of land along the shores of Lake Ontario, dilapidated old factories and warehouses have been renovated, turning this into one of Toronto's most fascinating areas. Apart from the restaurants, shops and vistas, there is also a variety of shows and cultural events that are the pride of Torontonians.

From Queen's Quay Terminal, head over toward the lake and the **Power Plant Contemporary Art Gallery** ★ *($4, students and seniors $2, free on Wed from 5pm to 8pm; Tue to Sun noon to 6pm, Wed noon to 8pm; 231 Queen's Quay W., ☎973-4949)*, a former power plant (surprise, surprise!) that is devoted to the exhibition and interpretation of modern painting, sculpture, photography, film and videographic work. This is a non-collecting gallery, with continuous travelling exhibits. Next door is the red-brick **Du Maurier Theatre Centre** *(231 Queen's Quay W. ☎973-3000)*, behind which is the **Tent in the Park**, where various concerts and plays are presented all summer long. A little further west is the **York Quay Centre ★** *(235 Queen's Quay W., ☎973-3000)*, with restaurants and other establishments. Be sure not to miss the **Craft Studio** *(York Quay Centre, free admission)*, where you can observe craftspeople working with glass, metal, ceramics and textiles and perhaps make some purchases.

Right near Lake Ontario, sailboats and motorboats can be rented at the **Queen's Quay Yachting** *($75 or more for three hours; 275 Queen's Quay W., ☎203-3000)*, with prices varying according to the size and type of boat. Sailing lessons are also offered. In the winter, the bay is transformed into a gigantic skating rink. You can rest at one of the many bars and restaurants of **Bathurst Pier 4**, which has water sports as its theme, or go on to explore some of the sailing clubs.

The very popular **Harbourfront Antique Market ★★** is open to visitors every day except Monday *(year-round, Tue to Sun 10am to 6pm, closed Mon; 390 Queen's Quay W. ☎260-2626)*. This makes for a most interesting visit. You can spend hours perusing the countless antique shops, each one guarding some treasure or marvel you simply cannot do without.

From Harbourfront Centre, it is just a few steps to the SkyDome and the CN Tower.

SkyDome ★★ *($9.50, children 4-12 $6, children 12-17, students and seniors $7, children under 3 free; guided tours every day 10am to 4pm; tour schedules may vary according to events; 1 Blue Jays Way, Suite 2100, ☎341-3663)*, the pride of Toronto, is the first sports stadium in the world with a fully retractable roof. In poor weather, four panels mounted on rails come together in 20 minutes, despite their 11,000 tonnes, to form the SkyDome's roof. Since opening in 1989, this remarkable building has been home to the American League's Toronto Blue Jays baseball team and to the Canadian Football League's Toronto Argonauts. The new **Air Canada Centre** *($9, students and seniors $7, children 12 and under $6; hourly tours Mon to Sat 10am to 3pm, Sun 11am to 3pm; 40 Bay St.,*

EXPLORING

☎815-5500) opened near the SkyDome in the former Postal Delivery Building in early 1999. It is now the home of the Toronto Raptors, one of two Canadian-based teams in the National Basketball Association, and the National Hockey League's Toronto Maple Leafs.

Depending on the requirements of different sports, the SkyDome can be converted quickly to welcome 52,000 baseball fans or 53,000 football fans. For special events, it can fit up to 70,000 people. For concerts and other events not requiring as great a capacity, out comes the Skytent, a giant cloth that divides the stadium to improve the sound quality. Finally, no spectator, even those who get stuck in the bleachers, need miss any of the action thanks to the Jumbotron, an enormous screen 10 metres high and 33 metres wide.

So that visitors can learn more about the SkyDome's technical aspects, guided tours are offered every day *(☎341-2770)*, lasting about an hour and a half. You will see a collection of objects excavated when the foundations for the new stadium were being built in 1986, as well as a 20-minute documentary film on the SkyDome's construction titled *The Inside Story*, which relates, perhaps with a bit too much drama, how architect Roderick Robbie and engineer Michael Allen developed the concept of the retractable roof. The tour also includes a visit to the press box and a peek into one of the corporate boxes; called SkyBoxes by the marketing people, these are rented for a mere $1 million for 10 years, not counting tickets, refreshments or food!

The **CN Tower** ★★★ *(observation deck: $15.99, seniors $13.99, children 4 to 12 $10.99; to go higher to the "Skypod" is an additional $4; summer, every day 8am to 11pm; winter, every day 9am to 10pm; Front St. W. at Blue Jays Way; ☎360-8500)*. No doubt the most easily recognizable building in Toronto, the CN Tower dominates the city from a height of 553.33 metres (1,815 feet), making it the highest observation tower in the world. Built by Canadian National Railways to help transmit radio and TV signals past the numerous downtown buildings, it has become one of the city's main attractions. To avoid long lines, it is best to go early in the morning or late in the day, especially in the summer and on weekends. Postpone your visit if it is overcast.

The foot of the tower offers a panoply of activities, including two motion **simulator theatres** *($7.50 for each 8-minute ride; summer, every day 10am to 9pm; winter, every day 11am to 7pm)* that put you in the centre of such cinematic dramas as "**Dinosaur Hunter**" and "**Comet Impact**". The Maple Leaf Cinema shows a 22-minute film called "**Momentum — Images of Canada**" *($7.50)*, and there is a pay-as-you-play games arcade called the Video Edge Arcade.

You can also climb to the observation deck in an elevator that lifts you from the ground floor at a speed of six metres per second, equivalent to the takeoff of a jet aircraft. Located 335.25 metres up and set on four levels, the observation deck is the nerve centre of the tower. The first floor houses telecommunications equipment, while the second floor has an outdoor observation deck and a glass floor for those who are not afraid of heights. The third floor has an indoor observation deck and elevators (for a $2.25 supplement) up to the **Space Deck**, floating 447 metres up and forming the world's highest public observation post, with splendid views, of course. On a clear day, you can see 160 kilometres away and even make out Niagara Falls. Finally, the fourth floor has a bar and restaurant with seating for up to 400 people. Because of the great height, you may feel the tower sway in the wind. This is perfectly normal and actually enhances the resistance of the entire structure.

To continue your tour of the waterfront, head west toward Fort York. By car, you can reach Fort York along Lakeshore Boulevard, turning right on Strachan, right on Fleet Street and left on Garrison Road. Streetcar number 511 along Bathurst Street also provides easy access.

It was on the shores of Lake Ontario, at **Fort York** *($5; summer, Mon to Fri 10am to 4pm, Sat to Sun 10am to 5pm; winter every day 10am to 5pm; 100 Garrison Rd., ☎392-6907)* that Toronto was born. Built in 1783 by Governor John Graves Simcoe in response to a looming American threat, Fort York was destroyed by American invaders in 1813 and rebuilt soon afterward. As relations with the United States improved rapidly, it gradually lost its purpose. In the 1930s, the city of Toronto renovated it extensively to turn it into a tourist attraction. Nowadays, Fort York is the site of the largest Canadian collection of buildings dating from the War of 1812. A visit includes a tour of the barracks, which are furnished as they were when they housed officers and soldiers, there is also a small museum with a short informative video on the history of the fort. Guides in period dress re-enact military manoeuvres in the summer.

Several years ago, Fort York was at the centre of another battle, this one pitting the city of Toronto against real-estate developers who wanted to move the site to make way for the Gardiner Expressway. The decision to preserve Fort York's authenticity was like a wake-up call for the city of Toronto, which began to see the importance of preserving the many pieces of history throughout the city, such as its splendid streetcar system. Though the expressway and warehouses that now surround Fort York are rather uninspiring and a far cry from the waterfront location it once enjoyed, it is interesting to see how Toronto has developed from this tiny fort into the sprawling metropolis it is today.

Continuing along Lakeshore Boulevard, head just a little further west, beyond the grounds of the Canadian National Exhibition, to Ontario Place.

Ontario Place ★ *(ages 6 to 54 $22, ages 4 and 5 and over 54 $11, children under 4 free; late May to Sep, 10am to midnight; 955 Lakeshore Boulevard W., ☎314-9900; from late May to early Sep, a bus service links Union Station with Ontario Place)*. Designed by Eberhard Zeidler, Ontario Place consists of three islands joined by bridges. Five structures are suspended several metres above the water and bustle with activities for the young and the not so young. An enormous white sphere stands out clearly from the other buildings; inside is the **Cinesphere**, an **IMAX cinema** *(☎965-7722)* with an impressive six-story-high movie screen.

Ontario Place has a marina with a capacity for about 300 boats, centred around the ***HMCS Haida***, a Second World War destroyer. If you have children, head to the **Children's Village**, with its playgrounds, pool, water slides, waterguns, bumper-boats, Nintendo centre, LEGO creative centre, cinema and other attractions. The not so young will appreciate the **Forum**, an outdoor amphitheatre with various musical shows each evening.

Canada goose

Take the time to stroll alongside the lake, enjoying the sun and the fresh air. This stretch of the Waterfront is a popular stomping ground for Canada geese.

 TOUR B: THE TORONTO ISLANDS ★ ★ ★

Originally, the Toronto Islands were nothing but a sandy peninsula called by the Mississauga Indians, "place of trees standing out of the water", and frequented by Lt.-Gov Simcoe in the summer of 1793. This sandbar did afford protection to the harbour, however, and thus contributed to the choice of York as the naval and military centre of Upper Canada. A violent storm in 1858 separated the islands from the mainland, and erosion, dredging, landfill and currents have since doubled their size. Today, these 17 islands are an idyllic collection of paths, beaches and cottages.

In the early 1800s, the islands became a residential community with homes on Centre, Ward's and Algonquin Islands. Though about one hundred private homes remain, the land here is officially park land and is administered by the Parks Department. An ongoing battle between city politicians and island residents over ownership of park land remains unresolved, though the residents are apparently not in any immediate danger of being expropriated. Provincial legislation has ensured that the community will continue at least until 2005. The residents, many of whom are former hippies and flower children, claim that the cottages are part of the islands' history and that their presence makes the park a safer place, while the politicians, who see these residents as squatters, like to point out the unfortunate handful of rather run-down dwellings. Be that as it may, this little bit of drama does make for interesting fodder.

A short 8-min **ferry ride** from Toronto Harbour will take you out to the islands *(open year-round; Metro Parks general information ☎392-8186; ferry return fares $5, seniors and students $2, children under 15 $1; schedule: first ferry to Ward's Island 6:35am, last return 11:30pm; first ferry to Hanlan's Point 8:30am, last return 10:15pm, 4:15pm with cars; first ferry to Centre Island 9am, last return 11pm; call for special departure times during the rest of the year ☎392-8193; to reserve picnic sites for large groups ☎392-8188)*. Three ferries, each departing from the Mainland Ferry Terminal at the foot of Bay Street, service the three biggest islands, Hanlan's Point, Centre Island and Ward's Island; bridges connect the other islands. Bicycles are permitted on all of these ferries, except, on occasion, the Centre Island ferry, which gets very crowded on weekends.

Two licensed restaurants are located on the islands, close to the Centre Island Ferry Dock, The Island Paradise Restaurant and The Iroquois Restaurant (see p 208).

You can explore the islands on foot, by bike, on in-line skates or aboard a trackless train that runs regularly between the Centre Island Dock and Hanlan's Point, offering free historical guided tours along the way. Enjoy the fresh air: the train is one of the only motorized vehicles on the islands.

Bikes can be rented at Hanlan's Point and at the pier, while canoes, rowboats and pedal-boats can be rented on Long Pond east of Manitou Bridge.

Whatever your mode of transportation, if you have young ones in tow, make your first and second stops at the **Centreville Amusement Area** *(free admission to grounds, charge per ride, day pass)* and **Far Enough Farm** *(late Apr to mid-May, Sat and Sun; mid-May to Sep, every day; ☎203-0405)* respectively. The

A mirrored skyscraper tower over Toronto's old city hall,
which dates from 1889. – *M. Grahame*

Skating beneath the arches of Nathan Phillips Square in front of New City Hall. – *G. Jones*

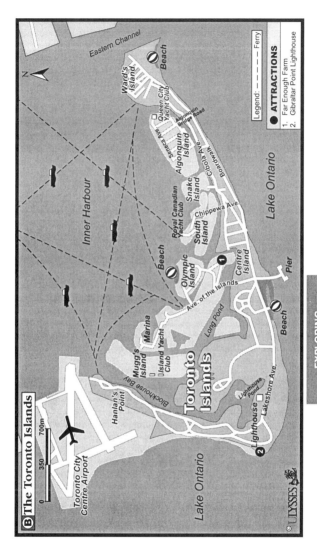

B The Toronto Islands

Legend: - - - - - Ferry

● **ATTRACTIONS**
1. Far Enough Farm
2. Gibraltar Point Lighthouse

Eastern Channel

Ward's Island

Beach

Queen City Yacht Club

Algonquin Bridge Road

Algonquin Island

Snake Island

Royal Canadian Yacht Club

South Island

Chippewa Ave.

Cibola Ave.

Boardwalk

Lake Ontario

Inner Harbour

Beach

Olympic Island

Ave. of the Islands

Centre Island

Pier

Beach

Marina

Long Pond

Mugg's Island

Island Yacht Club

Blockhouse Bay

Toronto Islands

Hanlan's Point

Lighthouse Pond

Lighthouse

Lakeshore Ave.

Toronto City Centre Airport

Lake Ontario

N

0   350   700m

© ULYSSES

EXPLORING

former is an old-fashioned amusement park built in 1833, one year before the town of York became Toronto. It boasts a classic ferris wheel, bumper cars, a log flume ride and a pretty 1890s merry-go-round. The latter is a petting zoo with barnyard animals, just a short distance beyond the amusement park, where the young ones can enjoy a pony ride.

Centre Island is and has always been the busiest of all the islands. In the 1950s, there were 8,000 people living here. The advent of Toronto Islands Park in the late 1950s and early 1960s, however, lead to the demolition of Centre Island's elegant resort hotels, theatres and shops.

The formal Avenue of the Islands extends across Centre Island from Manitou Bridge to the pier and the beach. It is lined with flower beds, reflecting pools, fountains and beautiful grassy expanses with signs inviting you to "please walk on the grass". These vast lawns are perfect for picnics. You can also continue to the end of the pier for an expansive view of Lake Ontario. From the pier follow the water and the beach to the west towards Hanlan's Point. Continue past the filtration plant and the Island Science School, where, incidentally, children can learn about life on the islands. The **Gibraltar Point Lighthouse** is the next big landmark. Built in 1806, it is Toronto's oldest remaining structure. Another sandy beach skirts the water's edge near the lighthouse, while just beyond it the trail forks. Keep left, close to the water, as you make your way to Hanlan's Point.

Hanlan's Point was originally known as Gibraltar Point and was the nucleus of York's (Toronto's) military defence mechanism. It was renamed when the Hanlans moved here in 1862. Their son Ned went on to become a championship rower. Landfill and bulldozing for Toronto Island Airport obliterated the little resort and the baseball stadium in which Babe Ruth hit his first professional home run. The beach and spectacular sunsets of Hanlan's are only slightly marred by the occasional passing plane. Aviation buffs might be interested to know that the former air terminal building of the airport, which now houses the administration offices, was recently declared a National Historic Site. It is the only such building still standing in Canada. The path ends at the ferry dock.

Retrace your steps, keeping to the left, close to the waters of Blockhouse Bay. You'll rejoin the main path again at the lighthouse; however, once at the filtration plant, turn left to follow Long Pond, where rowboats can be rented, and where the annual Dragon Boat Races (see p 258) are held. After passing the Manitou Bridge, you'll soon come upon St. Andrews-By-The-Lake Church, built in 1884 as part of the original cottage community. The sailing vessels moored to your left are part of the prestigious Royal Canadian Yacht Club, which is based here. Its presence, along with the Queen City Yacht Club on Algonquin Island, helps maintain the elegant and exclusive resort feeling of this part of the islands. Cross the bridge over to Algonquin Island to explore the pretty streets lined with cottages, several of which have been very well maintained. Street names remind visitors and residents alike that the original native inhabitants of this area also regarded the islands as a choice spot to relax.

Finally, make your way out to Ward's Island, where you'll not only find more quaint cottages but can also relax on some of the quietest and cleanest beaches on the islands. If you are lucky, one or both of the two small cafés run by island residents may be open. The Ward's Island Cafe is located close the ferry dock, while the Waterfront Cafe overlooks the boardwalk and Lake Ontario. The homes on Ward's and Algonquin are all privately owned, but they sit on land leased from Metro Toronto. The picturesque boardwalk follows the water all the way back to the pier, where you can drop off your rental bike before heading back to the city.

The ferry also runs in the winter (though less frequently), so you can visit the island year-round. Winter is actually a lovely time to come over as spectacular cross-country skiing and snowshoeing trails take the place of walking and jogging paths; there is also some great ice-skating. Summer, of course, remains the busiest time of the year as the paved, scenic trails that crisscross the islands are the delight of walkers, joggers, in-line skaters and cyclists. Remember that swimming is prohibited in the channels and lagoons. Tennis, frisbee-golf, softball diamonds and wading pools round out the other outdoor possibilities.

EXPLORING

Finally, one of the highlights of this urban oasis is certainly the spectacular view of Toronto, sparkling in the distance day and night.

TOUR C: THE THEATRE AND
FINANCIAL DISTRICTS ★★

Start at the corner of King and John. The stretch of King Street from here to Simcoe Street is also known as Mirvish Walkway (see p 102), after the father and son duo of discount-store magnates who refurbished the area by saving the Royal Alex from the wrecking ball and by filling in the empty warehouses with restaurants for theatre-goers.

The spanking new **Princess of Wales Theatre** *(300 King St. W., tickets: ☎872-1212)* was built in 1993 expressly for the musical *Miss Saigon* by none other than the Mirvishes. Though no tours are offered, it is worth taking a peak inside at the minimalist decor of moon and stars in the lobby, which is well-suited to the famous musical that still plays here.

● ATTRACTIONS

1. Princess of Wales Theatre	20. Scotia Plaza
2. Ed's Theatre Museum	21. Canadian Imperial Bank of
3. The Royal Alexandra	Commerce
4. Union Building	22. Royal Bank
5. Roy Thompson Hall	23. Canadian Pacific Building
6. Metro Hall	24. Trader's Bank
7. CBC Broadcast Centre	25. Bank of British North America
8. St. Andrew's Presbyterian Church	26. Number 15
9. Sun Life Tower	27. The Design Exchange
10. First Canadian Place	28. Royal Bank Plaza
11. Standard Life and Royal Trust	29. Union Station
12. Toronto-Dominion Centre	30. Royal York Hotel
13. Old Toronto Stock Exchange	31. Air Canada Centre
14. Bank of Nova Scotia	32. Canada Customs Building
15. National Club Building	33. BCE Place
16. Bank of Montreal	34. Hockey Hall of Fame
17. Canada Permanent Building	35. Bank of Montreal building
18. Northern Ontario Building	36. Hummingbird Centre
19. Atlas Building	37. St. Lawrence Centre

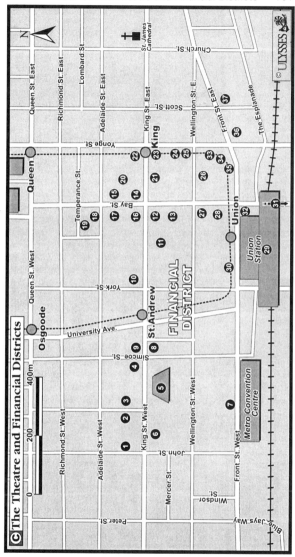

©The Theatre and Financial Districts

EXPLORING

© ULYSSES

Ed Mirvish

Ed Mirvish is a man of initiative. He was born in Virginia, but his family moved Toronto when he was nine years old. At the age of 15, his father died and Ed took over the management of the family grocery store. Mirvish's personal retail ventures would prove to be on a much grander scale, however. Garish yet delightful in all its neon splendour, his flagship **Honest Ed's** *(581 Bathurst St.)* discount store opened for business just below Bloor Street more than 40 years ago, and high volume and low markup have since been the foundations of his business. Shoppers profit from "daily door crashers" where 2-litre bottles of Coca-Cola might sell for 5¢. When zoning laws prevented Mirvish from razing the decaying mansions along Markham Street behind his store, he transformed them into **Mirvish (Markham) Village**. The buildings now house art galleries and bookstores. Mirvish is also known as a philanthropist of sorts. His growing interest in music, ballet and theatre prompted him to save the historic Royal Alexandra Theatre in 1963, and to purchase and refurbish the Old Vic in London, England. His son David now runs the Royal Alex (see p 102), and the pair recently built a brand new theatre, The Princess of Wales Theatre (see p 100) especially for the musical *Miss Saigon*.

Located upstairs from Old Ed's Restaurant is **Ed's Theatre Museum** *(open weekends only, 276 King St. W., ☎974-9378)*, where that consummate businessman, Ed Mirvish, displays his vast collection of theatre memorabilia for all to see, and to buy if you like, because yes, this is the "only museum in the world where everything is for sale"!

Continue to **The Royal Alexandra** ★★ *(260 King St. W., tickets: ☎872-3333)*. Plastered on the walls of Ed Mirvish's various food emporiums between the Princess of Wales and Royal Alexandra is a collection of newspaper articles attesting to the entrepreneur's various exploits. The Royal Alex, as it is more commonly known, was named after the king's consort. This is one of the most important theatres in the city and has been a favourite meeting place of Toronto's elite ever since it opened in 1907. Its rich Edwardian styling and beaux-arts decor of plush red velvet, gold brocade and green marble were

Roy Thompson Hall

restored in the 1960s by Toronto discount-sales magnate Ed Mirvish.

Just a few steps to the east and you'll find yourself in front of the offices of Swiss RE Holdings. This edifice is typical of the mini-Classic Revival palaces that were all the rage around 1907 when it was erected. Known as the **Union Building** *(212 King St. W.)*, it originally housed the Canadian General Electric Company.

Across the street rises **Roy Thompson Hall ★ ★** *(45-min guided tours Mon to Sat 12:30pm; $3; 60 Simcoe St., ☎593-4822)*, one of the most distinctive buildings in Toronto's cityscape. The space-age 40,000-square-foot mirrored-glass exterior was designed by Canada's Arthur Erickson and gets mixed reviews, having been compared to an upside-down mushroom and a ballerina tutu. The interior, however, is another story, boasting striking luminosity, a glamorous lobby and exceptional acoustics, which the resident Toronto Symphony and Mendelssohn Choir show off beautifully. Touted as the New Massey Hall while under construction, the hall was ultimately named after newspaper magnate Lord Thompson of Fleet, whose family made the largest single donation.

EXPLORING

A large courtyard stretches out to the west of Roy Thompson Hall and is bordered to the west by **Metro Hall** (facing the Princess of Wales), and to the south by **Simcoe Place** (the large square building to the left) and the **CBC Broadcast Centre** *(free guided tours available by appointment ☎205-8605, for information on free tickets for live tapings call ☎205-3700; 250 Front St. W.).* The Broadcast Centre opened in 1992 and quickly took its place on Toronto's skyline with its distinctive red grid-like exterior and angled façades. This is the headquarters of the English networks of the Canadian Broadcasting Corporation and the home of local French radio and television programming. A bright 10-story atrium is the focus of the lobby; free tours start here and the **CBC Museum** *(☎205-8926)* is also located here. Interactive displays highlight the history of radio and television in Canada. The Centre also houses the Granham Spry Theatre, where favourite programs are shown, and the Wayne & Shuster Comedy Wall of Fame.

Back on King Street, **St. Andrew's Presbyterian Church**, built in 1876, stands on the southwest corner of Simcoe Street. It used to share this intersection with Government House, Upper Canada College, and a rowdy watering hole, leading the corner to be known as "Legislation, Education, Damnation and Salvation". Today, its Scottish Romanesque Revival sandstone exterior contrasts sharply with the steel and mirrored glass that surround it on the way into Toronto's financial district. Ironically, the Sun Life Tower ensured the church's survival by paying some $4 million to build above and below it.

The walking tour now continues into Toronto's heart, the **financial district**, where the thing that makes many local residents run themselves ragged – money – is the leading preoccupation. The district extends between Adelaide Street to the north and Front Street to the south and between University Avenue to the west and Yonge Street to the east.

The intersection of King and Bay Streets is the symbolic and geographical centre of Toronto's financial district. The four corners of this intersection are occupied by four of Canada's five national banks: the Bank of Nova Scotia, on the northeast corner; the Canadian Imperial Bank of Commerce on the southeast; the Toronto-Dominion Bank on the southwest and the Bank of Montreal on the northwest.

Historically, high finance in Toronto has always been centred around this area. It all started at the intersection of Yonge and Wellington in the mid-1800s, when the only form of advertising available to financial organizations was architecture. Image was everything in those days, and a sense of solidity and permanence was achieved through majestic entrance halls, cornices, porticoes and the like. By the early 1900s the hub of the district had shifted north to King and Yonge, where the sleekness of Art Deco was in vogue. As the district expanded to the west, Bay Street's skyscrapers were built right up against the street, creating a northern version of the Wall Street canyon. In the last two decades, the steel and glass towers have become the centrepieces of vast windswept courtyards. In recent years these concrete parks have been in direct competition with the ever-expanding underground walkway system known as the PATH, and the debate continues as to the merits of this impersonal series of tunnels, which shuttle office workers hither and thither.

The first tower of steel and mirror, the **Sun Life Tower ★★** *(150-200 King St. W.)*, stands opposite St. Andrew's Church at the corner of Simcoe and King Streets. The sculpture in front of it is the work of Sorel Etrog. Continue along King Street to York Street. On the northeast corner stands the tower of marble known as **First Canadian Place ★**. Though its stark exterior and squat base are not very appealing, the interior commercial space is bright and airy. The **Toronto Stock Exchange ★★** *($5, seniors and students $3, children under 12 free; Mon to Sat 10am to 5pm, closed Sat in winter; no guided tours; 130 King St. W., ☎947-4676)* the focal point of Canadian high finance, is located inside. The Visitors' Centre is on the ground floor of the Exchange Tower, in the reception area. This is one of the more interesting stops in the district as visitors can watch the trading floor from an observation gallery.

Halfway between York and Bay, the **Standard Life** and **Royal Trust** buildings stand on the south side of King Street next to the impressive **Toronto-Dominion Centre ★★** *(55 King St. W.)*, on the southwest corner of King and Bay. The work of famous modernist Ludwig Mies van der Rohe, it was the first International Style skyscraper built in Toronto in the mid-1960s. These plain black towers may seem uninspiring, but the use of costly materials and the meticulous proportions have made T-D Centre one of the most renowned forms in Toronto's cityscape.

EXPLORING

The first phase of construction dates between 1963 and 1969, when two towers, 46 and 56 stories high, were erected. These modern towers gave rise to the construction of other buildings of this type in Toronto's city core, and elsewhere in Canada. In the 1970s and 1980s, three other towers (not designed by Mies van der Rohe) were built between King West and Wellington West Streets.

Stroll along Bay Street to see the beautiful Art Deco façade of the **Old Toronto Stock Exchange** *(234 Bay St.)*, which has been cleverly preserved and blends well with the surrounding skyscrapers. Its mural on the theme of "work" is especially interesting.

Continue a little further north along Bay Street

Occupying the northeast corner and extending along King is the **Bank of Nova Scotia ★** *(44 King St. W.)*, built in 1949-51 using Art Deco plans that had been shelved before the war. Heading north up Bay, you will come to the unassuming Neo-Georgian **National Club Building** *(303 Bay St.)*. The club was founded in 1874 to promote the Canada First movement, which challenged the notion of a union with the United States. On the west side of Bay is the former Trust and Guarantee Co. Ltd, now the **Bank of Montreal** *(302 Bay St.)*. A few steps farther north is the **Canada Permanent Building ★★** *(320 Bay St.)*. The splendour of the vaulted entrance and coffered ceiling seem to flout the hard times that were being ushered in in 1929, when the building was going up. The lobby is a triumph of Art Deco styling; don't miss the bronze elevator doors portraying figures from antiquity.

North of Adelaide, on the left, is the **Northern Ontario Building** *(330 Bay St.)*, a classic 1920s skyscraper. The **Atlas Building ★** *(350 Bay St.)* is next up the block. Its small lobby is decked out in lovely brass-work.

Retrace your steps and continue along King Street West

Turn left on Adelaide Street. Cross the back courtyard of the red-tinted trapezoid known as the **Scotia Plaza ★** *(30 King St. W.)* and walk through the lobby back to King Street. The façade of the Bank of Nova Scotia (see above) is visible inside this more recent addition, which fits into the surroundings harmoniously.

You will come to the **Canadian Imperial Bank of Commerce ★★** *(25 King St. W.)*, built between 1929 and 1931. With its 34 stories, it was once the tallest building in the British Empire. Today, this handsome Romanesque-Revival-style tower meshes well with its modern backdrop, Commerce Court. Step into the main hall to admire its stunning coffered ceiling, gilded moulding and wrought-iron details.

Nearby is the grand former head office of the **Royal Bank** *(2 King St. E.)*, now a retail store. Designed by Montréal architects Ross and Macdonald, it features classic Greek styling. Across King Street stands the **Canadian Pacific Building** *(1 King St. E.)*. Continuing down Yonge, you'll come to the **Trader's Bank** *(61-67 Yonge St.)*. With its 15 stories, it was Toronto's first real skyscraper when it was built in 1905. Ironically, its design sought to reduce the appearance of height in the building. The **Bank of British North America** building *(49 Yonge St.)* stands at the corner of Yonge and Wellington.

Go south on Yonge Street, then go west on Wellington Street.

Cross Yonge and Wellington Streets and make your way west along the latter. On the south side, at number 15, you'll find the oldest building on this tour. Originally the Commercial Bank of Midland District, then the Merchant's Bank, it is now simply known as **Number 15**, or depending whom you talk to, Marché Mövenpick (see p 210). Greek Revival in style, it was designed in 1845 by the same architect as St. Lawrence Hall (see p 117).

Turn left on Bay Street and walk to Front Street.

The Design Exchange *($5, seniors and students $3.50; exhibition hall: Tue to Fri 10am to 6pm, Sat and Sun noon to 5pm; 234 Bay St., ☎216-2160 for information)*. Known locally as the DX, the Design Exchange houses an exhibition hall, for which admission is charged, and the Design Effectiveness Centre, which is free and open on Saturdays as well. Exhibits of international and national designers are presented in the restored former Toronto Stock Exchange. Besides the latest in

EXPLORING

fashion, graphic design and ergonomics, the DX also boasts the original historic trading floor and spectacular murals and friezes.

Head back down Bay to Wellington for the next stop on the tour, the lavish and imposing **Royal Bank Plaza ★★** *(200 Bay St.)*. The gold-enriched mirrored exterior is like a breath of fresh air in the midst of the sober white-collar demeanour of Toronto's financial district, especially at twilight; the gold actually acts as an insulator, keeping the warmth in in the winter and the heat out in the summer. Two triangular towers are linked by a clear glass atrium abounding in lush tropical greenery, below which extends an underground shopping complex.

Make your way towards Front Street and Union Station.

Union Station ★★ *(65-75 Front St. W.)* dominates Front Street from Bay Street to York Street. It ranks first among Canadian railway stations for its size and magnificent appearance. It was built in the spirit of the great American railway terminals, with columns and coffered ceilings inspired by the basilicas of ancient Rome. Work on the station began in 1915 but was completed only in 1927. This was one of the masterpieces of Montréal architects Ross and Macdonald. Its façade on Front Street stretches more than 250 metres, hiding the port and Lake Ontario in the background.

The **Royal York Hotel ★** *(100 Front St. W.)* is a worthy introduction to downtown Toronto for anyone arriving by train at Union Station. Its message to new arrivals is clear: the Queen City is indeed a major metropolis that will play second fiddle to nobody. This hotel, the biggest in the Canadian Pacific chain, has more than 1,500 rooms on 25 floors. Like the station, it was designed by Montréal architects Ross and Macdonald. Here the château style of the railway hotels is combined with Lombard and Venetian elements (see p 189).

Heading south along York Street, you will reach the Air Canada Centre *(40 Bay St.)* (see p 91). Officially opened in 1999, it now houses the city's hockey team, the Toronto Maple Leafs.

Retrace your steps.

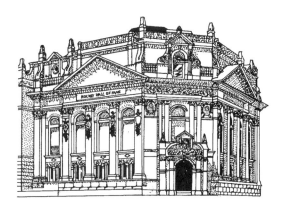

Hockey Hall of Fame

From the Royal York Hotel at the corner of York and Front Streets, continue east along Front Street. At the corner of front and Bay rises the Royal Bank Plaza (see above). Further along, the **Canada Trust Tower** is on the left and the **Canada Customs Building** on the right, at the southwest corner of Front and Bay.

Enter **BCE Place** ★★ by the courtyard located east of the Canada Trust Tower. BCE Place stretches from Bay Street to Yonge Street and is made up of twin towers linked by a magnificent five-story glass atrium supported by an enormous structure of white metal ribs. This bright and airy space is a delightful place to rest for a few moments or grab a bite from the ground-floor fast-food counters. For something unique, head instead to the **Marché Mövenpick** (see p 210), a happy blend of restaurant and market where diners move from stall to stall, choosing the dishes that seem most appealing. The Chamber of Commerce building, built in 1845, has been well preserved and blends harmoniously into its modern backdrop.

BCE Place also encloses the entrance to the famous **Hockey Hall of Fame** ★ *($12, seniors and children 4 to 18 $7, children under 4 free; Mon to Fri 10am to 5pm, Sat 9:30am to 6pm, Sun 10:30am to 5pm; 30 Yonge St., ☎360-7765, www.hhof.com)*, a veritable paradise for hockey fans. All sorts

EXPLORING

of items from the beginnings of this sport up to the present are on display. The layout includes 13 zones, which cover 51,000 square feet, the size of three NHL playing surfaces. Do not miss the Bell Great Hall, at the centre of which is the original Stanley Cup, North America's oldest professional sports trophy, donated by Lord Stanley of Preston in 1893. More than 300 plaques pay homage to the various players who have made their mark in professional ice hockey. Once inside the museum you'll see a reconstitution of the Montréal Canadiens' dressing room as well as some of hockey's most exciting moments on video screens. Other exhibits present the evolution of hockey equipment through the decades, with goaltender's masks, hockey sticks, skates and sweaters bequeathed by the greats.

Exit BCE Place onto Yonge Street.

At the corner of Yonge and Front Streets is the old building of the **Bank of Montreal ★★**. The Hockey Hall of Fame is actually located in this building, though the only entrance is through BCE Place. Built in 1886 by architects Darling and Curry, the Bank of Montreal building is one of the oldest 19th-century structures still standing in Toronto. Designed during a prosperous and optimistic period, its architecture conveys a sense of power and invulnerability that was typical of the era, with imposing masonry, splendid porticoes and gigantic windows. Until the construction of a new building in 1982, this was the Bank of Montreal's headquarters in Toronto.

At the southeast corner of Yonge and Front Streets is the **Hummingbird Centre**, also known as the **O'Keefe Centre**. With 3,200 seats, it is one of Toronto's most important theatre ballet and opera centres. One block east, the **St. Lawrence Centre** also serves as a site for many concerts and plays each year. Despite its imposing façade, it has a very intimate interior.

The eye-catching mural to the east is the starting point of the walking tour of the Old Town of York.

 TOUR D: OLD TOWN OF YORK ★

It was in the rectangular area formed by George, Berkley, Adelaide and Front Streets that Commander John Graves

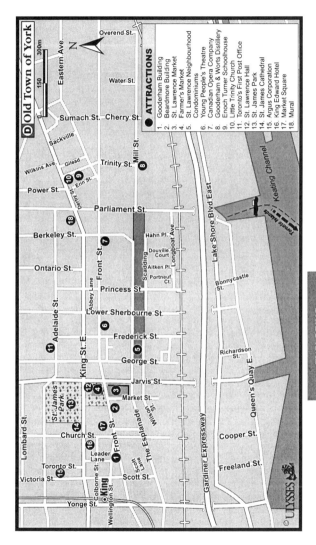

D Old Town of York

EXPLORING

● ATTRACTIONS

1. Gooderham Building
2. Beardmore Building
3. St. Lawrence Market
4. Farmer's Market
5. St. Lawrence Neighbourhood Condominiums
6. Young People's Theatre
7. Canadian Opera Company
8. Gooderham & Worts Distillery
9. Enoch Turner Schoolhouse
10. Little Trinity Church
11. Toronto's First Post Office
12. St. Lawrence Hall
13. St. James Park
14. St. James Cathedral
15. Argus Corporation
16. King Edward Hotel
17. Market Square
18. Mural

© ULYSSES

Hogtown

What may be Toronto's most typical Victorian factory stands at the corner of Frederick and Front Street. Built in 1867, the red-brick building with its yellow-brick window arches originally housed the William Davies & Co. pork packing plant, and its operations are what lent Toronto one of its early nicknames, "Hogtown."

Simcoe of the British army founded the town of York, better known today as Toronto, in 1793. This area near Lake Ontario was for many years the business centre of the growing city. At the end of the 19th century, economic activity slowly moved toward what is now known as the financial district (see p 104), leaving behind a partially deserted area. Like Harbourfront (see p 90), the St. Lawrence district has undergone major renovations over the last couple of decades, financed by the federal, provincial and municipal governments. Today a cheerful mixture of 19th- and 20th-century architecture characterizes an area where the city's various socio-economic groups cross paths.

Beyond Berczy Park is the amusing *trompe l'oeil* fresco painted on the back of the **Gooderham Building ★** *(49 Wellington St.)*. This mural, created by Derek Besant in 1980, has become a well-known sight in Toronto. Contrary to popular belief, it does not portray the windows of the Gooderham Building but rather the façade of the Perkins Building, located across the street at 41-43 Front Street East. The Gooderham is often called the Flatiron Building because of its triangular structure, recalling the shape of its famous New York namesake, which it predates by several years. The building's shape was dictated by the fact that it sits on a triangular lot at the corner of Wellington Street, which follows the grid pattern established by the British during the founding of York, and Front Street, which runs parallel to the north shore of Lake Ontario. Built for George Gooderham, a businessman who made his fortune in distilleries, this building stands out for its mural and for its castle-like architecture. It still houses many offices.

Gooderham Building

Look back now from where you came and contemplate the interesting vista formed by the Flatiron Building framed by the office towers of the financial district and the CN Tower.

Across Front Street, many of the gleaming façades that now harbour shops and cafes are those of one-time warehouses. The **Beardmore Building** *(35-39 Front St. E.)* is one of the more noteworthy of a series of buildings that once formed the heart of the warehouse district in the middle of the 19th century.

EXPLORING

At the corner of Jarvis Street is the **St. Lawrence Market ★★** *(91 Front St. E.)*. Built in 1844, it housed the city hall until 1904, the year Henry Bowyer Lane converted it into a public market. Expanded in 1978, St. Lawrence Market is famed today for the freshness of its fruits and vegetables, fish, meats, sausages and cheeses. Actually, this giant red-brick building completely envelops the former city hall, which is still perceptible in the façade. The best time to go is on Saturday, when the fish is freshest and area farmers arrive at 5am to sell their products across the street at the **Farmer's Market**. The **Market Gallery** on the second floor presents historical and contemporary exhibits on the ever-changing face of Toronto, with photographs, maps and paintings. The collection is part of the City of Toronto archives.

These days, the St. Lawrence neighbourhood is seen as a trendy area to live in. Named after a saint, like many of the working-class neighbourhoods in the area, St. Lawrence was a mainly Irish Protestant area of factories, warehouses, and simple housing. Until recently, these buildings stood neglected, but many have recently been or will be transformed into upscale condominiums and office space. One such project, aptly named the **St. Lawrence Neighbourhood Condominiums** (along The Esplanade, south of the market) and completed in 1982, has brought people back to this area. The place looks modern, yet its many low-rise buildings, designed by different teams of architects, retain a distinctly Victorian feel and blend harmoniously into the pre-existing urban landscape.

Walk back up to Front Street East on George Street or Frederick Street.

Toronto's **Young People's Theatre** *(165 Front St. E.)* is located a few steps to the east. What once provided shelter for the horses of the Toronto Street Railway Co. now sets the stage for excellent theatre productions for young people (see p 254).

The **Canadian Opera Company** *(239 Front St.E.)*, for its part, is located in an old factory built in 1888, which originally housed the Consumers' Gas Company. The lovely brickwork and stepped gables are an excellent example of how magnificent even a factory could be in the Victorian era. The motivation behind this grandeur is the same as that which prompted the opulence of the Old Bank of Commerce and the meticulousness of Toronto-Dominion Centre, both on King: the need to impress the customer. The factory has since been transformed into a rehearsal hall.

Continue along Front Street, turn right on Parliament, then left on Mill Street and walk one block to the Gooderham & Worts Distillery.

Gooderham & Worts Distillery *(55 Mill St.)*. Much of the area surrounding the Gooderham & Worts Distillery remains as it was in the mid-1800s and is a fine example of a typical Victorian working-class neighbourhood. Though several sectors have been transformed and gentrified, the distillery remains, and a stroll around it is like stepping back in time. Originally, grain was ground here, but soon after interests turned to distilling. Spirits still run the place (perhaps both figuratively and literally), as rum is produced from molasses here.

Walk up Trinity Street towards King Street.

Pretty little Trinity Street was once home to many poor Irish Protestant workers, who up until 1848 had to pay to send their children to St. James's school, something that many of them could not afford to do. In 1848, the Ontario government authorized free schooling, and many children that had simply gone without finally had access to free education. In Toronto, however, the city council found the notion too radical. Enoch Turner, a brewer and employer of many of the local residents, thus had Trinity Street School built in 1848 at his own expense. The charming soft yellow- and red-brick edifice was eventually transformed into a Sunday school for Trinity Church (see below) after being absorbed by the city in 1851, which finally conceded and accepted to offer free education. The **Enoch Turner Schoolhouse ★ ★** *(donations appreciated; Mon to Fri 10am to 4pm, weekends by appointment; 106 Trinity St., ☎863-0010)* is the oldest standing school building in Toronto, and the first free school in the city. It currently houses a small exhibit.

Just up the street, **Little Trinity Church ★** *(425 King St. E.)* was built for members of the local Anglican community, who could not afford the pew rents at St. James. The church, with its enchanting yet simple Tudor Gothic styling, occupies this corner almost magically.

EXPLORING

As you make your way back west along King Street East, you'll pass yet more factories and warehouses that have been rehabilitated as restaurants, cafés, office buildings and even the headquarters of the Toronto Star *(333 King St. E.)*, one of the city's daily newspapers. Notice the amusing **mural** ★ painted on the side of the building.

Did you know that Mr. Christie's cookies began in Toronto? Now one of the world's most renowned cookie manufacturers and owned by Nabisco brands, Mr. Christie's first bakery was here on King Street East. The horses that delivered the cookies were stabled at 95 Berkeley Street, just up from King, and the cookies were made farther along King at number 200. The bakery is no more, though; the building now houses the St. James campus of George Brown College.

Up on Adelaide Street stands the town of York's first bank, the **Bank of Upper Canada** *(252 Adelaide St. E.)*. At the time of its completion in 1827 the limestone structure dominated the unpaved streets of "Muddy York", as the town was known; the building certainly must have instilled hope and confidence in the residents of the fledgling city. The bank unfortunately failed in 1866, at which point the Christian Brothers moved in and started a Roman Catholic boys' school, the De La Salle Institute, which lasted until 1916.

At number 260 is **Toronto's First Post Office** ★ *(free admission; Mon to Fri 9am to 4pm, Sat and Sun 10am to 4pm; 260 Adelaide St. E., ☎865-1833)*. This old post office has been designated a national historic site. It was opened in 1843 during the British postal period, which lasted until 1851, when Canada Post came into existence. The place is still a working post office, with a clerk in period dress; besides the regular postal services, you can send a letter sealed with authentic be-ribboned hot wax.

Back down on King Street, the row of buildings at number 167-185, though constructed at different times, is the oldest "line" of buildings in Toronto. The yellow brick that you see on the façade of number 150 is common throughout Toronto. Fire ordonnances required the use of brick, and the "white" variety, as it was called at the time, was not only inexpensive because of the nearby claypits, but was also thought to resemble stone, which was much more costly.

Kitty-corner stands impressive **St. Lawrence Hall** ★ *(151 King St. E.)*, which was Toronto's community centre in the latter half of the 19th century. This Victorian structure was designed for concerts and balls. Among the celebrities who performed here were Jenny Lind, Andelina Patti, Tom Thumb and P.T. Barnum. For several years, St. Lawrence Hall was also home to the National Ballet of Canada.

Lovely **St. James Park**, a 19th-century garden with a fountain and seasonal flower beds, lies a few steps to the west. While seated on one of its many benches, you can contemplate **St. James Cathedral** ★★, Toronto's first Anglican cathedral, at the corner of Church and King Streets. Built in 1819 with help from a government loan and with the alms of the faithful, it was destroyed in the 1849 fire that levelled part of the city. The St. James Cathedral you see today was built on the ruins of its predecessor, according to a design by architect Frederick Cumberland, who wanted to invoke religious superiority. It has the highest steeple in all of Canada and the second highest in North America, after St. Patrick's Cathedral in New York. The yellow brick façade accentuates the gothic shapes of the cathedral, giving it a rather sober character. The interior is far more elaborate. The marble choir stall, where Bishop Strachan is interred, is truly magnificent.

Continue west along King Street, turning right at Toronto Street.

Toronto Street was one of the city's most beautiful streets in the 19th century. Nowadays, some buildings still provide a glimpse of the charm and elegance this street once radiated. Note the **Argus Corporation** building *(10 Toronto St.)*, with its portico of four symmetrical Ionic columns and its neoclassical architecture resembling a Greek temple. This building served as the Toronto post office, a customs office and a branch of the Bank of Canada before being transformed into offices.

Retrace your steps back to King Street.

The splendid **King Edward Hotel** ★★ *(37 King St. E.)* (see p 191), between Church Street and Leader Lane, was designed in 1903 by E.J. Lennox, architect of Old City Hall (see p 122), Massey Hall (see p 120) and Casa Loma (see p 155). With its Edwardian style, its wonderful mock marble columns on the

EXPLORING

ground floor and its magnificent dining rooms, the King Edward was one of Toronto's most luxurious hotels for nearly 60 years, until, with the decline of the surrounding area, it fell into disrepair. Today, with the revitalization of the neighbourhood, the King Edward is once again drawing a fashionable clientele with its superb rooms and its two wonderful restaurants.

Return now toward St. James Cathedral, in front of which extends the **Toronto Sculpture Garden**. Walk through the garden and back to Front Street, admiring the various sculptures along the way. Once back on Front, you'll find yourself at **Market Square ★** *(80 Front St. E.)*, right next to the city's first market. Of more recent construction, it was designed to blend in with the historic surroundings. Market Square houses numerous shops and luxury apartments.

 TOUR E: QUEEN WEST ★★

This tour starts at the corner of Yonge and Queen Streets, where Queen West begins. **The Bay** department store occupies the southwest corner and the whole south side of the street all the way to Bay Street. The building originally housed the Simpson's department store, until hard economic times forced its closure and most Simpson's stores became Bays. Simpson's was the largest retail establishment in Canada in 1907, when the nine-story addition along Queen was added. The original six-story building (1895) at Yonge and Queen features some lovely terra cotta decorations. An Art Deco addition in 1928 lead to glamorous renovations throughout the store, a fine example being the entrance at Richmond and Yonge.

Head north on Yonge Street. On the left is the exterior of the six-story shopping mecca, the Eaton Centre; on the right you'll soon come upon two more of Toronto's majestic theatres, the Elgin and Wintergarden and the Pantages.

Before visiting the Elgin and Wintergarden, take a look at the **Bank of Montreal** *(173 Yonge St.)* on the corner. This stylish Edwardian building dates from 1909.

The **Elgin and Wintergarden Theatres ★★** *(one-hour tours, $4, seniors $3; Thu 5pm, Sat 11am; 189 Yonge St., ☎314-2901*

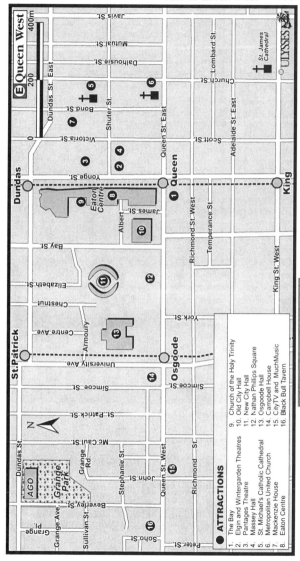

EXPLORING

● **ATTRACTIONS**

1. The Bay
2. Elgin and Wintergarden Theatres
3. Pantages Theatre
4. Massey Hall
5. St. Michael's Catholic Cathedral
6. Metropolitan United Church
7. Mackenzie House
8. Eaton Centre
9. Church of the Holy Trinity
10. Old City Hall
11. New City Hall
12. Nathan Phillips Square
13. Osgoode Hall
14. Campbell House
15. CityTV and MuchMusic
16. Black Bull Tavern

or 872-5555) together form the last operating double-decker theatre complex in the world. Opened in 1914, they began as vaudeville theatres; the Elgin downstairs was opulence galore, while the Wintergarden upstairs was one of the first "atmospheric theatres", with trellised walls and columns disguised as tree trunks supporting a ceiling of real leaves. After a stint as a movie house, these treasures were restored by the Ontario Heritage Centre and now once again serve as venues for live stage performances.

The **Toronto Historical Board** *(205 Yonge St., ☎392-6827)* presents ongoing exhibits on the history and development of the city of Toronto, as well as an exhibit celebrating the 200th anniversary of Yonge Street, the longest street in the world, with photographs, maps and drawings. The building is a former Bank of Toronto building.

Once the biggest vaudeville house in the British Empire, the **Pantages Theatre ★** *(one-hour tours Sat 10:30am; $4; 263 Yonge St., ☎362-3218)* had many reincarnations as a picture palace and then a six-theatre movie house. In 1988-89, it was restored to its original splendour. It is perhaps best-known, however, as the home of Andrew Lloyd Webber's *Phantom of the Opera*. This grandiose production is first-class, and the show and venue complement each other wonderfully.

Backtrack down Yonge Street, turn left at Shuter Street and walk two blocks to Massey Hall.

Massey Hall *(178 Victoria St., at Shuter St., ☎593-4828 or 872-4255)*, originally Massey Music Hall, is renowned for its exceptional acoustics. Though the Toronto Symphony Orchestra has moved out (see p 252), Massey Hall is still a venerable venue for musical acts.

Two of Toronto's great churches lie one block to the east.

Although there were relatively few Catholics in Toronto in the 19th century, they nevertheless had **St. Michael's Catholic Cathedral** *(57 Bond St.)* built between 1845 and 1867. This building lacks the presence of the Anglican cathedral or the nearby United church, and the sometimes overbearing architecture of Victorian Catholic churches is evident in the multiple openings of the spire, the massive dormers and the polychrome interior. The faux starred vault was completed in 1870. To the south, facing Queen Street, the **Metropolitan United Church ★** (1870) is seen as a challenge to both the St. James Anglican (see p 117) and Roman Catholic cathedrals and thus represents the commercial and social power of Toronto's Methodist community (the Methodists, along with the Congregationalists and two-thirds of the Presbyterians formed the United Church in 1925). Due to its grand proportions and location in the middle of a block-square park, it dominates the area.

Continue up Bond Street towards Dundas, stopping in at Mackenzie House along the way.

By 1837, fruitless attempts at establishing responsible government and growing impatience with England had left the Canadian colony in crisis. The colonial emancipation movement was lead by Louis-Joseph Papineau in Lower-Canada (Quebec) and by William Lyon Mackenzie in Upper Canada (Ontario). Mackenzie had arrived in Toronto from Scotland in 1820. Before becoming the city's first mayor, he ran a newspaper called *The Colonial Advocate*, which so enraged the Family Compact (see p 19), that his print shop was ransacked and his type dumped in Lake Ontario. After losing the mayorship in 1836, he lead an abortive rebellion against the oligarchy, then fled to the United States. **Mackenzie House ★** *($3.50, seniors and students $2.75, children 12 and under $2.50; Tue to Sun noon to 5pm; 82 Bond St., Dundas subway, ☎392-6915)*, a modest Georgian-style residence built in 1857, was offered to him by a group of followers upon his return in 1859. The Toronto Historical Board has since restored the house and now maintains a museum here. Guides in period dress re-enact the daily life of a middle-class Toronto household in the 1860s. The odd placement of the house is due to the fact that it was once part of a row of identical residences. It is furnished with antique furniture and also features a reconstruction of Mackenzie's print shop, complete with the offending printing press. Mackenzie's grandson was William Lyon Mackenzie King, Canada's longest serving Prime Minister.

Walk along Dundas to Yonge Street and turn left.

Even if you have no desire to go shopping, at least poke your head into the **Eaton Centre ★★**, which runs along Yonge

EXPLORING

Street between Queen and Dundas. And if you do need something, by all means linger in this glass-roofed arcade which even a few sparrows have decided is more pleasant than outside. Here, so-called streets have been stacked five-stories high and lined with pristine benches and trees. Look up and you will see Michael Snow's exquisite flock of fibreglass Canada geese, called *Step Flight*, suspended over the Galleria. Framed by two 30-story skyscrapers and two subway stations (Dundas and Queen Stations) and occupying six million square feet, the Eaton Centre contains more than 320 stores and restaurants, 2 parking garages and a 17-theatre cinema complex. It is also home to the **Thomson Gallery** *(9th floor of The Bay tower at the Eaton Centre)*, which exhibits the private collection of the exceedingly wealthy owner of The Bay and the *Globe and Mail*.

Once you've had your fill of the shops, exit the Eaton Centre via Trinity Square, at the northwest corner of the mall.

This lovely space was almost never created. The **Church of the Holy Trinity ★★** (1847), the **Rectory** (1861) and the **Scadding House** (1857) are some of Toronto's oldest landmarks, and the original plans for the Eaton Centre called for their demolition. Fortunately, enough people objected and the huge mall was built around the grouping. Holy Trinity was a gift from an anonymous woman in England who stipulated that free seating be guaranteed in the church. Its excellent acoustics helped create the beautiful music on the Cowboy Junkies album *The Trinity Session*. The rectory and the house of Rev. Henry Scadding, the first rector of Holy Trinity, complete the vista. The latter was moved to make way for the Eaton department store.

Head down James Street towards the back of **Old City Hall ★★** *(60 Queen St. W.)*, designed by E. J. Lennox in 1889. As you make your way around the building towards the front on Queen Street, look up at the eaves below which the architect carved the letters "E J LENNOX ARCHITECT" to ensure that his name would be remembered. Lennox won a contest to design the building but the city councillors denied his request to place his name on a cornerstone; in retaliation, he had disfigured versions of their faces carved above the front steps so that they would be confronted with their gargoyle-like selves every day! By the time all of these personal touches were revealed, it was too late to do anything about them.

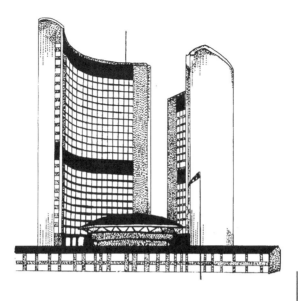

New City Hall

EXPLORING

The vast sandstone edifice was built on a square plan around a central square and is probably the most exacting example of Richardsonian neoclassicism in Canada. The style was developed in the 1870s and 1880s in the United States by architect Henry Hobson Richardson and was based on French Romanesque. It defined itself by a use of mass and volume and rough surfaces. The numerous vaulted openings are framed by small engaged columns, lending a medieval and picturesque air to buildings of this style. Its elegant clock tower rises above the centre of Bay Street, the hub of high finance in Toronto.

In 1965, the municipal administration of Toronto moved out of its Victorian "old" city hall and into **New City Hall ★★** *(100 Queen St. W.)*, a modernist masterpiece that quickly gained a certain notoriety and is as symbolic of Toronto as the CN Tower. A contest was held to choose an architect and the winner was Finn Viljo Revell, a master of Scandinavian postwar rationalist thinking. Its two curved towers of unequal length are like two hands protecting the saucer-shaped structure which houses the Council Room.

Stretching out in front of New City Hall is **Nathan Phillips Square ★**, a vast public space named after the mayor of Toronto who blessed Toronto with many new installations at the beginning of the 1960s. A large pool of water straddled by three arches is transformed into a skating rink in the winter. Nearby stands "The Archer", a sculpture by Henry Moore, and the Peace Garden, designed in 1984 by the Urban Design Group. This small green space serves as a frame for the Eternal Peace Flame, which flickers in a half-destroyed shack that reminds us of the effects of war and symbolizes the population's desire for peace.

Cast-iron gates enclose **Osgoode Hall ★★** *(116-138 Queen St. W.)* and its shaded garden, reminiscent of a royal palace of the British Empire, though it was originally built to house the Law Society of Upper Canada and the provincial law courts. Built in stages from 1829 to 1844 by different architects, its façade nevertheless forms a lovely ensemble. Its layout is in the Palladian style, though the decorative elements are those of an Italian Renaissance palace, as was the fashion with London high society at the time. The neoclassical vestibule and the magnificent law library can be visited by checking at the ticket office at the entrance.

Not far from Osgoode Hall, **Campbell House ★** *(160 Queen St. W.)* was the private club of a select group of Ontario lawyers, the Advocates Society. The house was built in 1822 for Judge William Campbell and is one of the oldest in Toronto. Its brick façade combines traditional Georgian elements with Adamesque fantasy, like the oval bull's-eye window of the pediment, which lightens the structure. The inside, open to visitors, is decorated with lovely woodworking and mantlepieces with delicate trimming typical of the art of the Adam brothers, the Scottish pair who swept Great Britain with their antiquated refinement at the end of the 18th century.

Make your way along Queen Street West, lined with trendy shops, cafés and bars for most of its length. It is also the home of **CityTV** and **Muchmusic** *(299 Queen St. W.)*, "the nation's music station". The former Wesley Building was built for a publishing company in 1913-15; note the grotesque readers and scribes that adorn its façade. Renovated in 1986 to accommodate Muchmusic, the Canadian counterpart to MTV, the building is now a beehive of activity, with "v-jays" often animating their shows right on the sidewalk and a televised fashion-show-cum-dance-party known as the "Electric Circus" every Friday night. Another intriguing feature is the Speakers' Corner video booth where you can request a video and applaud or criticize whatever cause you like, and maybe even end up on national television.

Stroll along **Queen West** ★★ and browse through the hip and avant-garde boutiques and bookstores. Queen Street Village, as it is often called, is touted as an "alternative shopping district", and while it has its share of the peculiar and underground, the last few years have seen the opening of several very mainstream clothing stores and cafes (places like The Gap, Roots and Second Cup spring to mind!). All the better, some might say, at least this way there is something for both the *artiste* and the conformist in you. Not to mention, when it comes to dining out, there are still as many unpretentious, simple eateries as there are places to see and be seen. There are even a few interesting architectural highlights, as most of these shops and restaurants occupy late 19th-century buildings where Victorian details survive on the upper floors.

The corner of Soho and Queen is often packed with motorcycles, the riders of which congregate at the **Black Bull Tavern** *(298 Queen St. W.)*. This tavern began as an inn way back in 1833. Number 371-373, now the Peter Pan Restaurant (see p 216), was built in 1890 and originally housed a grocery store. It boasts some lovely stained glass. Numbers 342 to 354 are collectively known as the Noble Block (1888), after Mrs. Emma Noble, a widow who once owned the property.

Queen Street West, west of Spadina, has yet to take on the slick "Queen Street Village" look that characterizes the couple of blocks to the east. The antique and junk shops, used record stores, and independent, family-run businesses still hold sway over the stretch between Spadina and Bathurst, but the territory is slowly being encroached upon by trendy bistros and funky nightclubs. This is certainly not a bad thing, but take this opportunity to stroll the sidewalks of Queen West and experience them before they are transformed forever.

EXPLORING

TOUR F: CHINATOWN AND KENSINGTON ★★★

Toronto has no fewer than seven recognized Chinatowns. The most vibrant and typical of these is explored in this walking tour. While the neighbourhood is presently centred around Spadina and Dundas, it actually started a few blocks east of there, near where New City Hall now stands. The construction of the municipal headquarters and the laying of Nathan Philips Square obliterated most traces of this original Chinatown; a few vestiges do remain, however, making this a good place to begin the tour. If you are setting out to visit this area on a Sunday, get an early start, for Sunday is the day when most Chinese families head out for brunch, though they call it dim sum, and there are no scrambled eggs or baked beans to wade through!

The area just south of New and Old City Halls was at one time a staging area for new immigrants to Toronto. Most of the new arrivals from China settled and established their businesses close by, thus founding the city's first Chinatown. At the northwest corner of Nathan Philips Square, if you look hard enough, you can find a small plaque commemorating the first Chinese hand-laundry in Toronto. Walking up Centre Street to Dundas Street, you'll notice that a few Chinese businesses remain.

Museum for Textiles ★ *($5, seniors and students $4, children under 12 free; Tue to Fri 11am to 5pm, Wed until 8pm, Sat and Sun noon to 5pm; 55 Centre Ave., ☎599-5515)* With 11 permanent exhibits, this museum tells you everything you ever wanted to know about textiles from around the world. Costumes, ceremonial cloths, tapestries, fascinating African story-telling cloth and rich embroideries are all on display. Devoted to non-western cultures, most of the exhibits are rather extraordinary.

Walk west along Dundas Street, across University Avenue towards McCaul Street.

The **St. Patrick's Chinese Catholic Church** *(131 McCaul St.)* stands at the corner of McCaul and Dundas Streets. The church originally served a mostly Irish congregation, but the parish changed considerably as Chinatown gradually moved

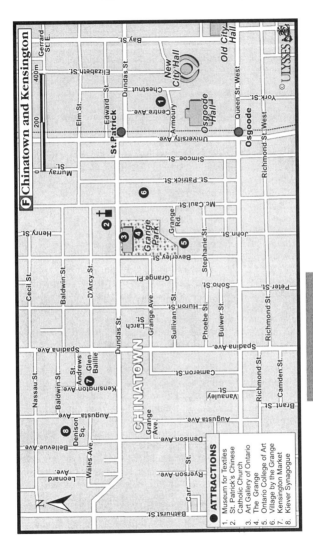

F | Chinatown and Kensington

● ATTRACTIONS

1. Museum for Textiles
2. St. Patrick's Chinese Catholic Church
3. Art Gallery of Ontario
4. The Grange
5. Ontario College of Art
6. Village by the Grange
7. Kensington Market
8. Kiever Synagogue

EXPLORING

westward. The original wooden chapel that stood on this site in the 1860s was among the first Roman Catholic churches in Toronto. The Romanesque Revival building before you today was erected in 1905.

The Art Gallery of Ontario is on the south side of Dundas, just west of McCaul Street.

The Art Museum of Toronto was founded in 1900, but was without a permanent home until 1913, when The Grange (see below) was bequeathed to the museum. A new building was added in 1918, and the first exhibition of Canada's renowned Group of Seven (see p 38) was held in 1920 at what was by then known as the Art Gallery of Toronto. A significant chapter in Canada's and Toronto's cultural histories was thus written. In 1966, the museum received provincial support and was officially re-baptized the **Art Gallery of Ontario** ★★★ *(permanent collection is "pay what you can", temporary exhibits have a separate varying fee; Tue to Fri noon to 9pm, Sat and Sun 10am to 5:30pm; 317 Dundas St. W., ☎977-0414)*. Successive renovations and additions over the years have each tried to reinvent the AGO, adding new elements and hiding old ones. The Gallery is now laid out in a collection of buildings, which were successfully united in 1989 by architects Barton Myers and Associates, and finally do justice to the splendid treasures they contain, collections donated by wealthy Ontarians over the years.

The 1989 renovations known as Stage III added close to 50 percent more exhibition space. The permanent collection is now installed chronologically from the 15th century to the present day. It features contemporary art, Inuit sculptures and the beautiful Tanenbaum Sculpture Atrium, where a façade of The Grange is exposed. The Henry Moore Sculpture Centre is one of the museum's greatest treasures. Donated by the artist himself, it is the largest public collection of Moore's work in the world. The Canadian historical and contemporary collections contain major pieces by such notables as Cornelius Krieghoff, Michael Snow, Emily Carr, Jean-Paul Riopelle, Tom Thomson and the Group of Seven — Frederick Varley, Lawren Harris, Franklin Carmichael, A. Y. Jackson, Arthur Lismer, J. E. H. MacDonald and Frank H. Johnson. The museum also boasts masterpieces by Rembrandt, Van Dyck, Reynolds, Renoir, Picasso, Rodin, Degas and Matisse, to name a few.

Adjacent to the Art Gallery of Ontario stands its original home, **The Grange ★** *(admission with AGO; May to Oct, Tue and Thu to Sun noon to 4pm, Wed noon to 9pm; Oct to May, Wed noon to 9pm, Thu to Sat noon to 4pm; 317 Dundas St. W., ☎977-0414)*. The Georgian-style residence was built in 1817-18 by D'Arcy Boulton Jr., a member of Toronto's ruling elite, the much-reviled Family Compact. The city of Toronto was barely thirty years old at the time, but by 1837, the year of Mackenzie's rebellion, The Grange had become the virtual seat of political power and thus symbolized the oppressive colonial regime in Upper Canada. In 1875, Goldwin Smith, an Oxford scholar, took up residence here. Seen as a liberal intellectual in his day, his suspicion of other religions and races have since revealed him to be a bigot. He nevertheless entertained some very eminent visitors at The Grange, including a young Winston Churchill, the Prince of Wales (later Edward VII) and Matthew Arnold. When Smith died in 1910, he willed the house to the Art Museum of Toronto, which occupied it for the next 15 years. The gallery then used it for offices until 1973 when its 1830s grandeur was restored and the whole house was opened to the public. It rear façade was integrated into the AGO's sculpture gallery in 1989. This gentleman's house, with its grand circular staircase and fascinating servant's quarters, was one of Toronto's first brick buildings.

The **Ontario College of Art** *(100 McCaul St.)* once occupied the look-alike building east of The Grange. The college's more recent addition faces McCaul Street. Its vibrant interior lay out features displays on animation, design, advertising art, tapestry, glassblowing, sculpture and painting.

Village by the Grange *(89 McCaul St.)* is an apartment and shopping complex with ethnic fast-food, shops and minor art galleries. Many rave about this spot's architecture and its hidden treasures, and while there are all sorts of neat things to be seen, smelled, eaten and purchased here, the commercial level is labyrinthine and in need of freshening up, and the fast-food is bit too fast in some places. For a quick break or bite to eat, though, it is perfectly fine.

After an edifying morning of art appreciation, make your way east along Dundas Street into the heart of Chinatown for some food and shopping.

EXPLORING

Bright colourful signs, packed sidewalks, Canto-pop piercing the air, racks of roasted ducks, the wonderful scents of fresh fruit or ginseng tea and the pungent odours of durian and fresh or dried fish; Chinatown is a feast for the senses in every way, so by all means, slow down and give yourself the time to soak up the atmosphere. Allow yourself to be drawn in by the marvellous and curious things you see in the shop windows; you won't regret it. Asian grocery stores, herb shops, tea shops and trading companies galore — not to mention the many divine little, and not so little, eateries — ensure that this tour will have something to please everyone! On Sundays, many restaurants serve dim sum (see p 222).

Just a few of the wonderful shopfronts you'll pass on the way are the Tai Sun Co. (407 Dundas St. W.) grocery store, which has a good selection of vegetables, especially mushrooms. A few doors down is the Ten Ren Tea House (454 Dundas St. W.), with green tea, black tea and oolong, plus miracle teas that promise to help you lose weight, among other things. You can also pick up a traditional clay teapot, and if you're lucky someone will be performing the ancient tea ceremony. Next door, WY Trading Co. has a wide selection of the latest Chinese records, CDs and tapes. The All Friends Bakery (492 Dundas St.) sells sweet and delicious lotus- or ginseng-filled moon cakes that are to die for.

The wonders continue on Spadina. Note the large yellow building at the southwest corner of Dundas and Spadina; it has a rather curious story. A series of failed businesses came and went, then reports of hovering ghosts finally prompted the building's owners to call in a feng shui specialist. Feng shui, which means "wind and water", is an ancient Chinese type of geomancy. An unbalanced alignment of doors and windows, design flaws or an incorrect lot placement can spell disaster for a building's success according to fung shui. In this case, the fung shui expert found that the billboard on the east side of Spadina just north of Dundas was reflecting negative energy onto the front of the building. A new door was therefore placed on the Dundas side of the building, thus relocating its front façade. Furthermore, the two stone lions on Spadina were put in place to guard the original entrance. The building has yet to house a successful business, and commercial activity here seems limited to the t-shirt and luggage vendor who essentially sells from the street.

At least three other commercial stops are in order on Spadina. The first one is the Great China Herbs Centre *(251 Spadina)*, where a Chinese doctor may be able to heal what ails you with a wonderful concoction prepared with the mysterious ingredients found in the hundreds of meticulously labelled drawers and jars that line the walls. These are weighed out on an old-fashioned scale and the price is clicked off with amazing rapidity on a real abacus. Your next stop should be Dragon City Mall *(280 Spadina)*, an Asian shopping mall with an interesting food court, among other things. Finally, be sure to stop in at one of the few old shops that have been here since the neighbourhood was almost exclusively Jewish.

Head west of Spadina towards Kensington Market.

Kensington Market ★★★ is located on Kensington Avenue, one street west of Spadina, between Dundas and Oxford Streets. This bazaar epitomizes Toronto's multi-ethnicity: what began as a primarily Eastern European market is now a wonderful mingling of Jewish, Portuguese, Asian and Caribbean cultures. The lower half of Kensington is mostly vintage clothing shops, while the upper portion boasts international grocers peddling fresh and tasty morsels from all over the world. Perfect for picnic fixings!

The run-down, yet jazzed-up old Victorian row houses and the sidewalks along Kensington from Dundas to St. Andrews are a gold-mine to those for whom all things old are like gold. Used Levi's, leather bomber jackets, sheepskin coats and psychedelic polyester shirts can all be bought for great prices. Courage My Love *(14 Kensington)*, Exile *(number 20)*, Black Market *(number 24)* and Noise *(number 47)* carry some unique merchandise. Besides the opportunity to complete your retro wardrobe, this part of Kensington also conceals treasures like incense, natural oils and exotic art.

Making your way north, you'll enter the more edible part of Kensington, where the treasures are just as exotic, if not more so! Creameries, fish markets, meat markets, cheese markets and spice markets fill the air with a bouquet of aromas. The window of Cheese from Around the World offers a sampling of the great prices and great selection inside. Mendel's Creamery, a veritable institution next door, sells great dill pickles, pickled herring and a wide variety of cheeses. Up on Baldwin Street,

EXPLORING

the catch of the day at the Madeiro Fish Market often comes from West Indian waters. The heaps of spices at Salamanca are just the thing to add that extra little zing to your favourite recipes.

Turn left on Augusta Avenue and right on Denison Square.

Built in 1927, the **Kiever Synagogue ★** *(28 Denison Sq.)* is one of the last synagogues in this area that still has regular services. At one time there were as many as 30 temples in this neighbourhood. Its geometric stained-glass windows provide inspiration to the Congregation Rodfei Sholom Anshei Kiev, which means Men of Kiev, as well as visitors.

Return to Augusta Avenue and turn left.

Around Baldwin Street, the sights and sounds of Portugal become ever more present at places like the Iberia Bakery and the Sagres Fish Market. To be sure you don't miss anything wander up to Oxford. Finally, make your way back to Spadina along Nassau Street, where still more unique shops and shopkeepers vie for your attention and your dollars.

Perhaps you have gathered the fixings for a fine homemade meal along this tour; if not, take a walk along Baldwin Street through Chinatown's residential area. Keep an eye out for the distinctive red and yellow banners on some of the houses, as well as the small medallions placed here and there on their façades to ward off the negative energy. This street is home to some fantastic little bistros and restaurants. See "Restaurants", p 222.

TOUR G: QUEEN'S PARK AND
THE UNIVERSITY OF TORONTO ★★★

Each of the ten provinces has its own legislative assembly. Ontario's is located in the **Provincial Parliament ★★** *(1 Queen's Park)*, located at the centre of Queen's Park in the middle of University Avenue. The red sandstone building (1886-1892) was designed in the Richardsonian neo-Romanesque style (see Old City Hall, p 122) by architect Richard A. Waite of Buffalo, who is also responsible for several Canadian buildings, including the old headquarters of the Grand Trunk Railway on McGill

Provincial Parliament

Street in Montreal (the Gérald-Godin building). Notice the amusing crowning towers of the central part of the parliament; they exhibit the inventiveness of 19th-century architects, who were preoccupied with eclecticism and the picturesque. Before entering, take a walk around the building to explore the typical 1890s public spaces with their intricately sculpted dark wood exteriors.

The forty or so buildings of the **University of Toronto** ★★ *(between Spadina Rd. to the west, Queen's Park Cresc. to the east, College St. to the south and Bloor to the north)* are spread about a vast and very green English-style campus. Awarded a charter in 1827, the institution didn't really get going until the construction of its first building in 1845 (no longer standing). However, religious rivalries slowed down the progress of the university as each denomination wanted its own institution for higher learning. In the following decade there were six universities, each one barely getting by. It wasn't until partial unification in the 1880s that the campus began to expand. Today, the University of Toronto is one of the most respected institutions of higher learning in North America.

EXPLORING

From Queen's Park Crescent West, walk around Hart House Circle.

Among the many university buildings, **Hart House** ★ *(7 Hart House Circle)* is particularly noteworthy. Its Great Hall is the social hub of the university. Donated by the Massey Foundation, Hart House was an undergraduate men's activity centre until 1972, when women were finally allowed to become members. It was designed by architects Sproatt & Rolph in the Gothic style; the Soldiers' Memorial Tower, by the same architects, was added in 1924.

Continue around the circle to King's College Circle.

The lovely Victorian **Students' Administrative Council Building** *(12 Hart House Circle)* was built in 1857. It is often called the Stewart Observatory after one of its reincarnations, but originally housed the Toronto Magnetic and Meteorological Observatory and stood on the other side of the Front Lawn. It was moved and reconstructed in 1908.

The oldest building of the original university is **University College** ★ *(15 Kings College Circle)*, built in 1859 by architects Cumberland and Storm. The result is a picturesque neo-Romanesque ensemble with remarkably detailed stone carving. The Norman portal is particularly magnificent. Neo-Romanesque was something new in Canada at the time and thus was not associated with any specific religious or social movements. It therefore met the needs of the university leaders, who wanted to create a secular environment, open to everyone. This philosophy did, however, lead some to refer to University College as the "godless college." **Knox College** *(23 King's College Circle/59 George St.)* has pretty leaded casement windows and a rough sandstone exterior. It is a favourite with movie producers.

The imposing circular hall where King's College Circle joins King's College Road is the university's **Convocation Hall** *(31 King's College Circle)*. Attached to this are the administrative offices of the university, located in **Simcoe Hall** *(27 King's College Circle)*.

Walk down King's College Road to College Street.

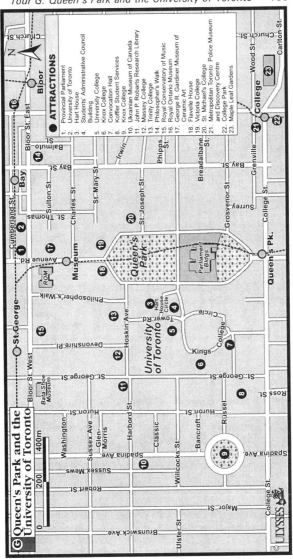

G Queen's Park and the University of Toronto

ATTRACTIONS

1. Provincial Parliament
2. University of Toronto
3. Hart House
4. Students' Administrative Council Building
5. University College
6. Knox College
7. Convocation Hall
8. Koffler Student Services
9. Knox College
10. Ukrainian Museum of Canada
11. John P. Robarts Research Library
12. Massey College
13. Trinity College
14. Philosopher's Walk
15. Royal Conservatory of Music
16. Royal Ontario Museum
17. George R. Gardiner Museum of Ceramic Art
18. Flavelle House
19. Victoria College
20. St. Michael's College
21. Metropolitan Toronto Police Museum and Discovery Centre
22. College Park
23. Maple Leaf Gardens

ULYSSES

EXPLORING

When the University of Toronto was founded in 1827 it sat at some distance from town. Access to the 160-acre wooded campus was gained along University Avenue and College Street, both private roads belonging to the university for some time. College was ceded to the city as a public thoroughfare in 1889. Among the huge pavilions that line the street today, the **Koffler Student Services** ★ *(214 College St.)* (1906) is particularly noteworthy. Originally the Public Reference Library, it owes its existence to American philanthropist Andrew Carnegie, who financed the construction of hundreds of public libraries in the United States and Canada.

Continue along College Street to Spadina, and turn right.

Spadina is 149 feet across, making it twice as wide as the rest of Toronto's early streets. The avenue was laid out in 1802 by William Warren Baldwin, whose house stood where Casa Loma now reigns. At the time, the road provided an unimpeded view of the lake and the burgeoning town of York to the south. As you look north now, however, you'll notice that the view is now broken by a crescent, in the middle of which stands a richly Victorian Gothic Revival building. This is the original **Knox College** *(1 Spadina Cresc.)*, founded in 1844 when Baldwin's granddaughter sold the land to this Presbyterian theological seminary. It was one of the many sectarian schools that would eventually join the University of Toronto. The college relocated to St. George street in 1915 (see further above).

Continue up Spadina to Harbord Street.

The **Ukrainian Museum of Canada** (Ontario Branch) *(free admission, donations appreciated; Tue to Fri 1pm to 4pm; 620 Spadina Ave., ☎923-3318)* presents the colourful heritage of the Ukrainian peoples who arrived in Canada with the opening of the west. Several stunning traditional costumes and Ukrainian Easter eggs make up part of the display.

Walk east along Harbord Street.

The Athletics Centre and New College are on your right, while further along, at St. George, where Harbord becomes Hoskin, is the **John P. Robarts Research Library** *(130 St. George St.)*. This strange-looking building is often referred to as Fort Book, and some architects say you have to see it from a helicopter to truly appreciate it... go figure!

Across St. George are the towers of the Newman Centre, next to which is **Massey College** *(4 Devonshire Place)*. Built in 1963, the latter successfully marries a medieval atmosphere with modern architecture.

Head over towards **Trinity College** *(6 Hoskin Ave.)*, which blends with Knox College, the Stewart Observatory and Hart House, all to the south (see further above), to create a romantic **ensemble of English Gothic buildings ★**. Designed by architects Darling and Pearson (1925), Trinity boasts a lovely chapel that is the work of Sir Giles Gilbert Scott, well known for his cathedral in Liverpool. These last four buildings, with their many stone ribs, leaded windows and peaceful courtyards, were inspired by the pavilions of Oxford and Cambridge.

Immediately to the east, stroll up the winding road called **Philosopher's Walk ★**. The Taddle Creek once flowed where the philosopher now walks, as the sounds of music students practising their scales at the Conservatory waft over the clamour of busy Bloor Street. A contemplative stroll next to the newly planted oak trees leads to the Alexandra Gates, which originally guarded the university entrance at Bloor and Queen's Park.

To the left along Bloor, you'll see the highly Victorian exterior of the **Royal Conservatory of Music** *(273 Bloor St. W.)*, with its dormers, chimneys and corbels. This building originally housed Toronto Baptist College.

Walk east along Bloor Street and turn left on Queen's Park to the entrance of the ROM.

The **Royal Ontario Museum ★★★** *($10, seniors and children $4, children $5, families $22; Mon and Wed to Sat 10am to 6pm, Tue 10am to 8pm, Sun 11am to 6pm; 100 Queen's Park, ☎586-5549 or 586-5551; Museum subway; parking is expensive)* is actually two museums in one since admission to the ROM, as it is called, also includes admission to the George R. Gardiner Museum of Ceramic Art (see below). Canada's largest public museum, as well as a research facility, the ROM preserves some six million treasures of art, archaeology and

EXPLORING

natural science. After extensive renovation and restoration and the opening of new galleries, the ROM is now able to display these treasures in a manner befitting their inestimable worth. Upon entering the impressive free-Romanesque-style building, visitors' eyes are drawn up to the Venetian glass ceiling, which depicts a mosaic of cultures. The ceiling is the only part of the museum that was not built using materials from Ontario. As you continue into the museum, your gaze will be drawn up once again by the towering totem poles flanking the lobby, one of which is 80 feet (24.4 m) tall, and whose top reaches just six inches (15.2 cm) below the ceiling! With exhibits on everything from bats to dinosaurs and Romans to Nubians, your first stop should be the Mankind Discovering Gallery, where the layout and workings of the ROM are explained. Visitors have a somewhat mind-boggling range of choices, including the Dinosaur Gallery, a favourite with amateur palaeontologists of all ages; the Maiasaurus exhibit, an ongoing project where onlookers can observe palaeontologists reconstructing a real dinosaur skeleton; the Evolution Gallery; the Roman Gallery, displaying the largest collection of its kind in Canada; the Textile Collection, one of the best in the world; the East Asian galleries, where you'll find one of the museum's most precious gems: the Chinese Art and Antiquities Collection, containing a Ming Tomb and the Bishop White Gallery, whose walls are covered with Buddhist and Daoist paintings; the Discovery Gallery, a treat for children, with hands-on displays featuring authentic artifacts; the Ancient Egypt Gallery and Nubia Gallery, which boast the consummate and ever-intriguing mummies and ancient relics; the Sigmund Samuel Canadiana Collection of decorative arts, recently relocated to the ROM from the campus of the University of Toronto; and the last big crowd-pleaser, the Bat Cave, a walk through an all too realistic replica of the St. Clair limestone cave in Jamaica, complete with all too realistic replicas of swooping bats. The possibilities of discovery and exploration at the ROM are endless!

Cross Queen's Park to the next attraction.

On the east side of Queen's Park Avenue, the **George R. Gardiner Museum of Ceramic Art ★★★** *($5, seniors, students and children $3, families $12, Tue are free; Tue 10am to 8pm, Wed to Sat 10am to 5pm, Sun 11am to 5pm; 111 Queen's Park, ☎586-8080)* boasts a striking collection of porcelain and pottery. Four galleries span history from the pre-Columbian

Mayans and Olmecs to European treasures of the last 500 years. These last pieces include Italian porcelain from the 16th and 17th centuries, Delftware from the 18th, as well as delicate pieces and whole services from such great names in china as Meissen, Derby, Doulton and Vienna. Particularly noteworthy is the renowned Swan Service – a stunning 2,200-piece set.

Make your way down Queen's Park to Queen's Park Crescent East.

Note **Flavelle House** ★ *(78 Queen's Park)* on the right. Built in 1901 for Joseph Flavelle, this was for many years the grandest of Toronto's mansions. It is now used by the university's faculty of law.

Continue around Queen's Park Crescent to Victoria College and St. Michael's College.

The rich, finely crafted Romanesque **Victoria College** ★ *(73 Queen's Park)* is very inviting for a scholarly building; it is just one of the buildings of Victoria University. This grouping, which includes Burwash Hall rimming the site to the east and north, Annesley Hall on Queen's Park and Emmanuel College to the west, is considered one of the finest on the University of Toronto campus.

The collection of buildings that make up the University of St. Michael's College occupy a lovely site at the corner of Queen's Park and St. Joseph Street. This Catholic school was founded by the Basilian Fathers from France; **St. Michael's College** *(50 St. Joseph St.)* and **St. Basil's Church** *(50 St. Joseph St.)*, both built in 1856, were its earliest buildings. The college was the first to affiliate itself with the University of Toronto in 1881, and thus claims the oldest buildings on campus. They predate University College (see above) by three years.

Walk down Bay Street to College Street.

The **Metropolitan Toronto Police Museum and Discovery Centre** ★ *(donations requested; every day 9am to 9pm; police headquarters 40 College St., ☎324-6201)* highlights policing from the era of Muddy York to the days of bicycle-riding cops.

Unique exhibits on how to find clues in blood and dirt samples at a crime scene, fingerprinting, famous crimes, old uniforms, a police cruiser and an old-fashioned paddy-wagon will make super-sleuths out of visitors. Young sleuths can even try to solve a crime.

Eaton's department store was originally located in a collection of individual buildings on Queen Street; then, in 1930, it moved to the Art Deco wonder at the corner of Yonge and College Streets, now called **College Park** *(444 Yonge St.)*. Much of the Art Deco detailing survived the successful transformation into shops, offices and apartments that followed Eaton's relocation when the Eaton Centre was built in 1977. These are visible on the shopping concourse, but above all in the superb seventh-floor concert hall. A pretty pool of water that becomes a skating rink in the winter is located in back.

Cross Yonge Street, where College Street become Carlton Street, and walk over to Church Street.

Toronto's Maple Leaf Gardens *(guided tours in summer only: $7, students and seniors $5, children 12 and under $4; Tue to Sat 11am, 12:30pm, 2pm, 3:30pm, Sun 12:30pm, 2pm, 3:30pm; 60 Carlton St., ☎815-5956)* was home to the National Hockey League's Toronto Maple Leafs for almost seven decades until early 1999. But although the Leafs have since moved to their new home in the Air Canada Centre (see p 91), many fans still associate the heart of their beloved Leafs with the Gardens. The start of the 1931 hockey season forced 700 workers to scramble to finish this yellow-brick box in just over 12 months! A 45-minute guided tour includes a stop at centre ice and a look at the dressing room.

 # TOUR H: BLOOR AND YORKVILLE ★

Start at the corner of Bloor and University Avenue, known as Avenue Road north of Bloor.

The Royal Ontario Museum (see p 137) lies on the southwest corner; across the street on the southeast corner is a neoclassical Revival building originally known as the Lillian Massey Department of Household Science, whose mandate

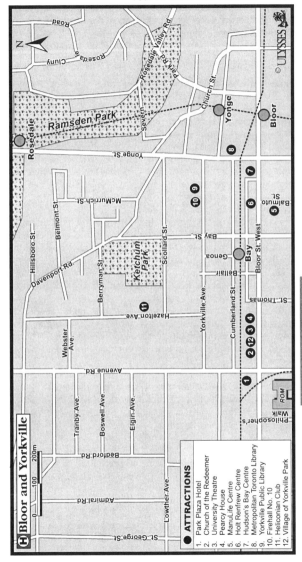

H Bloor and Yorkville

● **ATTRACTIONS**
1. Park Plaza Hotel
2. Church of the Redeemer
3. University Theatre
4. Pearcy House
5. ManuLife Centre
6. Holt Renfrew Centre
7. Hudson's Bay Centre
8. Metropolitan Toronto Library
9. Yorkville Public Library
10. Firehall No. 10
11. Heliconian Club
12. Village of Yorkville Park

EXPLORING

© ULYSSES

was the education of young women in the management of a household. More recently it housed the Provincial Ombudsmen, but is now the home of a mammoth Club Monaco clothing store!

Speaking of clothing stores, get set for a whirlwind shopping tour of posh Bloor & Yorkville!

This tour covers the area around Bloor and Yorkville, two names that are now synonymous with the expensive, the up-scale and the trendy. The area north and west of Bloor and Bedford was once the Village of Yorkville, incorporated in 1853 and existing as a separate town until 1883, when it was annexed to the city of Toronto. It was a stylish bedroom community that lay within a short distance of the growing metropolis to the south. However, the encroachment of that metropolis eventually saw the transformation of many of Yorkville's and Bloor's loveliest homes into office space and a relocation of the city's elite to more exclusive areas farther north. For the first half of this century this area was a middle-class suburb. The first signs of the area's trend-setting status began to appear in the postwar era, as the 19th-century residences were transformed into coffeehouses and shops, and Yorkville became the focus of Canada's folk music scene. The gentrification of the area took off in the seventies and eighties, and on Bloor Street multi-purpose complexes and high-rises have sought to make optimal use of now outrageously high rental costs.

The luxurious **Park Plaza Hotel** *(4 Avenue Rd.)* (see p 195), built in 1926, stands on the northwest corner of Avenue and Bloor. The rough stone walls, sweeping slate roof and belfry of the **Church of the Redeemer** *(162 Bloor St. W)* occupy the northeast corner. Rising behind it is the **Renaissance Centre**, which, though it dominates the church, also gives it a commanding presence over this busy corner. The **Colonnade**, to the east, was the first building on Bloor to combine commercial, residential and office space.

The stretch of Bloor Street from Queen's Park/Avenue to Yonge is a collection of modern office buildings, shopping malls and ultra-chic boutiques and galleries including such notables as Holt Renfrew, Chanel, Hermès, Tiffany's and Hugo Boss. According to some, Bloor Street is Toronto's Fifth Avenue, so

make your way along it as quickly or as leisurely as you wish
(see "Shopping" p 272). Most of Bloor Street's façades are
clearly more recent additions, though some have been
preserved and jazzed up in keeping with the chic boutiques that
have moved in. Two interesting buildings, however, await
transformation. The curved façade of the former **University
Theatre** *(100 Bloor St. W.)* and the modest red-brick Neo-
Georgian façade of **Pearcy House** *(96 Bloor St. W.)* are all that
remain of these two buildings, which now apparently house a
parking lot. At one time the plan was to transform the two into
the venue for Toronto's annual film festival, but for now,
parking is paying the bills.

East of Bay Street is the **ManuLife Centre** *(55 Bloor St. W.)*,
which combines residential, office and commercial space.
Streetfront shops line the sidewalk under the Centre's curious
cantilevered overhang. Across Bloor Street is the **Holt Renfrew
Centre** *(50 Bloor St. W.)*, home to this classy department store
as well as a shopping mall. Finally, the **Hudson's Bay Centre**
(2 Bloor St. E.) occupies the busy crossroads at Bloor and
Yonge.

*At Yonge Street, turn left and head towards the trendy
Yorkville area.*

Before hitting the shops, you'll come upon the **Metropolitan
Toronto Library** *(789 Yonge St.)* on the corner of Yonge and
Asquith, a large building of brick and glass that is very popular
with Torontonians. It does not look like much from the street,
but inside a profusion of plants and bright spaces make it feel
just like home. The building was designed by architect
Raymond Moriyama in 1973.

Heading west along Yorkville Avenue now, you'll come to the
grand **Yorkville Public Library** *(22 Yorkville Ave.)*, built in 1907
and remodelled in 1978. The bold porticoed entrance still
dominates the façade just as it did when this library served the
Village of Yorkville.

Right next door is the old **Firehall No. 10 ★** *(34 Yorkville Ave.)*,
built in 1876 and then reconstructed (except for the tower,
used to dry fire hoses) in 1889-90. This red and yellow brick
hose house once served the village of Yorkville and is still in
use. The coat of arms on the tower was salvaged from the

EXPLORING

town hall; the symbols on it represent the vocations of the town's first councillors: a beer barrel for the brewer, a plane for the carpenter, a brick mould for the builder, an anvil for the blacksmith and a bull's head for the butcher.

As you browse through the shops, take a look at the Georgian-style houses at **numbers 61-63** and **77**, the Queen Anne porch of **number 84**, the Victorian house that once served as the Mount Sinai Hospital at **number 100** (and is now awaiting the renovating hands of a good-willed developer) and finally the jazzed-up row of Victorian houses at **numbers 116-134**.

An exceptional collection of galleries, shops and cafés line Yorkville, Hazelton and Cumberland. More architectural gems, too numerous to list, remain on Hazelton Avenue. These have all been faithfully restored, some so well that they look like new buildings; nevertheless, the results are aesthetically pleasing and worth a look. Of particular note are **Hazelton House** *(33 Hazelton Ave.)*, which originally housed the Olivet Congregational Church at the end of the 19th century and now contains shops, galleries and offices, and the Carpenter Gothic-style **Heliconian Club**, a women's arts and letters club founded in 1909.

After exploring Hazelton Avenue, continue along Yorkville and turn left on Avenue Road.

If you have the time and the inclination you can explore the many lovely houses west of Avenue Road, between Avenue and Bedford. For the most part, they remain residential and the area is therefore indicative of what Yorkville was like before the developers and trendsetters.

The north side of Cumberland Street, between Avenue Road and Bellair Street, is lined with fancy boutiques and galleries, while the south side has recently been transformed into the **Village of Yorkville Park ★★**. This urban park, which lies over a subway station, is an uncommon demonstration of urban ecology, local history and regional identity. It is divided into 13 zones, each representing a different part of the province's geography. The huge boulder toward the centre is native Canadian-Shield granite. For more information on the park's layout, see p 180.

Toronto, the Canadian megacity, with its skyscrapers
and the famous CN Tower. – *T. B.*

Spadina Avenue – the main street of Toronto's largest Chinatown.
– *P. Quittemelle*

Looking south as you traverse the park, you can peer across the parking lot and through the façades of the University Theatre and Pearcy House (see above), two more pieces of Toronto's architectural heritage awaiting redevelopment.

 TOUR I: CABBAGETOWN ★★

Historically, Cabbagetown was delimited by the Don Valley, Parliament Street, Queen Street and Carlton Street. Nowadays, however, when people talk of Cabbagetown, they are most often referring to the community around Parliament Street (its commercial artery), which extends east to the Don Valley, and north and south between Gerrard and Bloor Streets. It was here that the poorest of the Irish immigrants — those that planted cabbages in their front lawns, thus giving the area its name — settled in the 1840s. These tiny, once run-down Victorians have now been gentrified, making this a lovely area for a stroll.

The land was originally set aside by Governor John Graves Simcoe as a government reserve, but was opened to subdivision in 1819. More than a century later, this working-class neighbourhood was seen as a dispensable slum when town-planners, keen on the new concept of urban renewal, razed most of the houses south of Gerrard Street and replaced them with government-subsidized housing called Regent Park. The project is now considered by many as an architectural failure.

Start on Gerrard Street in front of **Regent Park**. The buildings to the south of Gerrard are actually those of the Regent Park North public housing development; Regent Park South lies south of Dundas Street. Built in 1947 and 1957 respectively, the two-phase project is one of Canada's oldest such developments. Its design, based on the modernist principles of Le Corbusier and others, sought to protect residents from the surrounding slums and provide them with their own streets and parks, in effect with their own little community. In reality, however, as Robert Fulford a respected Toronto journalist points out, the design isolates residents and singles them out as second-class. There is nothing endearing about the self-contained parks, where the cars are more conspicuous than the trees. The buildings themselves are of plain red brick and lack

EXPLORING

any sort of adornment. Regent Park is worth a look, if only as a point of reference as you continue your tour through the charming Victorian neighbourhood that it partially replaced.

Make your way into the original Cabbagetown along Sackville Street.

The area to your left as you head north on **Sackville Street** was once occupied by the Toronto General Hospital. From 1855 to 1913, when it was demolished and rebuilt on University Avenue, the hospital covered four acres. Trinity College Medical School established itself close by in 1871 at 41 Spruce Street; the school was later absorbed by the University of Toronto. The red- and yellow-brick building has now been incorporated into a residential complex known as Trinity Mews. The house at number 35 was originally inhabited by Charles B. Mackay, a customs clerk, and later by the Dean of Medicine of Trinity. It is still surrounded by its original fence, built in 1867.

Turn back and head east along Spruce St. to Sumach St.

At the corner of Sumach are the **Spruce Court Apartments**. This was the city's first low-income housing project, and a successful one at that, with grassy courtyards, individual entrances and a very human scale. Clearly, the architects of Regent Park (see further above) didn't know a good thing when they saw it. Spruce Court is now a residential co-operative.

Walk up Sumach and turn right on Carlton Street.

The dignified Italianate villa at **397 Carlton** was built in 1883. At the time, the house stood alone on this block in an area that was still very much "the country". A sense of that rural atmosphere remains in the lovely expanse of green called **Riverdale Park ★★**, which unfolds north of Carlton Street.

Walk north through the park and note the classic gingerbread house to your left at 384 Sumach Street. It has come to be known as the **Witch's House ★** and anyone who has read Hansel and Gretel will know why.

Riverdale Park once covered 162 acres on both sides of the Don River. In 1898, Riverdale Zoo opened here with just two wolves and a few deer. The elephants and polar bears that

① Cabbagetown

0 200 400m

© ULYSSES

● ATTRACTIONS

1. Regent Park
2. Spruce Court Apartments
3. 397 Carlton
4. Riverdale Park
5. Witch's House
6. Riverdale Farm
7. Necropolis Chapel
8. Owl House Lane
9. 314 Wellesley Street
10. St. James Cemetery
11. St. James-the-Less Chapel
12. St. Enoch's Presbyterian Church
13. 37 Metcalfe Street
14. Hotel Winchester
15. First Church of the Christian Association
16. Allan Gardens-Tropical Plant Collection

EXPLORING

were eventually added needed more space and in 1978, were moved to the brand new Metro Toronto Zoo (see p 168) in Scarborough. The Riverdale facilities have since been home to the ponies, roosters and other barnyard critters of **Riverdale Farm ★★** *(free admission; 201 Winchester St., ☎392-0046)*, and will delight children. The zoo's original stone gates on Winchester Street now lead to the farm.

Polar Bear

North of Winchester Street extends another expanse of green. The **Necropolis** is one of Toronto's oldest nonsectarian burial grounds. It dates from the early 1850s and is the final resting place of William Lyon Mackenzie, the city's first mayor and leader of the rebellion of 1837 (see p 121) and George Brown, one of the fathers of Canadian Confederation. This city of the dead is ironically also a vibrant garden of sorts with an impressive collection of rare and exotic trees, shrubs and plants. Its most stunning feature, however, is its mortuary chapel, the **Necropolis Chapel ★★**, built in 1872. This wonderfully preserved High Victorian Gothic grouping is a true gem, with its patterned slate roof, tracery, ironwork and vine-covered exterior.

Continue up Sumach and turn right on Amelia Street.

Today, Cabbagetown is seen as the epitome of successful gentrification in Toronto. In the mid-1850s, however, some rather unsavoury elements contributed to the area's bad reputation: the Don River and the new Necropolis were both seen as threats to the water supply, while the Peter R. Lamb & Company factory buildings which once stood here were probably something of an eyesore, not to mention the stench that surely emanated from the production of glue, blacking, ground bone and animal charcoal that went on here.

Development in the area only started in earnest in the 1880s, when the factory burned down around the same time a second wave of immigrants from the British Isles hit Toronto.

The houses along **Wellesley Street** ★ were all built in the 1880s and 1890s for these new arrivals, who were generally better-off than those immigrants who settled a few blocks to the south in the original Cabbagetown. Many of these houses display either the Toronto Bay-'n'-Gable or the later Queen Anne style. The former applies to double and row houses and appeared all over the city toward the end of the 19th century. Its picturesque pointed gables, decorative bargeboards and polygonal bay windows are signatures of Toronto architecture. The latter is more elaborate, with towers, turrets, gables, dormers, bay windows and a combination of textures and materials, and is most often found on single detached dwellings.

One of the best examples of Toronto Bay-n-Gable stands at **398 Wellesley Street** ★. The Queen Anne style is represented by a simple condominium development at the end of **Owl House Lane**. The namesake house is adorned with a small owl and was once lived in by artist C. W. Jefferys.

Continuing along Wellesley Street you'll notice a row of simple gabled cottages running up a dead-end street called **Wellesley Cottages**. These former working-class dwellings are now modernized and highly-coveted properties. Continue up to **Alpha Avenue** where another row of low-slung cottages, these ones with mansard roofs, have been brightly revitalized.

Back on Wellesley Street, you'll soon come to the most typical Queen Anne house in the area at **number 314** ★. A variety of materials and a delightful arrangement of shapes and ornaments bear witness to the fact that the original owner was a stone-cutter.

Extending north and west of the corner of Parliament and Wellesley Streets is **St. James Cemetery** ★, Toronto's second Anglican cemetery, laid out in 1845. The wooded roads of this tranquil spot lead to the final resting places of Toronto's elite, many of whom erected some of the city's most elaborate monuments to the dead. The Toronto Historical Board has a list of the most prominent ones. Besides these, the cemetery also

EXPLORING

harbours what is considered one of the most praiseworthy church buildings in the country, **St.-James-the-Less Chapel ★★★** *(625 Parliament St.)*. Its sharp, lofty spire, severe roof line and diminutive base are simple but superb.

Make your way south along Parliament, Cabbagetown's main commercial artery. Turn left on Winchester and walk to Metcalfe Street.

Metcalfe Street ★★★ is perhaps the prettiest and most emblematic street of Cabbagetown. Lofty trees form a canopy over the street, which is lined with elegant iron fencing and rows of late-Victorian houses.

At the corner of Metcalfe and Winchester is the former **St. Enoch's Presbyterian Church** *(180 Winchester St.)*, built in 1891 in the Romanesque style. The Toronto Dance Theatre now occupies the building.

A surprising residence occupies **37 Metcalfe Street**. Successive additions and classic remodelling transformed an Italianate villa (1875) that fronted on Winchester Street into the Classic Revival edifice that now faces Metcalfe.

Making your way down Metcalfe towards Carlton you'll pass a neat Bay-n-Gable row on the right running from number six to 18, and a distinctive string of Queen Anne houses on the left from number one to 15.

Carlton Street ★★ marks the northern boundary of "Old Cabbagetown". Most of the homes here are considerably larger and more opulent than those whose front yards were filled with cabbages. Start around Rawlings Avenue and work your way west. Number 314, with its pretty mansard roof, was built in 1874; number 297 is an oft-photographed, lofty Queen Anne residence; the fine Gothic Revival house at number 295 had one of the first telephones in the city; across the street, numbers 294-300 are fine examples of late Bay-n-Gable; number 286 boasts some lovely ornamentations about its windows and door, and finally, note the decorative carved wooden porch of 280-282 Carlton.

Parliament Street is so named because it runs up from the site of the original Parliament Buildings. It is and has always been the neighbourhood's commercial artery. The Canadian Imperial Bank of Commerce building on the corner of Carlton and Parliament was designed by Darling & Pearson in 1905 in the Classic Revival style. Just north of Carlton is an early commercial block whose delightful façade features pretty arched-windows; the shopfront of **number 242 ★** is an original.

Walk up Parliament Street to Winchester Street.

The **Hotel Winchester** *(531 Parliament St.)*, built in 1888, originally housed the Lake View Hotel and was something of an attraction in its glory days, due to a lookout point set up atop the corner tower, which offered a view of the lake.

Turn left on Winchester Street.

The south side of Winchester is lined with some lovely row and single detached houses. The triple Queen Anne house at numbers 7-11 stands out for its brickwork (number five was actually rebuilt). The double house at number 13-15 is a typical Second Empire residence, with its imposing central block and decorative dormers.

Turn left and walk down Ontario Street.

Harmonious rows of a Bay-'n'-Gable houses line both sides of **Ontario Street ★★** between Aberdeen and Winchester. Below Aberdeen on the left, the picturesque pointed arches of the double house at 481-483 are typical Gothic Revival. The simple red-brick Gothic **First Church of the Christian Association** *(474 Ontario St.)* on the right was built in 1905.

Back on Carlton Street, make your way west to the limits of Cabbagetown.

Allan Gardens-Tropical Plant Collection ★★ *(free admission; Mon to Fri 9am to 4pm, Sat, Sun and holidays 10am to 5pm; ☎392-1111)* Bounded by Jarvis, Gerrard, Sherbourne and Carlton Streets, these old-style gardens are set in the middle of a lovely park on the edge of Cabbagetown. Among the garden's greenhouses is the Palm House, a grand Victorian greenhouse built in 1909. The collection includes tropical varieties and succulents, set on the former estate of George

EXPLORING

William Allan, a lawyer and former mayor of Toronto who married his way into the Family Compact (see p 19).

TOUR J: THE ANNEX ★★

Extending north and west from the intersection of Bloor Street and Avenue Road to Dupont and Bathurst Streets is an area that was annexed by the city of Toronto in 1887, and is now appropriately called The Annex. As this was a planned suburb, a certain architectural homogeneity prevails; even the unique gables, turrets and cornices are all lined up an equal distance from the street. Residents fought long and hard to preserve the Annex's architectural character, and save a few ugly apartment high-rises along St. George Street and Spadina, their efforts have been quite successful. The fact that this area remains essentially as it was 90 years ago is a testament to Torontonians burgeoning awareness of the historic value of their surroundings.

Start at the corner of St. George and Bloor Streets, just a few steps from the St. George subway station, at the new home of the **Bata Shoe Museum** ★★★ *($6, seniors and students $4, children $2, under 5 free, families $12; Tue to Sat 10am to 5pm, Thu until 8pm, Sun noon to 5pm; 327 Bloor St. W., ☎979-7799)*. The first museum of its kind in North America, it holds 10,000 shoes and provides an extraordinary perspective on the world's cultures. The new building was designed by architect Raymond Moriyama to look like a shoe box, and the oxidized copper along the edge of the roof suggests a lid resting on top. There are four permanent exhibits: "All About Shoes" is touted as a sumptuous feast of footwear with shoe

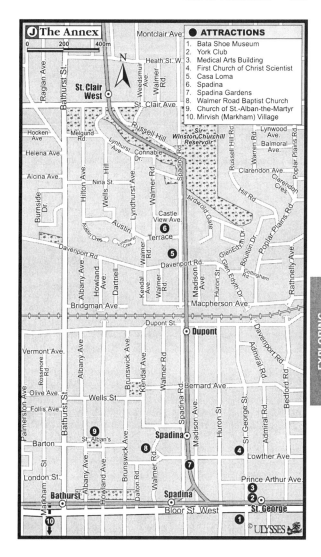

J The Annex

0   200   400m

N

Montclair Ave.

● ATTRACTIONS
1. Bata Shoe Museum
2. York Club
3. Medical Arts Building
4. First Church of Christ Scientist
5. Casa Loma
6. Spadina
7. Spadina Gardens
8. Walmer Road Baptist Church
9. Church of St.-Alban-the-Martyr
10. Mirvish (Markham) Village

© ULYSSES

EXPLORING

trivia, shoe history and shoes of the rich and famous; "Inuit Boots: A Woman's Art" takes a look at "Kamiks" and the importance of footwear in the Arctic; "The Gentle Step: 19th Century Women's Shoes" examines the evolution of women's footwear at the dawn of the modern age; and finally, "One, Two, Buckle My Shoe" exhibits illustrations of shoes from children's books. Some of the more memorable pieces of footwear on display include space boots of Apollo astronauts, geisha platform sandals and a pair of patent leather beauties that once belonged to Elvis Presley.

The impressive red brick and stone building kitty-corner to the museum, is now home to the **York Club ★**, but was once a private home. It is the most distinguished Richardsonian Romanesque house in Toronto and was built in 1889 for the wealthiest man in the province at the time, George Gooderham. The architect, David Roberts, also designed the distinctive Gooderham Building (see p 112), also known as the flatiron building, on Front Street. The York Club moved into the house in 1909, making it the first secular institution tolerated in the area.

The remnants of a wall that once surrounded George Gooderham's son's residence just to the north is now part of the Royal Canadian Yacht Club. This "city" clubhouse is of course secondary to the main Toronto Islands location. Across the street is the **Medical Arts Building** *(170 St. George St.)*, the area's first tall office building, built in 1929. Another Richardsonian Romanesque masterpiece occupies the northwest corner of St. George Street and Prince Arthur Avenue. With its characteristic wide round arches and ivy-covered tower, 180 St. George Street is quite handsome. Up at the corner of Lowther and St. George is the **First Church of Christ Scientist**, the first Christian Science church in Toronto, built in 1916.

Turn right on Lowther and left on Admiral Road.

Admiral Road is a peaceful street with some lovely Annex houses. A grand old tree (since taken down) about halfway up the block from Lowther and the curve of Davenport Road above Bernard Avenue explain Admiral's deviation from the strict grid pattern of the surrounding streets.

Casa Loma

Turni right at St. George Street and then left on Dupont Street.

Dupont marks the northern boundary of the area annexed by the city of Toronto in 1887. Grand old trees and typical Annex rows of houses frame this wide avenue.

Head east to Spadina, then turn right and walk beyond the train tracks to MacPherson Avenue. Turn left and then right on Walmer Road, cross Davenport and continue up Walmer Road to Austin Terrace and Casa Loma.

Canadians are known for their reserve, modesty and discretion. Of course there are exceptions to every rule and one of these is certainly **Casa Loma** ★★ *($9, seniors and children 14 to 17 $5.50, children 4 to 13 $5, children under 4 free; every day 9:30am to 4pm; 1 Austin Terrace, ☎923-1171)*, an immense Scottish castle with 98 rooms built in 1914 for the eccentric colonel Sir Henry Mill Pellatt (1859-1939) who made his fortune by investing in electricity and transportation companies. Pellatt owned, among others things, the tramways of São Paolo, Brazil! His palatial residence, designed by the architect

EXPLORING

of Toronto's Old City Hall, E.J. Lennox, includes a vast ballroom with a pipe organ and room for 500 guests, a library with 100,000 volumes and a fascinating cellar. The self-guided tour leads through various secret passages and lost rooms. Great views of downtown Toronto can be had from the towers.

To the east of Casa Loma, atop the Davenport hill and accessible by the Baldwin Steps, is **Spadina ★** *($5, seniors and youths 13 to 18 $3.25, children 4 to 12 $3, children under 4 free; Jun to Aug, Tue to Sun noon to 5pm; Sep to Dec, Mon to Fri noon to 4pm, Sat and Sun noon to 5:15pm, hours change in 2000; 285 Spadina Rd., ☎392-6910)*, another house-turned-museum of Toronto's high society. This one is smaller, but just as splendid for those who want to get a taste of the Belle Époque in Canada. It was built in 1866 for James Austin, the first president of the Toronto Dominion Bank, and the grounds include a solarium overflowing with luxuriant greenery and a charming Victorian garden, in bloom from May to September. The residence has been renovated several times and features several glassed-in overhangs, offering its owners panoramic views of the surroundings, which the natives called *Espanidong*, and the English *Spadina* (the correct pronunciation being *Spadeena*). Toronto Historical Board guides have been leading visitors on tours of the estate since 1982, when the last member of the Austin family left the house.

Return now to the Annex proper by taking Spadina Avenue all the way to Lowther Avenue.

As the main thoroughfare of the Annex, Spadina Avenue was one of the first streets to attract the attention of developers, who put up several rather ugly International Style box-like apartment buildings following World War II. Just south of Lowther, however, is an apartment house that merits our attention. Built in 1906, **Spadina Gardens** *(41-45 Spadina Ave.)* is still the classiest building of its kind on the street, despite more recent attempts to upstage it.

Continue west along Lowther Avenue, then north up Walmer Road.

The **Walmer Road Baptist Church** *(188 Lowther Ave.)* was once the largest Baptist church in Canada. It was founded by the uncle of artist Lawren Harris, one of the Group of Seven (see p 38). Winding Walmer Road is one of the more picturesque and prestigious-looking streets in the Annex; it also boasts some typical Annex houses like number 53, numbers 83-85 and finally the grand number 109.

Complete your stroll through the Annex by walking west along Bernard Avenue, around the park, along Wells Street and down Howland Avenue to Bloor Street. Only the splendid chancel of the **Church of St.-Alban-the-Martyr** ★ *(just before St. Alban's Sq.)*, what amounts to one quarter of the planned cathedral, was actually completed by the time the money ran out in 1891. This was to be the cathedral church of the Diocese of Toronto, an honour later bestowed on St. James Cathedral (see p 117).

Once at Bloor Street, turn right and walk to Honest Ed's and Mirvish Village (see p 102).

TOUR K: ROSEDALE, FOREST HILL
AND NORTH OF TORONTO ★★

The numbers following the attractions refer to the map of Tour K.

This tour explores two treasures in the vicinity of the Don River, the Ontario Science Centre and Todmorden Mills Park, then heads west into the posh residential neighbourhoods of Rosedale and Forest Hill, before finishing up with a collection of worthy attractions north of the city.

Since its opening on September 27, 1969, the **Ontario Science Centre** ★★★ *($10, ages 13 to 18 $7, ages 5 to 12 $6, free for ages 5 and under; every day 10am to 5pm, 770 Don Mills Rd., ☎429-4100, www.osc.on.ca)* has welcomed over 30 million visitors, young and old. Designed by architect Raymond Moriyama, it houses 650 different expositions. The best part about the centre is its many hands-on exhibits and experiments. These interactive exhibits are spread throughout 11 categories: The Living Earth, Space, Sport, Communication, Food, The Information Highway, Technology/Transportation, The Human Body, Science Arcade, Matter/Energy/Change, and Earth. One of the biggest crowd-pleasers is the electricity ball that stands your hair on end. Scientists at heart also discover the chemistry of cryogenics while the Starlab planetarium transports them to the four corners of the galaxy. They'll learn to make their own paper as well as about the evolution and the impact of the printing press on humanity. The steps involved in making metal objects are described at the foundry on site, and finally the numerous applications of lasers in the modern world are explored. In late 1996, the Science Centre opened its brand new OMNIMAX theatre, which is an improved version of the IMAX. Located at the entrance to the centre, the OMNIMAX seats 320 people under an enormous 24-m wide dome with a powerful hi-fidelity sound system. Admission is separate and reservations are recommended *(tickets: ☎696-1000)*.

Take Don Mills Road south to the Don Valley Parkway south, and take the Todmorden Mills Exit.

Todmorden Mills Heritage Museum ★ *($2.25, seniors and students $1.75, children 6 to 12 $1.25, under 6 free; May to Sep, Tue to Fri 11am to 4:30pm, Sat, Sun and holidays noon to 5pm; Oct to Dec, Mon to Fri 10am to 4pm; 67 Pottery Rd., ☎396-2819)* is an open-air museum with two restored Confederation (1867) houses, a former brewery and the Old Don Train Station, which once served both the Canadian National and the Canadian Pacific railroads. Todmorden Mills on the Don River was once inhabited by settlers from Todmorden Mills in England. The park that surrounds the museum is a lovely spot for a picnic.

Head west into Rosedale at Castle Frank Road.

One of Toronto's most distinguished and affluent neighbourhoods lies just north of the downtown area. **Rosedale** was not always a coveted address; the affluent folk that developers sought to attract here originally found Rosedale "too lonely" and "too far from town", furthermore it was "too difficult to find domestics" who would go there. It was not until the early 1900s that the majority of the houses were built, for the most part by a nouveau riche middle class, though some eminent surnames did find their way onto the Rosedale rosters, like Osler, Gooderham, Darling and Small.

Rosedale was named by Sheriff Jarvis' wife Mary, who delighted in the roses that grew wild in and around their house, the area's first, Rosedale Villa. Built overlooking the ravine, it was finally demolished in 1905. Following Mary's death in the

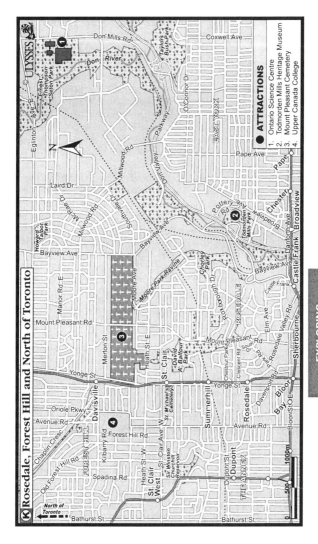

ATTRACTIONS

1. Ontario Science Centre
2. Todmorden Mills Heritage Museum
3. Mount Pleasant Cemetery
4. Upper Canada College

K Rosedale, Forest Hill and North of Toronto

EXPLORING

1850s, Jarvis laid out Park Road and began dividing up and selling off his domain. The surrounding estates followed suit, and slowly a handful of houses were built. Yet when Rosedale finally took off in the early 1900s, the inclination to sell off land remained as strong with the new arrivals, leading to further subdivisions. As a result, many of Rosedale's houses are built very close together and very near the street. There is also a distinct lack of continuity in the architecture, with houses of different styles located right next to each other. A walk through Rosedale's prettiest streets therefore offers an excellent opportunity to view a wide range of some of Toronto's loveliest residential architecture.

The land north of Bloor Street was claimed by Governor John Graves Simcoe in 1793 when he laid out the town of York. He named it Frank after his infant son and built a house on it which he called Castle Frank. The house burned down in 1829 after having been abandoned by Simcoe when he was called back to England in 1797. This part of Rosedale then passed into the hands of Francis Cayley, who called his rustic 120-acre estate Drumsnab *(5 Drumsnab Rd.)*. This domain was slowly parcelled off by land speculators though the house (built in 1834 and then added on to in 1856 and 1908) remains and is the oldest private residence in Toronto.

Take Castle Frank Road up to Elm Avenue.

Edgar Jarvis, Sheriff Jarvis' nephew, laid out Elm Avenue early in the development of Rosedale. He planted elm trees and built a fine residence in the hopes of attracting prospective buyers. His house still stands at the end of the street. Before coming to it though, note the house at 27 Sherbourne Street. Jarvis succeeded in selling this lot to the wealthy Gooderham family (see p 112) of distilling fame. This house was actually the second Gooderham mansion built on the lot; the first was demolished.

As you approach Mount Pleasant Road, Branksome Hall private girls' school is located on your right. The main building of the school is located on the other side of Mount Pleasant in the former residence of Edgar Jarvis, built in 1866. This fine Italianate house originally faced Park Road and was Jarvis' showpiece.

Head up Mount Pleasant Road and turn left on South Drive and left again on Park Road.

At 124 Park Road stands the first house built on the land divided up and parcelled off by Sheriff Jarvis. When this gracious Georgian house with the wrap-around veranda was built in 1855, it only had one storey.

Continue along Park and turn right on Avondale Road.

The area beyond the first intersection on the left marks the spot where "Rosedale Villa", Sheriff Jarvis' house, once stood. The house was built in 1821 and Jarvis moved in in 1824. He lived here until his wife's death in 1852. The house was demolished in 1905.

Crescent Road was one of the seven curving roads laid out by Jarvis when his property was subdivided for development. Follow it around to the right and return to Mount Pleasant Road.

Take Mount Pleasant Road up to Mount Pleasant Cemetery.

The first non-sectarian cemetery in Toronto was Potter's Field, which lay on the northwest corner of Bloor and Yonge. The growth of nearby Yorkville limited the available space in this cemetery, so the remains buried here were transferred to the new Necropolis, next to the Don River (see p 148). Soon that too proved too small and thus **Mount Pleasant Cemetery** *(bound by Yonge St., Bayview Ave., Moore Ave. and Merton St.)* was created in 1876. Its lovely landscaping quickly made it something of an attraction in Toronto, and it remains a tranquil and beautiful place for quiet contemplation. It boasts a lovely arboretum with native and introduced species, most of which are identified, as well as some extraordinary architecture. Since it developed from west to east, most of the historic personalities are buried closer to Yonge Street. The notable figures whose final resting places are in Mount Pleasant include William Lyon Mackenzie King, Canada's longest-running Prime Minister; Frederick Banting and Charles Best, who together discovered insulin; Glenn Gould, the world-renowned classical pianist, and Foster Hewitt, the voice of hockey who coined the phrase "he shoots, he scores!" The Eaton and Massey mausoleums are probably the most impressive in the cemetery,

EXPLORING

the former built with granite imported from Scotland, and the latter designed by E.J. Lennox.

As you continue north from Mount Pleasant towards North York, take a swing through **Forest Hill**, Toronto's other upscale residential neighbourhood.

Take Heath Street to Forest Hill Road and turn right.

The village of Forest Hill was incorporated in 1923 and later joined the City of Toronto in 1968. It became a memorable part of Toronto lore in 1982 when the city stopped collecting residents' garbage from their backyards; the rubbish now has to be left on the sidewalk out front, heaven forbid! Forest Hill has always been the home court of wealthy and influential Torontonians, most of whom reside in stunning Georgian Revival houses set on fittingly leafy lots.

Make your way up Forest Hill Road to Old Forest Hill Road.

On the right side of Forest Hill Road between Lonsdale and Kilbarry Roads is one of Canada's most respected private boys' schools, **Upper Canada College**. These hallowed halls have inspired some of Canada's greatest luminaries, including authors Stephen Leacock and Robertson Davies.

Turn left on Kilbarry Road and right on Old Forest Hill Road.

This winding road, which was once an Amerindian path, is lined with some of Forest Hill's most elegant residences. Make your way up to Eglinton Avenue, the northern boundary of Forest Hill. If you feel like doing a bit of shopping, head down Spadina Road towards St. Clair Avenue.

The **Beth Tzedec Museum** *(free admission; Mon, Wed, Thu 11am to 1pm and 2pm to 5pm, Sun 10am to 2pm; 1700 Bathurst St., ☎781-3511)* holds several curious and amusing treasures related to the Jewish culture and is certainly worth a visit if you're in the vicinity. It is located in the modern synagogue of the same name.

Continue north up Bathurst to Highway 401 and head east to Yonge Street to visit Gibson House.

The **Gibson House Museum** *($2.75, seniors and students $2.25, children $1.75, Tue to Fri 9:30am to 4:30pm, Sat, Sun and holidays noon to 5pm; 5172 Yonge St., ☎395-7432, North York Centre subway)*. David Gibson, a local surveyor and politician, and his family lived in this house in North York in the mid-1800s. Gibson was a staunch supporter of William Lyon Mackenzie, and was consequently exiled to the United States in 1837. He built this house upon returning from south of the border and finding his original house burnt to the ground by Family Compact supporters. At the time, the area was farmland with rolling fields as far as the eye could see. The house has been restored to that era, and guides in period dress re-enact the life and times of the Gibson family.

Head west on Highway 401, exit and head north on Bathurst Street.

Holocaust Education & Memorial Centre of Toronto *(free admission, donations appreciated; Mon to Thu 9am to 4pm, Fri 9am to 3pm, Sun 11:30am to 4:30pm; 4600 Bathurst St., ☎635-2883)*. This moving memorial pays tribute to the experiences of European Jews in World War II. The panorama of Jewish life in pre-Nazi Europe is particularly poignant.

Continue north up Bathurst Street to Finch Avenue. Head west on Finch to Jane Street.

Black Creek Pioneer Village *($9, seniors and students $7, children 5 to 14 $5, under 5 free; weekdays 9:30am to 4:30pm, weekends and holidays 10am to 5pm; 1000 Murray Ross Parkway, at Jane St. and Steeles Ave. W., ☎736-1733, from Finch subway station take bus 60 to Jane St.)* is about 30 minutes from downtown. Period buildings include an authentic mill from the 1840s with a 4-tonne waterwheel that grinds up to one hundred barrels of flour a day, a general store, a town hall, a print shop and a blacksmith; all of these are manned by friendly animators going about their business dipping candles, shearing sheep and baking goodies that you can sample. In the summer, enjoy a horse-drawn carriage ride, and in the winter bundle up for skating, tobogganing and sleigh rides.

Head north up Jane Street to Rutherford Road.

EXPLORING

The first one of its kind in the country, **Paramount Canada's Wonderland** *(Day Pass: ages 7 to 59 $43.27, seniors and children 3 to 6 $21.34, under 3 free; May, Sep and Oct, Sat and Sun 10am to 8pm; Jun to Labour Day, every day 10am to 10pm; 9580 Jane St., Vaughan, ☎905-832-7000 min from downtown, Rutherford exit from Hwy. 400 and follow the signs, or Yorkdale or York Mills subway then take special GO express bus)* is the answer if you have a day to kill and children to please. Gut-wrenching rides include the Vortex, the only suspended roller coaster in Canada, and the renowned Days of Thunder, which puts you behind the driver's seat for a simulated stock car race. The park also features a waterpark called Splash Works with 16 rides and slides, and live shows at the new Kingswood Theatre *(☎905-832-8131)*. Wonderland was recently purchased by Paramount, and Star Trek characters now wander through the park along with more Canadian idols like Scooby Doo and Fred Flintstone. The restaurant facilities may not be to everyone's liking, so pack a lunch.

Kleinberg's McMichael Collection of Canadian art lies about 45 minutes north of downtown Toronto.

The **McMichael Collection** ★ ★ ★ *($7; every day 10am to 5pm; take Hwy. 400, then Major Mackenzie Dr. to Islington Ave., 10365 Islington Ave., ☎905-893-1121)* houses one of the most magnificent collections of Canadian and native art in Canada and draws many visitors to the peaceful hamlet of Kleinberg on the outskirts of Greater Toronto. A magnificent stone and log house built in 1950s for the McMichaels is home to the collection. The McMichaels are great art-lovers, and their personal collection of paintings by the great Canadian masters is at the heart of the museum's collection today. The large and bright galleries present an impressive retrospective of the works of Tom Thomson and the Group of Seven. A visit here allows you to admire and contemplate some of the best works of these artists who strove to reproduce and interpret Ontario's wilderness in their own way. Inuit and native art is also well represented, notably the work of Ojibwa painter Norval Morrisseau, who created his own "pictographic" style.

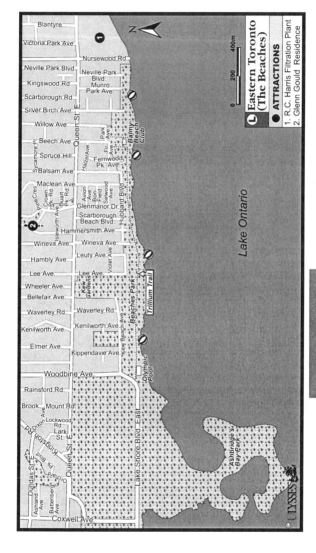

Eastern Toronto (The Beaches)

ATTRACTIONS
1. R.C. Harris Filtration Plant
2. Glenn Gould Residence

0   200   400m

Lake Ontario

Trillium Trail

Beaches Park

Kew Gardens

Olympic Pool

Ashbridge's Bay Park

Lake Shore Blvd. East

Queen St. E.

Blantyre
Victoria Park Ave.
Nursewood Rd.
Neville Park Blvd.
Neville Park Blvd.
Kingswood Rd.
Munro Park Ave.
Scarborough Rd.
Silver Birch Ave.
Willow Ave.
Beech Ave.
Spruce Hill
Balsam Ave.
Maclean Ave.
Glenmanor Dr.
Scarborough Beach Blvd.
Hammersmith Ave.
Wineva Ave.
Wineva Ave.
Hambly Ave.
Leuty Ave.
Lee Ave.
Lee Ave.
Wheeler Ave.
Bellefair Ave.
Waverley Rd.
Waverley Rd.
Kenilworth Ave.
Kenilworth Ave.
Elmer Ave.
Kippendavie Ave.
Woodbine Ave.
Rainsford Rd.
Brook Mount Rd.
Lockwood Rd.
Lark St.
Dundas St. E.
Ashland Ave.
Battenberg Ave.
Coxwell Ave.

Balmy Beach Club

Hubbard Blvd.
Kew Beach Ave.

Sycamore Pl.
Pine Cres.
Crown Pk. Rd.
Stuart Pk. Rd.
Isleworth Ave.
Halzel Ave.
Park Ave.
Fir Ave.
Fernwood Pk. Ave.
Avion Ave.
Bon-Field
Selwood Ave.
Violet Ave.

Kingston Rd.
Dixon Ave.
Orchard Pk. Blvd.

N

EXPLORING

© ULYSSES

TOUR L: EASTERN TORONTO

The Beaches

We say "Beaches" in the interests of conformity, clarity and perhaps tourism; however, in the interests of historical accuracy it should be noted that longtime residents are almost fiercely attached to what they feel is the neighbourhood's true name, "The Beach". The Beaches extend west from Woodbine Avenue to the R.C. Harris Filtration Plant, and north from the lake to Kingston Road.

In 1853, English soldier Joseph Williams built his domain here and called it Kew Farms. He changed the name to Kew Gardens in 1879, when the farm became a park that was all the rage with weary Torontonians. Soon these same city-dwellers began building cottages here (you'll notice that many of the neighbourhood's present houses are clearly winterized summer cottages). The reasoning for calling this place The Beaches is surely best supported by the fact that in those days there were actually three beaches: Kew Beach to the west, Scarboro Beach Park in the middle and Balmy Beach to the east.

Take streetcar 501 east along Queen Street to Woodbine Avenue.

Once at the beach the fun begins. A pretty wooden boardwalk runs the length of the beach, as does the **Trillium Trail**, a jogging and cycling path. A tennis club, lacrosse club and lawn-bowling club all face the beach. The green space to your left eventually opens up at Kew Gardens, which extends all the way up to Queen Street East. On Lee Avenue, which lines the park to the east, is the house built by Kew Williams, son of Joseph, at number 30.

If the prospect of warm sand, bright sun and a backdrop of sparkling waves carrying sailboats along the horizon appeals to you, then by all means hit the beach! The boardwalk continues all the way to Silver Birch Avenue and the Balmy Beach Canoe Club. From there, let the sand get between your toes and walk the few blocks to the **R.C. Harris Filtration Plant**, one of

Toronto's most evocative buildings and revered by some as its most imposing example of "engineering raised to art."

Walk up to Queen Street East and head west to experience a bit more of the "Beaches" way of life, complete with surf shops and sidewalk cafes. There is certainly a lot of window shopping to be done.

At Glen Manor Drive, turn right and walk up to Southwood Drive. Pianist Glenn Gould was a Beaches resident until his late twenties; his parents' house at **32 Southland Drive** is identified by a plaque.

Scarborough

A tour of Scarborough, you wonder? The reputation of this borough of Metropolitan Toronto, sometimes referred to as Scarberia, unfortunately precedes it! So why should you visit it? Well, despite its undistinguished strawberry-box bungalow houses, the city is also home to Metropolitan Toronto's spectacular zoo and to the majestic gray cliffs that earned it its name (Elizabeth Simcoe, the wife of Lt.-Gov. John Simcoe found they resembled those of Scarborough, England).

Four spectacular parks provide access to those fabled grey cliffs known as the Bluffs. Bluffers West Park, Scarborough Bluffs Park, Bluffers Park and Cathedral Bluffs Park. Each park boasts spectacular scenery over Lake Ontario and a wealth of outdoor possibilities.

From the Bluffs take Brimley Road north towards the centre of Scarborough.

Scarborough Historical Museum *($2, seniors and children $1; Apr to Jun and Sep to Dec, Mon to Fri 10am to 4pm; Jul and Aug, Wed to Sun 10am to 4pm; Thomson Memorial Park, 1007 Rd., ☎431-3441)* This outdoor museum features historical buildings and a display annex. The Cornell House of 1858 evokes rural life at the turn of the century; the McGowan Log House recreates an earlier time, that of the pioneers in the 1850s, and finally the Hough Carriage Works is an authentic 19th-century carriage shop.

EXPLORING

Continuing up Brimley Road, just north of Ellesmere Road, you'll come to Scarborough's town centre. Partly an attempt to shed its unfavourable image, the town centre was conceived in the late 1960s following the unveiling of New City Hall and the birth of Toronto's new public image. Architect Raymond Moriyama designed the exceptional **Scarborough Civic Centre** and thus gave the city core a focal point. Opinions are mixed as to the success of this building, which is nevertheless a lively place with its large square.

To reach the zoo, take McGowan Road up to Finch Avenue and head east. Continue along Old Finch Road to Meadowvale Drive and head south to the entrance.

Finally, for an enjoyable change of scenery just minutes from the heart of downtown Toronto, head to the **Toronto Metropolitan Zoo ★★** *($12, seniors and children 12 to 17 $9, 4 to 11 $7, under 4 free; every day Mar to May, 9am to 6pm; Jun to Aug, 9am to 7:30pm; Sep to Feb, 9:30am to 4:30pm; 361A Old Finch Ave., at Hwy. 401 and Meadowvale Rd.; ☎392-5900, www.torontozoo.com)*, where you can see some 4,000 animals from the four corners of the globe and take advantage of this lovely 300-hectare park. The African pavilion is particularly interesting, since it is located in a large greenhouse where the climate and vegetation have been recreated. Canadian wildlife is also well represented, and several species accustomed to the local climate roam free in large enclosures.

 TOUR M: NIAGARA FALLS ★★★

This tour covers the region to the west of the Niagara River, along the U.S. border. Control over this area was once crucial as far as shipping on Lakes Ontario and Superior was concerned, and the two forts that were built to protect it still stand on either side of the river. Nowadays, however, the region is best known for its wineries and orchards, and as the home of the extraordinary Niagara Falls, which have continued to amaze people of all ages and inspire lovers and daredevils for decades.

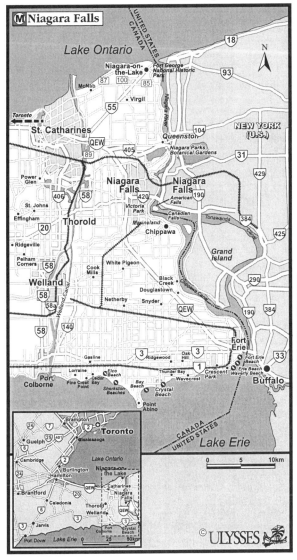

EXPLORING

Niagara-on-the-Lake ★★

The history of Niagara-on-the-Lake dates back to the late 18th century, when the town, then known as Newark, was the capital of Upper Canada from 1791 to 1796. Nothing remains of that time, however, for the town was burned during the War of 1812, which pitted the British colonies against the United States. After the American invasion, the town was rebuilt and graced with elegant English-style homes, which have been beautifully preserved and still give this community at the mouth of the Niagara River a great deal of charm. Some of these houses have been converted into elegant inns, which welcome visitors attending the celebrated Shaw Festival (see p 262), or simply lured here by the town's English atmosphere.

After the American Revolution, the British abandoned Fort Niagara, which stands on the east side of the Niagara River. To protect their remaining colonies, however, they decided to build another fort. Between 1797 and 1799, Fort George was erected on the west side of the river. Within a few years, the two countries were fighting again. In 1812, war broke out, and the Niagara-on-the-Lake region, which shared a border with the United States, was in the eye of the storm. Fort George was captured, then destroyed in 1813, only to be reconstructed in 1815.

At the **Fort George National Historic Park** ★ *($6, seniors $5, children $4, families $20; every day 10am to 5pm; Niagara Parkway S., ☎905-468-4257)*, you can tour the officer's quarters, the guard rooms, the barracks and other parts of the restored fort.

You can also visit the lovely, Georgian-style **McFarland House** *($1.75; late May through Jun, every day 10pm to 5pm; Jul to Sep, every day 10am to 5pm, by appointment during the rest of the year; Niagara Pkwy. S., 2 km south of town, ☎905-468-3322)*, built in 1800 for James McFarland and still decorated with furnishings dating from 1800 to 1840.

There are a number of vineyards in the Niagara-on-the-Lake region, large, striped fields all along the side of the highway. Some of these offer tours:

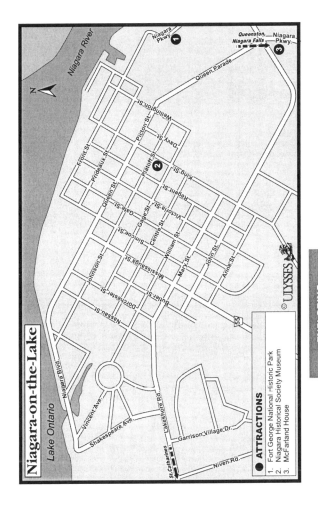

Niagara-on-the-Lake

Lake Ontario

● **ATTRACTIONS**

1. Fort George National Historic Park
2. Niagara Historical Society Museum
3. McFarland House

© ULYSSES

EXPLORING

Hillebrand Estates Winery
Highway 55
Niagara-on-the-Lake
☎905-468-7123

Konzelmann
1096 Lakeshore Rd.
Niagara-on-the-Lake
☎905-935-2866

Stonechurch
Route 87
Niagara-on-the-Lake
☎905-935-3535

Château des Charmes
1025 York Rd.
St. David (near Queenston)
☎905-262-5202

Continue heading south on the Niagara Parkway, which runs alongside the Niagara River to Queenston.

Queenston

A pretty hamlet on the banks of the Niagara River, Queenston consists of a few little houses and verdant gardens. It is best known as the former home of Laura Secord.

Farther south, you'll reach the foot of Queenston Height. If you're feeling energetic, you can climb the steps to the statue of Isaac Brock, a British general who died in this area while leading his men to victory during the War of 1812. This spot also offers a splendid **view** ★ of the region.

Keep heading south to Niagara Falls.

Niagara Falls ★★★

The striking spectacle of the Niagara Falls has been attracting crowds of visitors for many years, a trend supposedly started

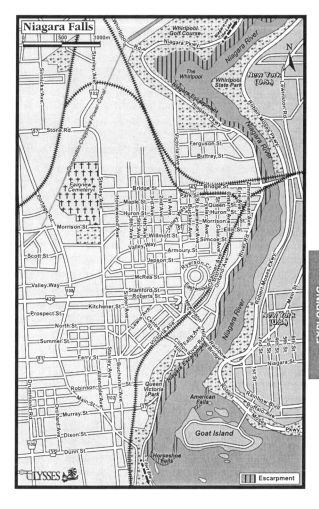

EXPLORING

when Napoleon's brother came here with his young bride. Right beside the falls, the town of the same name is entirely devoted to tourism, and its downtown area is a series of nondescript motels, uninteresting museums and fast-food restaurants, accented by scores of colourful signs. These places have sprung up in a chaotic manner, and no one seems to have given a second thought to aesthetics. There's no denying that the Niagara Falls are a natural treasure, but the town is best avoided.

The **Niagara Falls ★★★** were formed some 10,000 years ago, when the glaciers receded, clearing the Niagara Escarpment and diverting the waters of Lake Erie into Lake Ontario. This natural formation is remarkably beautiful, with two falls, one on either side of the border. The American Falls are 64 metres high and 305 metres wide, with a flow of 14 million litres per minute, while Canada's Horseshoe Falls, named for their shape, are 54 metres high and 675 metres wide, with a flow of 155 million litres of water per minute. The rocky shelf of the falls is made of soft stone, and it was being worn away at a rate of one metre per year until some of the water was diverted to the nearby hydroelectric power stations. The rate of erosion is now about 0.3 metres per year.

It would be hard not to be impressed by the sight of all that raging water plunging into the gulf at your feet with a thundering roar. This seemingly untameable natural force has been a source of inspiration to many a visitor. In the early 20th century, a few daring souls tried to demonstrate their bravery by going over the falls in a barrel or walking over them on a tightrope, resulting in several deaths. In 1912, these types of stunts were outlawed.

In 1885, **Victoria Park ★** was created in order to protect the natural setting around the falls from unbridled commercial development. This beautiful green space alongside the river is scored with hiking and cross-country ski trails.

There are **observation decks ★★★** in front of the falls, which can also be viewed from countless other angles; read on...

The *Maid of the Mist* ★ *($10.65; May to Oct, departures every 30 min; 5920 River Rd., ☎905-358-5781)* takes passengers to the foot of the falls, which make the boat seem very small indeed. Protected by a raincoat from getting drenched during the outing, you can view the American side of the falls and then the Canadian side, right in the middle of the horseshoe.

If you climb to the top of the **Skylon Tower** *($7.95; every day from 8am on; 5200 Robinson St., ☎905-356-2651)*, you can **view the falls** ★★ at your feet, a truly unique and memorable sight. You will enjoy a similar view from the **Minolta Tower** *($6.95; every day from 9am on; 6732 Oakes Prom., ☎905-356-1501)*.

The **Spanish Aero Car** *($5.25, children $2.65, Mar to Nov, 10am to dusk; Niagara Pkwy., ☎877-642-7275)* offers a bird's-eye view of the falls from a height of 76.2 m.

For a closer look at the falls, head to the **Table Rock Panoramic Tunnels**, which lead behind the Canadian side.

How about soaring through the air over the falls? You can do just that, thanks to **Niagara Helicopters** *($85; every day from 9am on, weather permitting; 3731 Victoria Ave., ☎905-357-5672)*.

An **elevator** transports visitors all the way down to the rapids *(Great Gorge Adventure $5; May to Oct from 9am on; 4330 River Rd., ☎905-374-1221)*.

Niagara has countless museums, some of little interest. A number of them are located in the downtown area known as Clifton Hill.

If you have a little time to spare, visit the Niagara Falls Museum *($6.75; May to Sep every day 9am to 10pm, Oct to Apr 10am to 5pm; 5651 River Rd., ☎905-356-2151)*, which has a collection ranging from Egyptian mummies to souvenirs of daredevils who have tried to conquer the falls.

The **Imax Theatre** *($7.50; May to Oct every day; 6170 Buchanan Ave., ☎905-358-3611)* shows a giant-screen film on the falls.

If you'd like to forget about the falls for a little while and watch some performing sea-lions, dolphins and whales instead, head to **Marineland** *(prices vary, $26.95 during summer; May to Oct*

EXPLORING

*10am to 5pm, Jul and Aug 9am to 6pm; 7657 Portage Rd.,
☎905-356-9565).* The little zoo and carousels are sure to be a
hit with the kids.

Toronto's Top Attractions for Children

Pioneer-living has always fascinated children, so why not take a
trip out to **Black Creek Pioneer Village** (see p 163)?

Underground tunnels and an old-fashioned stable keep younger
minds occupied at **Casa Loma** (see p 155).

The opportunities for discovery at the **CN Tower** extend as far
as the eye can see and sometimes that can be all the way to
Niagara Falls. The glass floor of the second-floor observations
deck is especially mind-boggling for the little ones (see p 92).

Soldiers in full dress, authentic military buildings and the heat of
battle make **Fort York** an exciting place for children (see p 93).

Harbourfront has something to please everyone. Besides the two
festivals — Zoom! International Children's Film Festival and the
Milk International Children's Festival, created especially for kids
— there is the Craft Studio, where artists can be observed at
work (see p 90).

Hockey is Canada's national sport, and just about every child has
his or her favourite player and team. What better way to please
the next great one than to take him or her on a tour of the
Canadiens dressing room and let them see the real Stanley Cup!
All this is possible at the **Hockey Hall of Fame** (see p 109).

Sports fans will delight in the opportunity to visit the dressing
rooms of the Toronto Raptors at the **SkyDome** (see p 91) and
the Toronto Maple Leafs at and Raptors at the **Air Canada Centre**
(see p 91).

Besides the exceptional collections of animals from around the
globe, sure to thrill younger animal lovers, the **Metro Toronto
Zoo** also has an area called Littlefootland where children can get
a closer look at some tamer animals like bunnies, ponies and
sheep (see p 168).

Children can play detective for a day as they analyze blood and dirt samples and solve a crime at the **Metropolitan Toronto Police Museum & Discovery Centre** (see p 139).

Vibrant **Nathan Phillips Square** is the setting for all sorts of concerts, markets and a skating rink in winter (see p 124).

Ontario Place is an obvious thrill for children, in particular the Cinesphere with its exciting line-up of 3-D movies (see p 94). Along the same lines but with dolphins and whales, **Marineland** (see p 175) is sure to please the young ones.

Fun and discovery are paramount at the **Ontario Science Centre**; one of the biggest crowd-pleasers is definitely the static ball that makes your hair stand on end. The new Cinesphere promises to be very popular (see p 157).

Paramount Canada's Wonderland is another full-day activity that no child will refuse (see p 164).

There are samples at the **Redpath Sugar Museum**, where kids can see how the sweet stuff is made (see p 88).

Riverdale Farm is close to downtown and there is no admission fee. Children will love the friendly barnyard animals (see p 148).

Wonderfully mysterious things like dinosaurs and mummies are just some of what the **ROM** has to offer (see p 137).

The beach, seagulls, ducks, Far Enough Farm and the Centreville Amusement Park make **Toronto Islands** the perfect escape for parents and kids (see p 95).

Young People's Theatre puts on productions just for children (see p 254).

EXPLORING

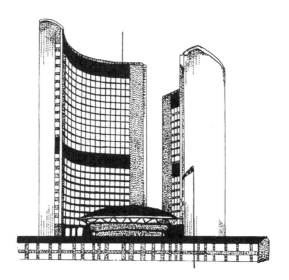

OUTDOORS

Today's Metropolitan Toronto began as a collection of small, previously independent villages and is therefore graced with hundreds of lovely parks encompassing the city's largest natural areas, and many of which include heritage buildings. Over 80 kilometres of maintained trails beckon to walkers, joggers, cyclists and in-line skaters. The outdoor possibilities are endless.

 PARKS

High Park *(☎392-1111)*, located in the western part of the city and bounded by Bloor Street to the north, The Queensway to the south, Parkside Drive to the east and Ellis Avenue to the west, is Toronto's Central Park. It is accessible by both subway (Keele or High Park stations) and streetcar (College or Queen). As Toronto's largest park, High Park features tennis courts, playgrounds, bike paths, nature trails and a swimming pool; skating and fishing on Grenadier Pond; rare flora; wildlife indigenous to the area plus animal paddocks where buffaloes, llamas and sheep are kept; a beach on Lake Ontario and "Dream in High Park" (see p 255), a version of Shakespeare in the park. Historic **Colborne Lodge** *(adults $3.50, seniors and students $2.75, children $2.50; May to Oct, Tue to Sun noon*

Buffalo

to 4pm; Jan to Apr, weekdays only; year-round for booked groups; these hours change often so call ahead; High Park, ☎392-6916) is also located in the park. Built in 1837, this Regency-style residence was built and inhabited by architect John Howard. Its lovely three-sided veranda once offered clear views of Lake Ontario and the Humber River. Howard deeded 67 hectares to the City of Toronto in 1873. The other 94 hectares that make up High Park were acquired separately. The house is now open to the public and run by guides in period dress. The nearby **Howard Tomb and Monument** is surrounded by an iron fence that was designed by Christopher Wren and once helped guard St. Paul's Cathedral in London, England.

The **Village of Yorkville Park** *(Cumberland St. between Avenue Rd. and Bellair St.)*, a new addition to Toronto's cityscape, is a fascinating example of urban ecology. Divided into 13 sectors, it represents local history and regional identity. A walk through the park from west to east begins in the Amelanchier Grove and leads through the Heritage Walk (Old York Lane), the Herbaceous Border Garden, the Canadian Shield Clearing & Fountain, the Alder Grove, the Ontario Marsh, the Festival Walk, the Cumberland Court Cross Walk, The Crabapple Orchard, The Fragrant Herb Rock Garden, The Birch Grove and the Prairie Wildflower Gardens before ending up in the Pine Grove. The highlight of the walk is certainly the village rock in the Canadian Shield sector. The rock is approximately one billion years old and weighs 650 tonnes. It comes from the area northeast of Gravenhurst, in the Muskoka Lakes region of northern Ontario.

Allan Gardens *(between Dundas, Gerrard, Sherbourne and Jarvis streets)* is a pretty city park with a lovely old Victorian greenhouse overflowing with brightly coloured flowers year-round.

The Don River Valley wends its way through Toronto to Lake Ontario and harbours a network of beautiful parks linked by bridges and trails. **Edwards Gardens** *(parking at Leslie St. and Lawrence Ave. E.; ☎397-1340)* is one of Toronto's first garden parks and features rock gardens, perennials, rose gardens, small waterfalls and dense forest. The river flows south past **Wilket Creek Park** and **Ernest Thompson Seton Park**. The Ontario Science Centre overlooks the latter. Near Don Mills Road, **Taylor Creek Park** extends to the east all the way to Warden Woods. All of these parks are wonderful places for walking, bicycling, jogging, cross-country skiing and even bird-watching.

Scarborough Bluffs Park and **Cathedral Bluffs Park** command breathtaking views of Lake Ontario from atop the scenic bluffs, while **Bluffer's Park** and **Bluffer's West Park** offer beautiful, spacious beaches and picnic areas.

Toronto Islands Park is on a group of 17 islands collectively known as the Toronto Islands, a short eight-minute ferry ride from Toronto Harbour. Three ferries, each departing from the Mainland Ferry Terminal at the foot of Bay Street, go to the islands. See p 95 for a walking tour of the islands.

 OUTDOOR ACTIVITIES

 Bicycling

The **Martin Goodman Trail**, a 22-kilometre jogging and cycling path, follows the shore of Lake Ontario from the mouth of the

Humber River west of the city centre, past Ontario Place and Queen's Quay to the Balmy Beach Club in The Beaches. Call ☎392-8186 for a map of the trail.

Bicycle and jogging paths also weave their way through Metropolitan Toronto's parks. For maps and information on the trails call ☎392-8186.

Toronto Island Bicycle Rental
Centre Island, ☎203-0009
$5 an hour, tandem $11 an hour.

Wheel Excitement
5 Rees St. (south of the SkyDome), ☎260-9000

 In-line Skating

Toronto's streets may be a bit hazardous for this sport, but the scenic paths on the Toronto Islands and near the water in The Beaches, or at the parks near the Bluffs, are ideal.

Wheel Excitement
5 Rees St. (south of the SkyDome), ☎260-9000
This shop rents skates and all the necessary equipment (pads) and offers lessons. You will need at least three hours to tour the islands.

 Ice Skating

There are several enchanting places to go ice-skating in the city. These include the rink in front of New City Hall, Grenadier Pond in High Park and York Quay at Harbourfront. For information on city rinks call ☎392-1111.

 Golf

There are five municipal golf courses (two executive and three regulation), which operate on a first-come, first-served basis. The **Don Valley Golf Course** *(☎392-2465)* is a challenging regulation course with several water and bunker hazards.

For something more challenging, take a little jaunt out to Oakville, to the **Glen Abbey Golf Club** *(green fees and cart $225, discount rates in off-season and on weekends after 2pm $115; ☎905-844-1800)*. This spectacular course was the first to be designed by Jack Nicklaus. The rates are high, but it's a real thrill to play where the pros play. The Canadian Open Championship is held here.

  ## Hiking and Cross-Country Skiing

Trails crisscross the **Toronto Islands** (see p 181).

Toronto's many ravines are wonderful places to explore by foot or on skis. A lovely trail begins in **Edwards Gardens** and meanders along the **Don River** to **Taylor Creek**. Pedestrians can access the Don River Valley from Leslie Street between Lawrence and Eglinton, from Gateway Boulevard behind the Ontario Science Centre, from Moore Avenue near Mount Pleasant Cemetery and from the Gerrard Street overpass.

Much more pristine than the Don River Valley, **Highland Creek** to the east of Scarborough is also lined with scenic walking trails. This area is known for its spectacular fall colours. The woodsy trails of **Morningside Park** are perfect for cross-country skiing.

ACCOMMODATIONS

This chapter suggests several different types of accommodations, listing them in the same order as the tours, and according to price, beginning with the least expensive.

Travellers will discover a large variety of hotels and inns in all categories in Toronto. Rates vary greatly from one season to the next, and are much higher during the summer, but usually lower on the weekends than during the week. Finally, remember that the weeks of the Caribana festival (end of July and beginning of August) and the film festival (early September) are particularly busy; we recommend making reservations long in advance if you plan to be in Toronto during these events. In the off-season, it is often possible to obtain better rates than those quoted in this guide. Several establishments also offer discounts to automobile club members and corporate employees. Make sure to ask about these discounts, as they are easy to obtain.

As far as bed and breakfasts are concerned, a few addresses are listed here; otherwise, check the list on p 77 for associations that can organize this type of accommodation.

Prices are for one standard room for two people during the high
season, not including taxes.

$	less than $50
$$	$50 to $75
$$$	$75 to $125
$$$$	$125 to $175
$$$$$	more than $175

TOUR A: THE WATERFRONT

The **SkyDome Hotel** *($$$$; ≡, ℛ, ≈, ⊘, pb, △, tv; 1 Blue Jays
Way, Toronto M5V 1J4, ☎341-7100 or 800-441-1414,
≈341-5091)* has 346 rooms with panoramic views and also
offers its customers 70 rooms facing the inside of the stadium.
The latter cost more, but what a view! The hotel has a choice
of restaurants and a bar that also offers a view of the playing
field. The modern rooms are adequate, but nothing special.
Valet service and room service are available day and night.

If you like the sea, you will feel at home at the **Radisson Plaza
Hotel Admiral** *($$$$; ≡, ⊛, ≈, pb; 249 Queen's Quay W.,
Toronto M5J 2N5, ☎203-3333 or 800-333-3333, ≈203-3100)*.
The decor of this charming hotel displays a seafaring motif,
with the rooms giving guests the impression they are aboard a
cruise ship. The view of the bay from the fifth-floor pool is
quite magnificent. Regular shuttle service is offered between
the hotel and the downtown area.

The **Westin Harbour Castle** *($$$$$; ≡, ≈, ℛ, ⊘, pb, △, tv;
1 Harbour Square, Toronto M5J 1A6, ☎869-1600 or
800-228-3000, ≈869-0573)* used to be part of the Hilton hotel
chain. In 1987, Westin and Hilton decided to swap their
respective Toronto hotels. Located in a calm and peaceful spot
on the shore of Lake Ontario, the Westin Harbour Castle is just
a few steps from the Harbourfront Centre and the ferry to the
Toronto Islands. To help guests reach the downtown area, the
hotel offers a free shuttle service; it also lies along a streetcar
line.

Ulysses's Favourites

For the location:
> Toronto Marriott Eaton Centre (p 191)
> Westin Harbour Castle (p 186)
> Royal York Hotel (p 189)
> Sheraton Getaway (p 201)

For the view:
> Westin Harbour Castle (p 186)
> SkyDome Hotel (p 186)

For Victorian charm:
> The Beaconsfield (p 191)
> Beverly Place Bed & Breakfast (p 193)
> The Amblecote (p 198)

For history buffs:
> Royal Meridian King Edward Hotel (p 191)
> Royal York Hotel (p 189)

For the utmost in luxury:
> Sutton Place Hotel (p 194)

For budget travellers:
> St. George Campus (p 193)

For long term stays:
> Victoria's Mansion (p 195)

TOUR C: THE THEATRE AND FINANCIAL DISTRICTS

Global Village Backpackers *($; sb/pb, ℝ, K; 460 King St. W., Toronto M5V 1L7, ☎703-8540)* is housed in what was once the infamous Spadina Hotel. Now totally refurbished as a youth hostel, it is located right in the theatre district, just three blocks from the trendy, artsy area of Queen West. It is Toronto's largest international traveller's hostel, with 200 beds. Its dormitory-style accommodations lend it a great atmosphere for students.

To enjoy a pleasant hotel located in the heart of downtown, just a few steps from the Royal York Hotel and a few minutes' walk from the waterfront, head to the **Strathcona Hotel** *($$$; ≡; 60 York Street, Toronto M5J 1S8, ☎363-3321, ⇒363-4679)*.

⛭ The **Executive Motor Hotel** *($$$; pb, ≡; 621 King St. W., Toronto M5V 1M5, ☎504-7441)* is one of the best budget choices downtown. It has free parking and is right on the transit line. Complementary morning coffee and doughnuts are provided. Located a short walk or streetcar ride from the CN Tower, SkyDome, the theatre district and the trendy Queen West area.

The **Hotel Victoria** *($$$; pb, ℛ, ℝ, tv; 56 Yonge St., Toronto M5E 1G5, ☎363-1666, ⇒363-7327)* has a wonderful location, midway between the financial district and Union Station. The hotel offers simple rooms at very affordable prices. Although it does not have its own parking area, this should not be a problem, as there are a number of public parking lots nearby.

The **Crowne Plaza Toronto Centre** *($$$$; ≡, ⊛, ≈, ℛ, ⊘, pb, △, tv; 225 Front St. W., Toronto M5V 2X3, ☎597-1400 or 800-HOLIDAY, ⇒597-8128)* is connected to the Convention Centre, making this a very busy spot at times. It lies just a few steps from the CN Tower and the SkyDome. The lobby is attractively decorated in magnificent polished bronze, pink marble and cherrywood.

Toronto Colony Hotel, Downtown City Hall *($$$$-$$$$$; pb, ≡, ≈, ℛ, ⊛, ℝ, K, △, ⊘; 89 Chestnut St., Toronto M5G 1R1, ☎977-0707)* is located in the centre of Toronto's financial district, just steps from Nathan Phillips Square and City Hall, the Eaton Centre and the theatre district. A short walk away are trendy Queen Street West, the SkyDome and the CN Tower. The hotel has two restaurants, two pools and a health club.

The **Holiday Inn on King** *($$$$-$$$$$; pb, tv; 370 King St. W., Toronto M5V 1J9, ☎599-4000, ⇒599-7394)* has rooms with pleasant, modern decor but no special charm. Some have balconies.

🦑 With its renovated guest rooms, 34 banquet rooms (each decorated differently), and 10 restaurants, it is easy to understand why the **Royal York Hotel** *($$$$$; ≡, ≈, ⊘, pb, △, tv; 100 Front St. W., Toronto M5J 1E3, ☎863-6333, 800-828-7447 or 800-441-1414)* is one of Toronto's most popular hotels. The impressive, sumptuously decorated lobby is an indication of the elegance of the rooms.

The **Toronto Hilton International** *($$$$$; ≡, ⊛, ≈, ℜ, ⊘, pb, △, tv; 145 Richmond St. W., Toronto M5H 2L2, ☎869-3456 or 800-445-8667, ⊷869-1478)* resembles many other Hilton hotels, with its pastel decor. It offers comfortable, clean, well-equipped rooms. Many visiting sports teams stay at the Hilton, among them the Montreal Canadiens, the Los Angeles Kings and the Oakland A's.

🛏 TOUR D: OLD TOWN OF YORK

Hostelling International *($; K, tv, ℜ; 76 Church St., M5B 1Y7, ☎971-4440 or 800-668-4487, ⊷368-6499)* offers 175 beds in semi-private rooms or dormitories at very affordable prices. Guests will find a television lounge, a laundromat, a kitchen and a restaurant with a pool table and dart board, as well as an outdoor terrace.

Jarvis House *($$; tv, ≡, ⊛, K, P; 344 Jarvis St., M4Y 2G6, ☎975-3838, ⊷975-9808)* offers 10 spotless rooms, each with a private bathroom. This newly renovated Victorian house also offers laundry service and full or continental breakfasts.

St. Lawrence Residences *($$ bkfst incl.; sb; 137 Jarvis St., M5C 2H6, ☎361-0053)* provides B&B-, hotel- or dorm-style rooms. The rooms are bright and airy at this downtown establishment which is close to the Eaton Centre, Yonge Street, the financial district and many restaurants.

🦑 **Ambassador Inn Downtown Toronto** *($$$-$$$$$ bkfst incl.; sb/pb, ≡; 208 Jarvis St., M5B 2C5)* is an elegant, upscale B&B in a 20-room Victorian mansion with fireplaces, a cathedral ceiling, gabled roof, stained glass windows and skylights. Options include private or shared bathrooms, air conditioning and colour cable television.

Best Western Primrose Hotel *($$$-$$$$; pb, ≡, ≈, ℜ, △, ℰ; 111 Carlton St., Toronto M5B 2G3, ☎977-8000 or 800-268-8082)* is located in the heart of downtown Toronto, opposite Maple Leaf Gardens. It has spacious rooms with two double beds or a king size bed and a sofa, meeting rooms, saunas, an exercise room, a lounge and an outdoor pool.

Cawthra Square Bed & Breakfast *($$$-$$$$ bkfst incl.; sb/pb, ≡, ℜ, K; 10 Cawthra Sq., Toronto M4Y 1K8, ☎966-3074 or 800-259-5474)* comprises two elegant Victorian and Edwardian homes are in the heart of Toronto's gay village, near Church and Wellesley. It has grand principal rooms, continental breakfast rooms and guest rooms, and private bathrooms and terraces are available.

French hotel chain **Novotel** *($$$-$$$$; ≡, ⊛, ℜ, ℰ, pb, △, tv; 45 The Esplanade, Toronto M5E 1W2, ☎367-8900 or 800-668-6835, ≈360-8285)* enjoys an ideal Toronto location, just minutes from Harbourfront, the St. Lawrence and Hummingbird centres, and Union Station. Comfort is assured at this hotel, except perhaps for the rooms facing The Esplanade, whose peace and quiet may be disturbed by sounds from the outdoor bars.

The **Quality Hotel by Journey's End** *($$$$; ≡, tv, pb; 111 Lombard St., Toronto M5C 2T9, ☎367-5555, ≈367-3470)* caters to people who want simple but comfortable rooms at a reasonable price.

The **Ramada Hotel and Suites** *($$$$; ≡, ≈, ℜ, ℰ, pb, △; 300 Jarvis St., Toronto M5B 2C5, ☎977-4823 or 800-272-6232, ≈977-4830)* squeezes about 100 rooms into a rather small space, but it manages to retain a special old-world charm. Rooms are small but very comfortable, and the service is excellent.

The **Cambridge Suites Hotel** *($$$$$ bkfst incl.; ≡, ≈, ⊛, K, ℝ, ℰ, pb, △, tv; 15 Richmond St. E., Toronto M5C 1N2, ☎368-1990, ≈601-3751)* offers sumptuous 51-square-metre (nearly 550 square feet) suites, all equipped with a microwave oven, a refrigerator and a complete sets of dishes. Deluxe suites have a whirlpool bath.

ACCOMMODATIONS

Built in 1903, the **Royal Meridian King Edward Hotel** *($$$$$; ≡, ℜ, Ⓒ, pb, tv; 37 King St. E., Toronto M5C 1E9, ☎863-9700 or 800-5245-5843, ⊷367-5515)* is the oldest hotel in Toronto and still one of the most attractive. Rooms at this very elegant spot each have their own character but do not, unfortunately, offer much in terms of views. The magnificent lobby and the two ballrooms make up for this, however. Airport buses stop here regularly.

TOUR E: QUEEN WEST

Located in the heart of the trendy Queen West area, the **Alexandra Apartment Hotel** *($$; pb, ≡, ℜ, K; 77 Ryerson Ave., Toronto M5T 2V4, ☎504-2121 or 800-567-1893)* has comfortable studio suites equipped with kitchenettes, bathrooms, colour cable television, air conditioning, direct dial telephones and laundry facilities. Parking is available.

The **Beaconsfield** *($$$-$$$$ bkfst incl.; tv; 38 Beaconsfield Ave., Toronto M6J 3H9, ☎535-3338)*, a superb Victorian house dating from 1882 in a quiet little neighbourhood near Queen Street, is a good place to turn if you are looking for something different from the big hotels. Rooms are charming and imaginatively decorated. Perhaps best of all, though, are the delightful breakfasts accompanied by music.

The **Sheraton Centre Toronto** *($$$$$; ≡, ≈, ℜ, Ⓒ, pb, △, tv; 123 Queen St. W., Toronto M5H 2M9, ☎361-1000 or 800-325-3535, ⊷947-4801)* is an enormous complex including 40 shops, restaurants and bars as well as two movie theatres. This very comfortable hotel has many rooms, the most attractive of which are in the two towers, reached by private elevators. The lobby is this hotel's most astonishing feature, with its magnificent two-acre indoor garden. Guests also have access to the network of indoor passageways linking many downtown points.

If you prefer to have everything under the same roof, the **Toronto Marriott Eaton Centre** *($$$$$; ≡, ≈, ℜ, ⊛, △, Ⓒ, pb, tv; 525 Bay St., Toronto M5G 2L2, ☎597-9200, ⊷597-9211)* fits the bill. Linked to the famous Eaton Centre, a shoppers' mecca and one of the city's main attractions (see p 121), the Marriott

Hotel offers huge, well-equipped rooms (they even have irons and ironing boards). If you wish to relax, there are two ground floor lounges, one with pool tables and televisions.

 TOUR F: CHINATOWN AND KENSINGTON

Grange Apartment/Hotel *($$; pb, ≡, ℝ, K; 165 Grange Ave., Toronto M5T 2V5, ☎603-7700)*. Located downtown, near Chinatown, Kensington and Queen Street West, the affordable rooms are comfortable and air conditioned ,with colour tv, telephone, laundry rooms and parking available.

The **Metropolitan Chestnut Park** *($$$$$; ≡, ≈, ⊘, pb, △, tv; 108 Chestnut St., Toronto M5G 1R3, ☎977-5000 or 800-668-6600)* is one of the biggest additions to the Toronto hotel scene. Entering the lobby, you will discover an inviting atrium, giving you an idea of what to expect in the thoroughly pleasant rooms.

 TOUR G: QUEEN'S PARK AND
THE UNIVERSITY OF TORONTO

The Admiral House *($; sb, ℝ, K; 32-34 Admiral Rd., Toronto M5R 2L5, ☎923-4799)* rents out furnished rooms, shared kitchens with bathrooms and laundry facilities to students and post-graduates year-round. There is a television lounge on every floor. Located on the Bloor Street subway line, right near the University of Toronto and a five-minute walk from the Annex.

Massey College — University of Toronto *($ bkfst incl.; sb/pb, ℛ, ℝ, K; 4 Devonshire Pl., Toronto M5S 2E1, ☎978-2892)* is a college residence with 75 rooms surrounding a beautiful courtyard, offering a quiet escape in the middle of downtown Toronto. Breakfast is included on weekdays. Available only from May to July.

The Residence College Hotel *($; sb, ≡, ≈, ℝ, K, ⊘; 90 Gerrard St. W., Toronto M5G 1J6, ☎340-3750)* has furnished rooms with shared kitchen, bathroom and laundry facilities. Daily, weekly and monthly rates are available. Located on Gerrard Street near Bay, it is within walking distance of the transit system, shopping and the Eaton Centre.

Centre Island bursts into bloom in the summer.
– *Walter Bibikow*

The Rolling Stones are immortalized in this mural on Yonge Street.
– *Walter Bibikow*

The famous Niagara Falls,
one of the natural wonders of the world. – *T. Bognar*

The **Neill Wycik College Hotel** *($-$$; ℛ, △; 96 Gerrard St. E., Toronto M5B 1G7, ☎977-2320 or 800-268-4358, ⇝977-2809)* opens its student residences to travellers from mid-May to mid-August. Rooms are simple and offer only the basics, but guests have room-cleaning service, a television lounge and a laundromat at their disposal.

Morning Glory *($$ bkfst incl.; 486 Manning Ave., Toronto M2G 2V7, ☎533-6120)* Bed and Breakfast occupies a charming Edwardian house with pretty stained-glass windows and big, comfortable rooms. Weather permitting, you can have your breakfast on the outdoor terrace. Outdoor parking is available.

From May to August, at the **St. George Campus** of the **University of Toronto** *($$; K, ℛ, ℛ, ⊘; 214 College St., Toronto M5T 2Z9, ☎978-8045, ⇝978-1616)*, you will find an excellent, low-cost alternative to expensive hotels. The university has lodgings that can accommodate four to six persons, and all come with a fully equipped kitchenette. They are located near a cafeteria, a pub and a physical fitness centre.

If you are visiting Toronto during the summer months and want a clean, economic place to sleep, you can take advantage of the 425 rooms at **Victoria University** *($$ bkfst incl.; ⊘, tv; 140 Charles St. W., Toronto M5S 1K9, ☎585-4524)*. A laundromat, cafeteria and sports facilities are at guests' disposal.

🦫 **Beverly Place Bed & Breakfast** *($$-$$$ bkfst incl.; sb/pb, ≡; 235 Beverly St., Toronto M5T 1Z4, ☎977-0077)*. This 1887 Victorian house has been restored to its original beauty, complete with exquisite antique furnishings. Awarded the Government of Canada Tourism Ambassador Certificate, it is centrally located, near the University of Toronto campus, Chinatown and the cafés and shops in the Annex.

The **Bond Place Hotel** *($$$; ≡, ℛ, tv; 65 Dundas St. E., Toronto M5B 2G8, ☎362-6061, ⇝360-6406)* is doubtless the best located hotel for enjoying the rhythm of the city and mixing with the varied throng at the corner of Dundas and Yonge.

🦫 The **Delta Chelsea** *($$$$$; ≡, ⊛, ≈, ℛ, ⊘, pb, tv; 33 Gerrard St. W., M5G 1Z4, ☎595-1975 or 800-268-1133,*

ACCOMMODATIONS

585-4362) is very popular with visitors and justly so, for it offers comfortable rooms at reasonable prices, and guests under 18 can share their parents' room free of charge. The new tower draws business travellers thanks to its business centre equipped with ergonomically designed chairs, fax machines and telephones.

The **Sutton Place Hotel** *($$$$$; ≈, ℛ, ⊘; 955 Bay St., Toronto M5S 2A2, ☎924-9221 or 800-268-3790, ≈924-1778)* boasts a solid reputation for luxury and the highest standards of quality and service, and all this ideally located near Queen's Park, the Royal Ontario Museum and the shops of Bloor and Yorkville. Each of the rooms and suites comes with bathrobes, a hairdryer, a mini-bar, an in-room safe, computer connection and voice-mail. The suites also have a full kitchen and a stunning antique decor.

 TOUR H: BLOOR AND YORKVILLE

The **Comfort Hotel Downtown** *($$$; pb, ℛ, ≡; 15 Charles St. E., Toronto M4Y 1S1, ☎924-1222 or 800-228-5150)* is near Bloor Street's upscale shopping district, and a block from the central intersection of Yonge and Bloor. This newly renovated hotel has elegantly decorated rooms.

Days Inn – Toronto Downtown *($$$; pb, ≡, ≈, ℛ, ℝ, ⊘; 30 Carlton St., Toronto M5B 2E9, ☎977-6655 or 800-329-7466)* offers decent, affordable hotel accommodation. It is just half a block from the subway and within walking distance of Yonge Street and the Eaton Centre. Indoor pool, sauna and in-room movies are at guests' disposal.

Howard Johnson Inn Yorkville *($$$ bkfst incl.; pb, ≡, ℝ; 89 Avenue Rd., Toronto M5R 2G3, ☎964-1220 or 800-654-6423)* is a quaint, 71-room hotel located in the trendy Yorkville area. It is a little less expensive than some of the five-star hotels in the area, but is still just a step from the shop-lined streets of Yorkville and Bloor and some of Toronto's finest galleries.

Marlborough Place *($$$; bkfst incl.; sb/pb, ≡; 93 Marlborough Ave., Toronto M5R 1X5, ☎922-2159)* is a B&B in a charming

1880 Victorian townhouse located near the fashionable Yorkville shopping area. Spacious loft, twin beds, private bathroom and deck.

Quality Hotel Midtown *($$$; pb, ≡, ℛ; 280 Bloor St. W., Toronto M5S 1V8, ☎968-0010 or 800-424-6423)* is right on fashionable Bloor Street West, amidst shops, museums and the beautiful, tree-lined grounds of the University of Toronto. The many restaurants found in the Annex area are an easy walk away. Rooms are clean and spacious, and the hotel is located near the city's transit system.

Near the stylish boutiques and swank restaurants of Yorkville is the **Venture Inn** *($$$$ bkfst incl.; 89 Avenue Rd., Toronto M5R 2G3, ☎964-1220, ⇔964-8692)*. While it is perhaps lacking some of the charm of other neighbourhood institutions, its rooms are comfortable and reasonably priced. As if to compensate for its lacklustre exterior, its interior is warmly and tastefully decorated. Its furniture is mostly pine, creating a more rustic ambiance, thus distinguishing it from other establishments in this category.

Victoria's Mansion *($$$$; tv; ℝ; 68 Gloucester St., M4Y 1L5, ☎921-4625, ⇔925-0300)* is a beautiful turn-of-the-century home located on a quiet street close to lively neighbourhoods, just a few streets south of Bloor. Its elaborate exterior gives a somewhat inaccurate idea of its modestly decorated interior and plainly furnished suites. Vicotria's is particularly well suited for long-term stays, since each room has a kitchenette and desk, offering a level of comfort similar to a small apartment.

The rooms at the **Park Hyatt** *($$$$$; ≡, ℛ, ⊘, pb, tv; 4 Avenue Rd., Toronto M5R 2E8, ☎924-5471 or 800-977-4197, ⇔924-4933)* have been tastefully renovated – even the bath-rooms, which are now covered in marble. It has a very pleasant location, in the heart of Yorkville, just a few minutes' walk from the Royal Ontario Museum.

If you are looking for top-of-the-line luxury, the **Four Seasons Hotel Toronto** *($$$$$; ≡, ⊛, ≈, ℛ, ⊘, pb, tv; 21 Avenue Rd., Toronto M5R 2G1, ☎964-0411 or 800-268-6282, ⇔964-2301)* is one of the most highly rated hotels in North America. This spot lives up to its reputation, with impeccable service and beautifully decorated rooms. It also has a sumptuous ballroom with Persian carpets and crystal chandeliers. The hotel restaurant, **Truffles** (see p 229), boasts Uffizi sculptures of two wild boars at the entrance, and will satisfy your appetite with some of the best food in Toronto.

Just a few steps from the Royal Ontario Museum and from Yorkville Street, the **Inter-Continental Toronto** *($$$$$; ≡, ≈, ℜ, ⊘, pb, △, tv; 220 Bloor St. W., Toronto M5S 1T8, ☎960-5200, ≈920-8269)* is sure to seduce you with its vast, tastefully decorated rooms and its exemplary service.

 ## TOUR I: CABBAGETOWN

Set close to charming Cabbagetown, the **Homewood Inn** *($$ bkfst incl.; tv, ℜ, P; 65 Homewood Ave., Toronto M4Y 2K1, ☎/≈920-7944)* boasts an excellent location and Victorian charm.

The Mulberry Tree *($$ bkfst incl.; sb, ≡, ℜ; 122 Isabella St., Toronto M4Y 1P1, ☎960-5249)* is on shady, tree-lined Isabella Street, near Cabbagetown, the gay village and the upscale shopping area at Yonge and Bloor. It is a downtown heritage home with a touch of European flair, has a guest lounge, free parking and sauna and 24-hour coffee and tea.

A charming, inexpensive option near Rosedale is the **Hotel Selby** *($$-$$$ bkfst incl.; ≡, ⊘, K, P; 592 Sherbourne St., Toronto M4X 1L4, ☎921-3142 or 800-387-4788, ≈923-3177)*. There are senior, student and weekly rates, as well as laundry facilities.

An 1871 Historic House *($$$ bkfst incl.; sb/pb, ≡, ℜ; 65 Huntley St., Toronto M4Y 2L2, ☎923-6950)* is located between the Yonge and Bloor shopping area and Cabbagetown, and it is an easy walk to either. This sunny, comfortable, antique-filled home has hardwood floors, a whirlpool bath and antique wicker furnishings.

TOUR J: THE ANNEX

ACCOMMODATIONS

The Global Guest House *($$; =; 9 Spadina Rd., Toronto M5R 2S9, ☎923-4004, ⇒923-1208)* is a popular, inexpensive and ecologically sound alternative, ideally situated just north of Bloor Street. The nine rooms are all spotless and simply decorated.

Lowther House *($$ bkfst incl.; tv, =; 72 Lowther Ave., Toronto M5R 1C8, ☎323-1589 or 800-265-4158, ⇒962-7005)* is a charming, beautifully restored Victorian mansion in the heart of the Annex and just minutes from many of the city's best sights. A double whirlpool bath, sun room, fireplace, claw-footed tub and delicious Belgian waffles are just some of the treasures that await visitors at this home away from home. Private and shared bathrooms.

Philomena & Dave Bed & Breakfast *($$ bkfst incl.; sb, =, ℝ, K; 31 Dalton Rd., Toronto M5R 2Y8, ☎962-2786 or 888-272-2718)* is an elegant, affordable home located at the fringe of the Annex area, at the intersection of both the east-west and north-south transit lines. It has oak woodwork, stained-glass windows and comfortable beds.

Annex House Bed & Breakfast *($$-$$$ bkfst incl.; pb, =, ℝ, K; 147 Madison Ave., Toronto M5R 2S6, ☎920-3922)* is located among beautiful Victorian and Georgian homes in the tree-lined streets of the Annex, and is within easy walking distance of Bloor Street's many restaurants and the transit line.

A lovely Georgian house with two elegant white columns accommodates the **Palmerston Inn** *($$$ bkfst incl.; 322 Palmerston Blvd., Toronto M6G 2N6, ☎920-7842, ⇒960-9529)* Bed and Breakfast. Located on one of the city's few quiet streets, this establishment offers eight rooms for non-smokers only, five of them air-conditioned and all decorated with period furniture.

Antique furnishings and leaded-glass windows contribute to the beautiful surroundings at the **Terrace House B&B** *($$$ bkfst incl.; =, pb; 52 Austin Terrace, Toronto M5R 1Y6, ☎535-1493,*

☞535-9616), located close to Casa Loma. Friendly hosts and the resident cat will make you feel at home.

 The **Amblecote** *($$$ bkfst incl.; 109 Walmer Rd., Toronto M5R 2X8, ☎927-1713)* Bed and Breakfast is a little jewel hidden in the trendy Annex district west of Yorkville, on a quiet street lined with stately homes. Dating from the early 20th century, this superb house has been fully renovated after a period of neglect. The new owners, Paul and Mark, worked hard to restore it to its former glory. There are beautiful antiques throughout. The guest rooms at either end are especially splendid, bright and spacious.

TOUR K: ROSEDALE, FOREST HILL AND NORTH OF TORONTO

YWCA Woodlawn Residence *($-$$ bkfst incl.; sb/pb; 80 Woodlawn Ave. E., Toronto M4T 1C1, ☎923-8454)* is a women's residence located south of St. Clair Avenue and Yonge Street, just north of the Summerhill subway station. Dormitory-style accommodation is available for travellers, with up to 10 women in one room. There are also private rooms with either a shared or private bathroom. Breakfast is included.

The **Vanderkooy Bed & Breakfast** *($$ bkfst incl.; sb/pb, ≡; 53 Walker Ave., Toronto M4V 1G3, ☎925-8765)* is in Toronto's upscale, residential, tree-lined Rosedale neighbourhood, just a five-minute walk from the Summerhill subway station and a 15-minute walk from Yonge and Bloor. There are a resident cat and a pond in the garden, and the owners have a penchant for jazz music.

Yonge Street Bed & Breakfast *($$-$$$ bkfst incl.; sb/pb, ≡; 3266 Yonge St., Toronto M4N 3P6, ☎481-2206)* is located north of downtown on the Yonge Street corridor, with access to the transit system. Private rooms with private bathrooms and parking are available. Only a short walk from great restaurants and shopping.

TOUR L: EASTERN TORONTO

Scarborough

The **University of Toronto Scarborough Campus** *($$$; R, K, ⊘; 1265 Military Trail, Scarborough M1C 1A4, ☎287-7369, ≈287-7667)* offers four- and six-person townhouses, complete with private bathrooms and fully-equipped kitchens from mid-May to the end of August. Located east of downtown, near the Metropolitan Zoo, this spot is ideal for families. The university's sports facilities are available to guests, and there is a snack bar on campus. Bring your own towels, and take note that there are no televisions, no room phones or pool, and no pets are allowed.

You can enjoy the pleasure of a traditional country inn just minutes from Toronto, at Scarborough's **Guild Inn** *($$$; ≈, ℜ; 201 Guildwood Pkwy., Scarborough M1E 1P6, ☎261-3331, ≈261-5675)*. Thirteen rooms occupy the original 1930s building set amidst a lush green forest; another 67 occupy an adjoining modern wing. The utmost in romance and charmp; a must!

The Beaches

Balmy Beach in the Beaches Bed & Breakfast *($$ bkfst incl.; ≈; 107 Dixon Ave., Toronto M4L 1N8, ☎690-8254 or 888-423-3337)* is right on the Beaches waterfront. This B&B is in a restored Victorian home with a homey atmosphere and breakfast consisting of freshly-baked bread, home-made muffins, fruit jams and freshly ground coffee. Parking available.

Craig House Bed & Breakfast on the Beach *($$ bkfst incl.; sb/pb, R, K; 78 Spruce Hill Rd., Toronto M4E 3G3, ☎698-3916)* is in the popular Beaches neighbourhood by the lake, where visitors can enjoy the boardwalk, bicycling and in-line skating paths, a yacht club, shopping and sidewalk cafés galore. This home is surrounded by gardens. There are private or shared bathrooms and kitchen facilities are available. Free parking.

Beaches Bed & Breakfast *($$ bkfst incl.; sb/pb, ≡, ℝ, K; 174 Waverly Rd, Toronto M4L 3T3, ☎699-0818)* is a charming and unusual home right in the heart of the Beaches neighbourhood, close to the lake, parks, shops, cafés and the streetcar to downtown. Cats share the home with guests and the breakfast each morning is tasty and nutritious.

WEST OF THE CITY

For an alternative to the big, expensive hotels, try the **Marigold Hostel** *($ bkfst incl.; 2011 Dundas St. W., Toronto M6R 1W7, ☎536-8824 after 7pm)*. This charming little hotel is often filled with young travellers and students who prefer to save a bit of cash and will forego a private bathroom. All of the rooms are dormitory style.

Islington Bed & Breakfast House *($$ bkfst incl.; sb, ≡; 1411 Islington Ave., Toronto M9A 3K5, ☎236-2707)* is located west of the city in one of Toronto's prestigious real estate neighbourhoods near the Humber Valley. Just steps away from the subway line for downtown. Free parking. No smoking.

Old Mill Manor *($$ bkfst incl.; pb; 100 Old Mill Rd., Toronto M8X 1G8, ☎233-7460)* is a charming Georgian home in the historical parkland setting of Old Mill, overlooking the Humber River. It is 15 minutes to the city or to the airport by car, and some shops, restaurants and movie theatres are within walking distance.

Novotel Mississauga Hotel *($$$; pb, ≡, ≈, ℛ, ☺; 3670 Hurontario St., Mississauga L5B 1P3, ☎905-896-1000 or 800-NOVOTEL)* lies just west of the city, in the suburb of Mississauga. Located in the heart of Mississauga City Centre, restaurants and shopping are close at hand and the airport is just a short drive away. An exercise room, sauna, racquetball, indoor pool, whirlpool and free airport shuttle are available here.

NEAR THE AIRPORT

Close to the airport, the **Best Western Carlton Place Hotel** *($$$-$$$$; ≡, ⊛, ≈, ℛ, ◌, tv, pb; 33 Carlson Court, Etobicoke*

M9W 6H5, ☎*675-1234 or 800-528-1234,* ⇒*675-3436)* offers decent, comfortable rooms at reasonable prices.

Ramada Hotel Toronto Airport *($$$-$$$$ bkfst incl.; pb, ≡, ≈, ℜ, ☻, △, ⊘; 2 Holiday Dr., Toronto M9C 2Z7,* ☎*621-2121 or 800-2RAMADA)* is five minutes from the airport and offers complementary shuttle service and free parking. It features a health club, sauna, whirlpool, indoor/outdoor pool and licensed dining room.

Regal Constellation Hotel *($$$-$$$$ bkfst incl.; pb, ≡, ≈, ℜ, ☻, △, ⊘; 900 Dixon Rd., Toronto M9W 1J7,* ☎*675-1500 or 800-268-4838)* is a large hotel, convention and trade-show facility near Pearson International Airport. It has an impressive array of amenities, including a heated indoor/outdoor pool, beauty salon, travel agency, four restaurants and a lounge.

Holiday Inn Select Toronto Airport *($$$$ bkfst incl.; pb, ≡, ≈, ℜ, ☻, △, ⊘; 970 Dixon Rd., Toronto M9W 1J9,* ☎*675-7611 or 800-HOLIDAY)* has a sauna, health club, heated indoor/outdoor pools, whirlpool, parking and a licensed dining room. There is a snooker lounge with light dining and a bar, billiard tables, dart boards and a library. Pets are allowed.

🦐 For middle-budget travellers, **Quality Suites** *($$$$ bkfst incl.; ≡, ℜ, pb, tv; 262 Carlingview Dr., Etobicoke M9W 5G1,* ☎*674-8442 or 800-228-5151)* offers pleasant, unpretentious rooms. Although it is a little far from the airport, this place offers one of the best quality-to-price ratios in the area. A regular bus links the hotel and the airport every half-hour.

The **Sheraton Gateway Hotel at Terminal Three** *($$$$$; ≡, ☻, ℜ, ⊘, pb, tv; P.O. Box 3000, Toronto AMF L5P 1C4,* ☎*905-672-7000 or 800-565-0010,* ⇒*905-672-7100)*, linked directly to Terminal 3 at Toronto's Pearson International Airport, is the best located hotel for in-transit passengers. It has 474 attractively decorated rooms and is fully soundproofed, with panoramic views of the airport or the city.

ACCOMMODATIONS

RESTAURANTS

Toronto is a city abounding in opportunities to sample its culinary delights. As a cosmopolitan metropolis with myriad cultures and neighbourhoods brushing up against one another, its restaurants, which serve cuisines from all over the world, are as diverse as its population. Certainly Toronto offers plenty of fine dining opportunities, with prices to match, but even the pennywise can find unique and interesting eateries within their budget. The restaurants that follow are presented in the order of the tours outlined in this guide (see p 87) to make it easier to find them, no matter where you are in your exploration of Toronto.

Prices are for a meal for one person including taxes, but excluding drinks and tip.

$	less than $10
$$	$10 to $20
$$$	$20 to $30
$$$$	more than $30

RESTAURANT INDEX BY TYPE OF CUISINE

RESTAURANTS

RESTAURANTS

 TOUR A: THE WATERFRONT

Spinnaker's *($$$; 207 Queen's Quay W., ☎203-0559)* has a sprawling, 200-seat patio right on the waterfront in Queen's Quay Terminal. With a super modern design incorporating lots of stucco, wild colours and architectural shapes, it achieves a sort of eclectic Mediterranean bistro aesthetic. The executive chef specializes in seafood, but a variety of other dishes are served as well.

Right next to Spinnaker's in Queen's Quay Terminal, **The Boathouse Bar and Grill** *($$$; 207 Queen's Quay W., ☎203-6300)* has a nautical look, with lots of brass accents. It has an outdoor patio and serves roadhouse fare — steak, potatoes and pasta.

Pearl Harbourfront Chinese Cuisine *($$$; 207 Queen's Quay W., ☎203-1233)* is a somewhat formal restaurant, also in the Queen's Quay Terminal. Its many skylights make the room open and airy. The staff is very attentive. The Chinese specialties, including delicious chicken and prawn dishes, are cooked with market-fresh food.

Imagine savouring a meal and a bottle of wine, with a panoramic view of Toronto and Lake Ontario as the backdrop. The **360 Restaurant** *($$$$; CN Tower, 301 Front St. W., ☎362-5411)*, which revolves atop the CN Tower, offers fine dining and undoubtedly the most spectacular views in town.

Planet Hollywood *($$-$$$; 277 Front St. W., ☎596-7827)*, the giant American chain, goes for Hollywood glitz with movie memorabilia, flashing lights and big-screen televisions. Situated at the base of the CN Tower, it mainly attracts tourists. The food, however, isn't quite as glamourous as the restaurant tries to be. The typical American fare of burgers, pasta and sandwiches is over-priced and mediocre.

Toronto's **Hard Rock Cafe** *($$; 1 Blue Jays Way, in the SkyDome, ☎341-2388)*, like other locations of this worldwide chain, is a tribute to the greats of rock and roll. The walls and ceiling are covered with paraphernalia that once belonged to the likes of Paul McCartney and Janis Joplin. With a view of the Skydome's playing field, a meal here can be an experience to remember. The usual burgers and fries make up the menu.

Wayne Gretzky's *($$; 99 Blue Jays Way, ☎979-PUCK)* may be the last place to get close to the Great One, now that the stick-handling virtuoso has retired. Just around the corner from the CN Tower, this mega-sized sports bar seats hundreds and is a veritable shrine of Gretzky memorabilia, with displays of sweaters, trophies and skates. The rooftop Oasis patio has a rock waterfall and fake palm trees, and serves up barbecue food such as burgers and ribs from an open grill. A good selection of pasta rounds out the regular pub fare on the rest of the menu.

TOUR B: TORONTO ISLANDS

A few steps from the amusement park on the Toronto Islands, the **Iroquois** *($; ☎203-8795)* restaurant is often invaded by crowds of happy children who come for a pizza or a hamburger.

People go to the **Island Paradise Restaurant** *($$$; next to the Centre Island ferry, ☎203-0245)* for its spectacular views of Lake Ontario and of Toronto, which can be enjoyed while

Ulysses's Favourites

For the finest dining:
Truffles (p 229)

For the innovative cuisine:
Fez Batik (p 216), North 44 (p 233)

For the interesting selection:
Marché Mövenpick (p 210)

For the atmosphere:
Select Bistro (p 216), Nothing in Common (p 232),
The Paddock (p 219) and C'est What (p 212)

For the view:
360 Restaurant (p 208)

For the decor:
Addis Ababa (p 221), Bombay Palace (p 213),
Nothing in Common (p 232) and Fez Batik (p 216)
and Flo's Diner (p 227).

For breakfast or brunch:
Café du Marché (p 214)

For afternoon tea:
Queen Mother Café (p 215)

For the price:
Epicure Café (p 217)

For sports fans:
C'est What (p 212)

For the terrasse:
Spinnaker's (p 207)

For people-watching:
Café Nervosa (p 227)

For the desserts:
Bibiche Bistro (p 235)

RESTAURANTS

savouring a chicken dish or a steak. Open until the departure of the last ferry.

TOUR C: THE THEATRE AND FINANCIAL DISTRICTS

At the **Marché Mövenpick** *($$-$$$; inside BCE place at Front and Yonge, ☎366-8986)* you can serve yourself from an array of gourmet food counters, offering everything from freshly-made sushi to fresh pasta and salads. The only challenge is choosing between so many dishes, as each is as tempting as the next. This spot is very popular and often has line-ups, particularly during lunch hour (see also p 228).

Some establishments have continuously pleased their customers for decades. Such is the case of **Shopsy's** *($-$$; 33 Yonge St., ☎365-3333)*, a delicatessen that opened in 1921 and has captured the hearts and stomachs of Torontonians with its traditional breakfasts and its hot dogs. The deli is located a few steps from the Hockey Hall of Fame, at the corner of Yonge and Front streets.

As the name suggests, **Acqua** *($$$; BCE Place, 10 Front St. W., ☎368-7171)* takes water as its main theme. While observing the fine and rather unusual decor of this fashionable restaurant, you will enjoy succulent dishes drawn from the culinary traditions of the Mediterranean and California.

Toronto and Montreal: these long-time rivals have one good thing in common – **Moishes** *($$$; 77 Adelaide St. W., ☎363-3509)*. Its in-house specialty, a tender, succulent steak, will delight any gourmet. A quiet ambiance and impeccable service add to your dining experience.

Mövenpick Restaurant *($$$; 165 York St., ☎366-0558)* serves the same delicious Swiss specialties as the Marché (see further above) but with table service and without the hectic cafeteria ambiance. Their all-you-can-eat weekend brunches are fabulous as well.

The **Mercer Street Grill** *($$$$; 36 Mercer St., ☎599-3399)* is a well-known trendy, upscale restaurant in Toronto's theatre district. The decor is modern and funky, the fare a unique Asian fusion including sushi desserts.

The strip along King Street between John and Peter streets is popular with both the theatre and after-work crowds. **Fred's Not Here** *($$$; 321 King St. W., ☎971-9155)* has a crisp look, with white tablecloths and glass sculpted decor. There is a fixed-price dinner menu for $19.95, but you can also order à la carte. The spicy home-made jalapeno corn bread will keep you going while you decide. Among the menu items: grilled baby octopus served on glass noodles; lamb satay with peanut sauce; baked lobster and crab soup. The atmosphere is civilized, although noise from The Red Tomato, the bar below, can get quite loud.

Hey Lucy *($$; 295 King St. W., ☎408-3633)* puts a little panache into pizza-eating, with exposed brick walls and a wood-fired pizza oven. Suits and theatre-goers congregate within or on the sidewalk patio out front for nachos or fresh mussel appetizers, a choice of gourmet salads, 16 different kinds of pizza, and pasta including seafood linguine. They even have a dessert pizza: a wood-fired crust baked with cinnamon and brown sugar, topped with raspberry sauce, fresh fruit and whipped cream.

You can't miss **N'Awlins Jazz Bar and Grill** *($$-$$$; 299 King St. W., ☎595-1958)* — it's the one with the piano hanging above the door outside! The place has a loungy atmosphere reserved for a hip, sophisticated crowd. There are excellent live jazz players every night, providing the musical soundscape while you sample the menu of tasty gourmet pasta and meat dishes.

Fenice *($$; 319 King St. W., ☎585-2377)* invites you to enjoy delicious Italian dishes prepared with fresh ingredients, and to delight in a warm atmosphere, cradled by the sounds of classical music.

The famous Honest Ed Mirvish will take you on a trip back in time to the good old days of the Victorian era at **Ed's Warehouse** *($$-$$$; 270 King St. W., ☎977-3939)*, decorated with plenty of antique items. Remember, everything at Honest Ed's is for sale; do not hesitate to ask the price if something catches your eye. Besides the decor, this restaurant, spread over five floors in two buildings, will satisfy every craving: it includes Ed's Chinese, Ed's Seafood, Old Ed's, Ed's Italian and Ed's Folly.

The **Whistling Oyster Seafood Café** *($-$$; 11 Duncan St., ☎598-7707)* has a daily happy hour, but not for alcohol. Here, it's bargain-priced seafood and Thai-inspired items that bring people in. A few examples: a half-dozen fresh oysters cost just over $6, New England clam chowder is $2, and you pay only $4 for grilled chicken and shrimp satay. The place is located in the basement of the same building where The Filet of Sole is found, and has a casual, loungy atmosphere.

Acme Bar and Grill *($$; 86 John St., ☎340-9700)* is the place for sports lovers and attracts a big crowd after a Blue Jays game lets out at the nearby SkyDome. Rows of TVs and the requisite big screen are all here. Its big draws: more than 90 single malts, many of them for less than $5, and over 50 sizzling hot sauces to put a bit of fire into your meal. The fare is typical sportsman's food: burgers, which are nothing to write home about, and succulent ribs, a much better choice.

Plantation *($; 121 King St. W., ☎861-0808)* is an ideal place to stop and savour a coffee or a dish made from fresh, quality ingredients. High ceilings, large windows, and fresco replicas all make this a fine place to eat.

 TOUR D: OLD TOWN OF YORK

In response to Toronto's growing infatuation with good coffee, **Starbucks** *($; 81 Front St. E., ☎955-9956)*, the famous Seattle-based chain, has recently opened several branches in Toronto. With its excellent coffee, it has become so popular among Torontonians that it is sometimes hard to find a seat.

C'est What *($$; 67 Front St. E, ☎867-9499)*. A wonderful medley of cuisines is served into the wee hours at this before-and after-theatre stop. The exciting menu features exotic salads and original sandwiches. The ambiance is almost pub-like, with cozy chairs, board games and mood music that runs the gamut from folk to jazz.

Café Victoria *($$$-$$$$; Royal Meridian King Edward Hotel, 37 King St. E., ☎863-9700)* is sure to enchant you with its classic decor and its intimate tables, spaced evenly within a vast dining room. The meal, a veritable feast ending with a delicious dessert, is sure to be memorable.

🍽 A few steps from St. Lawrence Hall, you can enjoy Italian food worthy of the finest palates at **Biaggio** *($$$; 155 King St. E., ☎366-4040)*. This elegant restaurant serves some of the best fresh pastas in town. After struggling to settle on one of the very tempting dishes, you can choose from among an excellent selection of wines. Fortunately, the server will be able to help you.

You are sure to be satisfied at **Le Papillon** *($$-$$$; 16 Church St., ☎363-0838)*, whose menu offers a tempting variety of dishes combining the delicacies of French and Québecois cuisines. The *crêpes* are especially good.

Sushiman Japanese Restaurant *($$; 26 Richmond St. E., ☎362-8793)* serves excellent sushi and tempura at reasonable prices, with a traditional sushi bar and Japanese decor. Lunchtime specials draw a crowd that usually packs the place at midday.

🍽 **The Bombay Palace** *($$-$$$; 71 Jarvis, ☎368-8048)* has a dimly lit, ornate interior decorated with typical Indian art. It manages to transcend the bright lights and tacky dinette sets which typify so many of Toronto's Indian restaurants. White tablecloths and uniformed waiters give it a reserved air, but the food is excellent and well-priced. There is an extensive menu as well as a steaming buffet table.

🍽 **Young Thailand** *($$-$$$; 81 Church St., ☎368-1368)* is a large, bustling Thai eatery with a menu so involved you will need some time to get through it all. It has a decent wine list, dainty appetizers and a plethora of delicious Thai specialties, from green mango salad to marinated fish to shrimp coconut curries.

Golden Thai *($$-$$$; 105 Church St., ☎868-6668)* is just a few doors up from Young Thailand and offers similar fare at

RESTAURANTS

similar prices. It, too, is a popular dinner spot with a spectrum of Thai cuisine offerings.

The **Senator** *($$$$; closed Mon; 249 Victoria, ☎364-7517)* has survived the recent explosion of the Toronto restaurant scene and still serves one of the best steaks in town. Classy, refined setting.

The **Salad King** *($; 335 Yonge St., ☎971-7041)*, tucked on the corner of Yonge and Gould streets, is a place so unassuming that it would be easy to walk by it if you weren't looking for it. The food, however, which is ordered cafeteria-style from an open kitchen, is worth stopping for. The ambience scores low (most of the tables are in a dim, windowless room), but the authentic Thai fare is excellent and one of the best deals in town. Primarily a lunch counter, it is closed in the evenings.

Hard Rock Café *($$; 283 Yonge St., ☎362-3636)* is in the heart of Toronto's downtown core. Directly opposite the Eaton Centre, this tourist hot-spot lives up to its reputation, with memorabilia and paraphernalia honouring decades of rock and roll history. The fare is typical American burgers and fries.

Café du Marché *($-$$; 45 Colborne St., ☎368-0371)* serves only breakfast and lunch (it closes at 3pm), but is excellent value for your money. There is both a take-out counter and a dining room serving soups, salads, sandwiches, quiches, omelettes, entrees and a scrumptious selection of desserts.

Walking upstairs into the **Cyberland Café** *($; 257 Yonge St., 2nd floor, ☎955-9628)* across from the Eaton Centre is like entering a futuristic, cosmic lounge. Loud, spacy, electronic music fills the stairwell and the ceiling is a montage of planets and stars. This cyber café has dozens of computer terminals and mediocre food, including nachos and watery salads, in case you get peckish in cyberspace.

 TOUR E: QUEEN WEST

Queen Street West is at the heart of Toronto's nightlife, and is animated day and night with a mix of people, from club kids to underground music-lovers to restaurant-goers looking for a

night out in the hip part of town. The strip is peppered with
dozens of interesting, funky restaurants, representing a whole
range of cuisines. Most are in the middle price range, but there
are some true gems with alluringly cheap prices as well.

Between University and Spadina

Queen West divides into a few distinct areas. The stretch from
University Avenue to Spadina Avenue is the most gentrified,
with a café or restaurant every few feet, nestled between
major retailers such as the Gap and HMV records. The following
are some of the area's best choices:

Babur *($$; 273 Queen St. W., ☎599-7720)* is a typical Indian
restaurant with specialties from different parts of India — from
chicken tandoori to paneer korma. The vegetable pakoras
(deep-fried Indian fritters) make a savoury appetizer. Like many
of the restaurants on Queen West, Babur gets very busy,
especially on the weekends, so it's a good idea to reserve
ahead of time.

The interior of **Tiger Lily's Noodle House** *($$; 257 Queen St.
W., ☎977-5499)* is simple, almost pristine, with miniature
potted plants on each table, and lightning-fast service.
Ambrosial Thai and Chinese soups are served, arriving in
something more akin to a serving dish than a soup bowl, and
large enough for a meal. Soup may be the specialty here, but
the menu is rounded out with a tasty array of noodle dishes.

Queen Mother Café *($$-$$$; 210 Queen St. W., ☎598-4719)*
is owned by the same people who run the popular Rivoli
restaurant and bar down the road. Hardly a place for afternoon
tea, the Queen Mum serves up an eclectic range of dishes from
Laos and Thailand. Cozy booths and tables fill three rooms and
there is a small patio out back. Their Pad Thai has been a
favourite since long before every other place on the street was
serving it, and the sticky rice with peanut sauce is a pure
delight. There is an extensive menu of specials every day, and
the desserts from Dufflet Pasteries (one of the city's finest
bakeries) are divine.

RESTAURANTS

🥢 **Fez Batik** *($$$; 129 Peter St., ☎204-9660)* is the newest hot spot on the block, as a pair of successful local restaurateurs recently transformed a club into what is now a Moroccan-themed dinner lounge. It's a large, three-level space with a massive sculpted Buddha head dominating the entrance, and a lounge area where couches are piled high with Moroccan cushions. The food is an outstanding fusion of culinary styles, from Moroccan to Japanese, as artfully displayed as they are carefully prepared. The friendly, hipster-type servers will bring you fresh bread with a delicious tapenade of roasted tomatoes, olives and garlic as you pore over the enticing menu. In addition to a fine wine list, there are more than 40 types of tea to choose from.

🥢 Upon entering **Le Select Bistro** *($$$; 328 Queen St. W., ☎596-6405)*, you will be surrounded by jazz that makes it tempting to stay for hours. But this Parisian-style bistro offers more than a warm, relaxing atmosphere. It also has a mouth watering menu that draws a clientele of connoisseurs. There is something to please you at all times of year, especially in the summer when you can enjoy the inviting outdoor terrace.

Peter Pan *($$$; 373 Queen St. W., ☎593-0917)* has a beautiful 1930s decor and serves delicious and imaginative dishes. Pasta, pizza and fish take on an original look here. Service is distinguished.

There is nothing quite like a good *sushi* or *sashimi* of the type prepared at the **Sushi Bistro** *($$$; 204 Queen St. W., ☎971-5315)*. Sitting at the sushi bar, you can watch the chef prepare these delicious mouthfuls of raw fish with a stunning degree of skill. To end the evening on a festive note, you can take the stage at the *karaoke* bar.

🥢 The **Bamboo** *($$; 312 Queen St. W., ☎593-5771)* restaurant is one of Queen Street's most colourful spots. To reach the dining rooms, you have to squeeze through a narrow passageway linking the "temple" to the street. You can then choose between a two-level outdoor terrace or one of two indoor dining rooms. This one-of-a-kind restaurant, with food running the gamut from Caribbean to Malay to Thai and Indonesian flavours, also offers shows. You can enjoy specialties such as *satay* (chicken brochettes with spicy peanut sauce) before heading out onto the dance floor and swaying your hips to the captivating rhythms of reggae or salsa.

Tortilla Flats *($$; 429 Queen St. W., ☎593-9870)* is a Tex-Mex emporium near the corner of Queen and Spadina decorated with bright colours and typical Mexican trinkets. There are a bar, booths, tables and a patio at the back. The food is passable Tex-Mex — lots of cheesy burritos, nachos, enchiladas and fajitas. Try their head-clearing, fiery-hot Jalapeno Poppers – whole jalapeno peppers stuffed with cream cheese, breaded and deep fried. There are excellent drink specials on certain days of the week, so look for their two-for-one margarita days!

Between Spadina and Bathurst

The stretch between Spadina and Bathurst maintains the original Queen Street charm, with discount fabric stores, used book stores and dollar stores. However, as the trendy part of Queen West spreads further west, a number of choice eateries have opened up in this area:

Taro Grill *($$; 492 Queen St. W., ☎504-1320)* is one of those places you go not only to eat but also to be seen. This is one of the trendier places in town. The spectacle is complete with the chef visible in the open kitchen.

Cavernous and austere decor, exquisite presentation, attitude, mood lighting and an interesting interpretation of southwestern cuisine: that pretty much sums up the dining experience at **Left Bank** *($$; 567 Queen St. W., ☎504-1626)*.

The **Epicure Café** *($$; 512 Queen St. W., ☎504-8942)* has a warm, bistro-like atmosphere, with two levels and two patios – one right on Queen and a quieter outdoor retreat on the rooftop. The fixed-price meals are all under $10 and include a variety of pastas or delicious burgers (veggie or beef) with salad or crispy fries. Fried Cajun calamari and mussels provençale add a French-Louisiana element to the fare. A variety of beers are on tap and there is a cappuccino bar.

Home cooking is a hit at **The Butler's Pantry** *($; 484 Queen St. W., ☎504-3414)*, which recently moved to Queen from Toronto's Polish neighbourhood. The menu includes a selection of hearty items (many of them vegetarian), ranging from spinach casserole to curry pie, all for under $7. The airy interior has a domed ceiling painted with angelic frescoes, and a loyal crowd gathers here for cheap, robust meals.

Toronto's café scene has exploded in the last five years, and you can't walk more than a block or two in any of the main areas without stumbling upon a unique, independent coffee house serving gourmet brews. **The Lost Camel** *($; 559 Queen St. W., ☎703-5275)*, with its couches, art-adorned walls and accommodating staff feels more like a living room than a lunch spot. It serves generous, healthy sandwiches and salads and the coffee is good and strong.

Across the street, **Tequila Bookworm** *($; 490 Queen St. W., ☎504-7335)*, which doubles as a café and used bookstore, has no sign outside. You will recognize it by the racks of magazines, shelves of books and the intoxicating aroma of fresh-brewed coffee. High ceilings and art hanging from the exposed brick walls give it an artist's-loft atmosphere. In addition to fancy coffee and fresh-squeezed juices, there are salads, sandwiches on focaccia bread and a selection of bagels and cream cheese to choose from.

Pizza aficionados can find their heaven at **Amato** *($; 534 Queen St. W., ☎703-8989)*, where a $3 slice constitutes a quarter of a large pizza. Every day, there are at least a dozen gourmet pizzas to choose from, ranging from your standard pepperoni pie to vegan pizzas, white pizzas (no tomato sauce), and pizzas with snazzy toppings like artichoke hearts, feta cheese and spinach. Amato also has a cozy sit-down section at the back with large comfortable booths where you can order delectable pastas, salads, focaccia sandwiches and pizzas.

Azul *($; 181 Bathurst St., ☎703-9360)*, tucked around the corner from Queen on Bathurst Street, exudes a casual, laid-back air, with walls covered in burlap and a coffee table scattered with magazines in one corner. But the owner/chef has managed to combine a casual atmosphere with three impressive menus (with separate spreads for brunch, lunch and dinner). No matter which meal you try, the emphasis is on healthy, with lots of veggie options and a selection of virtuously wholesome vegetable and fruit juices and smoothies. Enticing drinks such as Mind Fuzz Be Gone (carrot, apple, ginger, beet and a shot of gingko) live up to their names.

Not long ago, **The Paddock** *($$$; 178 Bathurst St., ☎504-9997)* was a notorious saloon-style drinking hole — one of those places your mother warns you about. Now totally refurbished, it's a warm, jazzy den where the neighbourhood's thirtysomethings go for fine dining. The portions are small but beautifully presented, and include treats such as sweet-potato and Gorgonzola crumpet with baby greens and mesquite-smoked steak with potato gaufrette and grilled peppers. The place becomes a cocktail lounge in the evenings.

RESTAURANTS

West of Bathurst

Once you go west of Bathurst, you cross into yet another chapter of the Queen Street scene. Since it's further from downtown, this is more of a fringe part of town, and interesting interior decor shops and second-hand record stores give the area its character. But three or four blocks west of Bathurst, there is a cluster of unique and well-priced restaurants serving quality fare.

The **Vienna Home Bakery** *($; 626 Queen St. W., ☎703-7278)* looks like it should be in a small town in northern Ontario, rather than a stone's throw from Queen and Bathurst. This simple, cozy lunch counter is characterized by its pale pink walls and the smell of fresh bread baking. Vegan home-made soups are prepared fresh every day and the bread is always straight from the oven. They also make sandwiches and some of the best pie in town.

La Hacienda *($-$$; 640 Queen St. W., ☎703-3377)* is a trendy local hangout, serving decent Mexican fare at bargain prices. It is dimly lit inside, the walls are decorated with the work of local photographers and artists, and there is a large, shady back patio open in the summer months. The music is loud and the service is slow, but it's a great place to immerse yourself in Queen West's artists' and musicians' milieu.

Future Bakery *($; 735 Queen St. W, ☎504-8700)* is a lofty café where the air is infused with the wonderful aromas of bread baking and coffee brewing. You can stop in for picnic fixings, stay for a piece of one of the sumptuous cakes or pies or settle in for a hearty meal of varenyky, cabbage rolls and borscht. You can even just sit and enjoy a good book and a coffee in peace for hours on end! See also p 231.

Cities *($$$; 859 Queen St. W., ☎504-3762)* exemplifies the joy of cooking and eating. The menu and the decor are both exceptionally imaginative. Very good value considering the variety and freshness of ingredients. Good wine list.

Gypsy Co-Op *($$-$$$; 815 Queen St. W., ☎703-5069)* is a hipster mainstay in this part of town. The restaurant serves a fancy fusion menu, including a mezes-type appetizer of roasted garlic gloves, feta cheese, designer greens with balsamic vinaigrette and fresh kalamata olives. The back half is a loungy bar, with couches, comfy chairs and some of the city's best DJs. The noise and smoke from the bar can cloud the dining experience, so if you're looking for dinner and conversation, go early.

Squirly's *($$; 807 Queen St. W., ☎703-0574)* has a casual atmosphere and menu of pizzas, pastas, stir-fries, quesadillas and hamburgers, which you can enjoy without emptying your pockets. It's just dingy and artfully decorated enough to double as a cool late-night drinking spot. Don't expect to find any fine wines here, and the music can get loud after 11pm. The back room, with its red velvet sofas and candlelight, is a casual, intimate den that turns into a patio when the roof comes off in the summertime.

Terroni *($$; 720 Queen St. W, ☎504-0320)* is a long, narrow, gourmet pizzeria with wooden booths surrounded by shelves crammed with Italian groceries. There is also a tiny patio at the back. Italian salads, sandwiches and pizzas are made fresh with top-quality ingredients (interestingly, they don't serve pasta). Frequented by those in the local arts scene, this is the place to linger over an espresso, surrounded by the area's actors, photographers and artists. Worth noting: They don't accept credit cards.

Across the road from Terroni (see above), the candle-lit **Citron** *($$; 813 Queen St. W., ☎504-2647)* has more of an air of casual sophistication than some of its neighbours. The staff is friendly and relaxed and an open kitchen ensures that the small room is always filled with delicious aromas. A near-perfect salad with organic greens, grilled pears, walnuts and feta and starters such as vegetable Thai bundles in rice paper with peanut sauce set the tone for the main dishes, which are very reasonably priced and include a vegetarian North African stew and Asian chicken with toasted sesame seeds. A variety of fine wines are available by the glass.

Dufflet Pasteries *($; 787 Queen St. W., ☎506-2870)* is a cake shop that makes some of the most divine cakes, tarts and pies in the city. Its goods fill the dessert cases of a number of restaurants, but there's nothing like getting it from the source. You can buy an entire cake for a special occasion, or sit in the bright little shop sipping a cappuccino or café latte while you indulge in sinfully sweet delights.

Just west of Trinity Bellwoods Park, **Swan Restaurant** *($$; 892 Queen St. W., ☎532-0452)* attracts the local film and theatre people with a taste for fine food. The long, narrow space is filled with retro-style booths and cool, jazzy music. The brunches are a step above most in the city, and include fresh shellfish (it's an oyster bar, and you can watch the chef shucking them fresh). The menu is an exquisite roster of delicacies, including home-made soups served with Portuguese bread.

Next door to Swan (see above), **XXX Diner** *($; 894 Queen St. W., ☎536-2822)* (known to regulars as "Triple X") is a more casually cool café, where dog walkers from the nearby park are welcome to bring their pooches. The weekend brunches (featuring Tex-Mex egg-oriented dishes such as breakfast burritos) are a unique experience, as there's a live DJ spinning trancey drum 'n' bass tunes.

If a daringly different atmosphere is what you're looking for, **Addis Ababa** *($; 1184 Queen St. W., ☎538-0059)*, much farther along Queen, is an intoxicatingly heady den that serves up traditional Ethiopian cuisine. Dinner is a communal rite, as the spicy dishes come on a platter shared by everyone at the table. Diners eat with their hands, scooping up the food with *injera* — the flat, crepe-like Ethiopian bread. Clouded by the smoke of burning frankincense and animated with African music, its tables are covered in colourful woven tablecloths, the walls in wooden carvings and paintings from Ethiopia.

 TOUR F: CHINATOWN AND KENSINGTON

Not surprisingly, there are many Chinese, Vietnamese and Japanese restaurants in Chinatown, particularly along Spadina Avenue from Queen to College streets and along Dundas Street from Spadina to University.

Pho Hung Vietnamese Restaurant *($; 350 Spadina Ave., ☎593-6274)* on Spadina at Baldwin, affectionately known as the "laughing cow" due to its chuckling bovine logo, serves up good bargain Vietnamese food, complemented by cheap beer.

For stellar lunchtime bargains, try the **Shanghai Restaurant** *($; 409 Spadina Ave., ☎596-7311)*, just south of College on Spadina, for a heaping plate of food, including a choice of dishes from chicken balls to sweet and sour pork. You can get a bowl of hot and sour soup and a spring roll for under $4.

Thai Dynasty *($-$$; 440 Spadina Ave., ☎961-4400)* is one of the few Thai eateries on the Spadina strip. The interior is slightly gaudy and overdone, but the food is good, spicy Thai cuisine, with interesting appetizers such as soy-soaked mung-bean glass noodles in deep-fried wonton wrappers with a sweet and sour dipping sauce, and tasty entrees like pineapple red-curry chicken.

Just around the corner, **Peter's Chung King** *($-$$; 281 College St., ☎928-2936)* serves up the almost-forgotten Chinatown culinary tradition of sizzling Szechuan. Long an institution in this part of town, Peter's has a nondescript ambience and indifferent staff, and although the food still rates well, you've got to put in a special request to get your Szechuan spiced flame-red chilli hot like it should be.

Happy Seven *($-$$; 358 Spadina Ave., ☎971-9820)* is another Chinatown institution, and like so many others it has glaring lighting but pristine cleanliness. There are a dizzying 212 items to choose from on the menu, including dozens of soups and at least 30 seafood selections, all served in generous portions.

Lotus Garden Vietnamese Vegetarian Restaurant *($; 393 Dundas St. W., Unit G, ☎598-1883)* is a unique Vietnamese eatery that attracts younger types who come for its soya and tofu dishes, salads and soups. There is no MSG used in the cooking and very little salt. Some dishes are made with organic vegetables.

🦐 On certain days, the little **Lee Garden** *($$; 331 Spadina Ave., ☎593-9524)* restaurant is so crowded you may believe all of China has squeezed in here. People come for the delectable Chinese cuisine, especially the seafood and duck dishes.

The Lucky Dragon *($; 418 Spadina Ave., ☎598-7823)* is typical of Spadina's Chinese restaurants, with bright lights, plain decor and a massive fish tank. The menu is extensive, with hundreds of selections drawing on culinary traditions from all over China, including spicy specialty rices with such toppings as squid in chilli and garlic sauce, and whole braised fish in a soy-ginger sauce.

Swatow *($; 309 Spadina, ☎977-0601)* is a no-fuss eatery with an extensive menu that is guaranteed to satisfy your palate. There is nothing fancy about this place, but you can't beat it for its genuine Cantonese cooking served up fast and good, just like in China.

🦐 Toronto is home to many excellent Chinese restaurants, but few can compare to **Lai Wah Heen** *($$$; 108 Chestnut St., Metropolitan Hotel, ☎977-9899)*. Its menu features mostly Cantonese *haute cuisine*. Remarkable attention to detail is shown in both preparation and presentation. A place of great refinement for its food, decor, and service. Dim Sum is also served in the afternoons.

Despite its proximity to Chinatown, **Oasis** *($$; 294 College St., ☎975-0845)* leaves the Asian cuisine behind, and instead offers tapas with a twist. You can order a number of small dishes, but the chefs add their own creations, like jerk chicken kebabs and

Thai coconut rice balls, to the Spanish fare. The interior is fairly shoddy and casual but the food is good, and it's cheap.

Located right in the heart of Kensington Market, the **Moonbean Café** *($; 30 St. Andrew St., ☎595-0327)* is a pleasant café with a light menu of sandwiches and a breezy outdoor patio, perfect for watching the colourful activity in the market. Iced mocaccinos and fresh carrot and beet juices are just some of their specialties, and beer and wine are served as well.

Baldwin Street

Baldwin is a shaded street removed from the hustle and bustle of Chinatown's main drags but crowded with trendy, popular eateries. In the summertime, most of its restaurants have sunny outdoor patios.

Margaritas *($$; 14 Baldwin St., ☎977-5525)* provides quite an escape with its infectious Latin music and its tasty dishes including Toronto's best *nachos* and delicious *guacamole*. This piece of Mexico will transport you far from the rush of urban Toronto.

The **Bodega** *($$$; 30 Baldwin St., ☎977-1287)* serves resolutely gastronomic French dishes made with the freshest of ingredients. The wall coverings, the lace and the music that wafts across the dining room help create an authentic French atmosphere.

Caffé La Gaffe *($$$; 24 Baldwin St., ☎596-2397)* is housed in a converted store on Baldwin. Known as "the Gaffe," it attracts both the Queen West and student crowds to its front and back patios. Most things in the interior are mismatched – from the shaky chairs to the art on the walls. Patrons are greeted with a basket of Portuguese corn bread to start, before digging into seafood appetizers and hearty pastas and pizzas for the main course.

TOUR G: QUEEN'S PARK AND THE UNIVERSITY OF TORONTO

College Street is the best place in this area to stroll around and soak up the lively atmosphere. Although the area (along College west of Bathurst) is known as Little Italy, and indeed is infused with Italian culture from generations of immigrants, it has been transformed in recent years into a trendy spot with dozens of restaurants serving all sorts of cuisines. There are as many bars as restaurants (some places are both), so the area attracts a lot of students and is busy well into the night.

Kalendar Koffee House *($$; 546 College St.,* ☎*923-4138)* has an ornately decorated dining room with burgundy walls, gold-leaf mirrors and seductive low lighting. Smooth jazz music adds to the air of sophistication. Kalendar's specialties are its regal-sounding "scrolls" — pockets of light pastry folded around fillings such as chicken breast, snow peas and julienned carrots with a sweet curry sauce – and Italian sausage with parmesan and sun-dried tomatoes in spicy tomato sauce. It also serves designer greens, such as the artichoke heart salad with a light poppy-seed dressing, and tasty, thin-crusted pizzas. Aside from the waiters, who can be a little pretentious, it's the perfect setting for an intimate dinner.

El Bodegon *($$; 537 College St.,* ☎*944-8297)* is awash in typical South American decor: village scenes are painted in primary colours on orange stucco, sombreros and pan flutes hang from the walls and fake parrots hover on perches beneath a ceiling of plastic vines. Peruvian music compounds the thematic effect. An impressive list of seafood-rich broths is upstaged only by the calamari, grilled to tender perfection. A host of hearty, simple Peruvian dishes, such as *ceviche*, hearty meat stews and tortillas (thick omelettes) round out the menu, which also includes inexplicably disparate items such as pasta, BLT sandwiches and wonton soup.

Neither the menu nor the interior of **Utopia Café and Grill** *($-$$; 585 College St.,* ☎*534-7751)* is remarkable at first glance, but the dark wood, low lighting and candles on each of the tables give this small place a warm ambience. Quiet strains of North African and new-age music waft around the eight to ten tables, while a grey cat patrols the floor. Both the beef burger and the all-natural veggie burgers are savoury delights, and the fries are a perfect crispy brown. Utopia's fare of home-made charbroiled hamburgers, grilled chicken breast, smoked salmon sandwiches, burritos, quesadillas and New York strip sirloin may not be unique, but quality makes up for originality, and the meals are excellent value.

Bar Italia *($$; 582 College St., ☎535-3621)* is a sleek, swanky pasta spot attracting beautiful people until the wee hours. Mirrors at eye level running all the way around the restaurant's simple wood booths make it easy to check out and be checked out. Sandwiches on panini are gourmet affairs, and the pastas are quite rich, in cream and gorgonzola cheese sauces. Home-made Italian ice creams is a sweet ending to the meal.

Bertucci's *($$; 630 College St., ☎537-0911)* is a friendly little Italian restaurant with very simple decor. People come not for the decor, however, but to eat delicious pasta dishes while enjoying a level of service worthy of the finest hotels.

The friendly **College Street Bar** *($$; 574 College St., ☎533-2417)* boasts a tasty Mediterranean menu and lively atmosphere. This hot spot is frequented by a young crowd, and many people just stop in to have drinks and soak up the atmosphere.

Soft lighting, crisp white tiles, fresh-cut flowers and simple chairs with gold-stencilled white slipcovers come together to create a romantic ambiance in which to enjoy the Italian specialties at **Pony** *($$; 488 College St., ☎923-7665)*. The veal and calamari are particularly noteworthy.

A little beyond what is normally thought of as the "fashionable" section of College, **Café Societa** *($$-$$$; 796 College St., ☎588-7490)* is a chic spot, slick in its white and chrome design, with a clientele to match. The inside is tiny, with just 10 tables, so it's a squeeze when it's full, which is most of the time. The menu is seasonal, but features main courses with daily fish and meats (there are few vegetarian options on the menu), and dishes such as sterling salmon with an olive tapenade or roasted Japanese eggplant lasagna.

There is nothing quite like a tender grilled sirloin steak the way it is done at **Barberian's** *($$$$; 7 Elm St., toward Bay and Dundas, ☎597-0225)*. Steak dominates the menu at this restaurant, which may seem a little scanty to anyone hoping for other choices. It is preferable to reserve in advance.

 Although there is but one restaurant on College serving Caribbean fare, **Irie Caribbean Restaurant** *($-$$; 808 College St., ☎531-4743)* happens to make some of the best rotis in the city. Frequented mainly by a West Indian crowd, its authenticity is hardly suspect. A jerk chicken salad is accented with heaps of tropical fruits, and in addition to the delicious rotis, there are spicy main dishes cooked island-style, such as steamed red snapper and jerk specialties.

TOUR H: BLOOR AND YORKVILLE

Amid the designer shops in the Yorkville district, you may be surprised to discover **Flo's Diner** *($; 10 Bellair St., ☎961-4333)*, a traditional diner complete with booths and bottomless cups of coffee. Here, you will feel for a minute like you're back in the '50s. The food is typical diner-style, with burgers, fries and milkshakes, and in the summer you can sun yourself on the rooftop terrace.

You'd have to be looking for **Little Tibet** *($$; 81 Yorkville Ave., ☎963-8221)* to find it, tucked unassumingly in a Yorkville basement. Its interior is hardly gloomy, however, decorated in bright yellows and blues, and the food makes the search worthwhile. Extremely reasonably priced for this swank area, the appetizers include *thang*, a clear, salty soup with spinach, and steamed beef and vegetable dumplings with hot sauce. Among the main courses are sliced beef marinated with ginger and garlic, and a sort of Himalayan stew — beef simmered with baby potatoes and onions.

The patio at **Café Nervosa** *($$-$$$; 75 Yorkville Ave., ☎961-4642)* is a prime spot from which to watch the Yorkville socialites pass by. The interior has that trendy modern jungle look going on, with lots of leopard prints and wrought iron. Upper-crust guests from the nearby Four Seasons Hotel vie with American tourists for table space from which they can see and be seen while enjoying average fare of fancy salads, pastas and pizzas. There are live jazz performances on Thursday and Friday nights.

It is really worth taking the trouble to find **Jacques L'Omelette**, also called **Jacques Bistro du Parc** *($$-$$$; 126-A Cumberland Ave., ☎961-1893)*. This charming little spot is located upstairs in a fine Yorkville house. The very friendly French owner offers simple but high-quality food. The fresh Atlantic salmon and the spinach salad are among the pleasant surprises on the menu.

Acquazzurra *($$$; 137 Avenue Rd., ☎920-4946)* is a lively place with a Mediterranean theme to the menu. Appetizers include smoked salmon carpaccio, caprese salad and crispy calamari. Main dishes are predominantly pastas, dished up in huge portions on jumbo-sized plates, but there's a bit of Spain thrown in as well with the heaping plate of *paella* with chicken, sausage, mussels and vegetables, and daily fish specials.

Mövenpick *($$$; 133 Yorkville Ave., ☎926-9545)* is a big, tastefully decorated Swiss restaurant with innovative dishes and reasonable prices for what you get. The decadent Sunday brunch buffet here is a must, but there can be a long wait.

With a funky 1960s decor, **Opus** *($$$; 37 Prince Arthur, ☎921-3105)* serves refined and modern cuisine described as "contemporary Canadian," mixing traditional recipes with other culinary traditions. Exceptional wine list.

Remy's *($$$; 115 Yorkville Ave., ☎968-9429)* is the ideal spot to rest after a hot summer day. Sit out on the terrace and try the chicken with peanut sauce, a true delight.

Sassafraz *($$$; 100 Cumberland Ave., ☎964-2222)* is a big bar and bistro with bay windows looking out onto the street to catch the passing scene. The decor is in shades of pink, with wooden floors and furniture. On the left, a pleasant dining room with modern furnishings and lighting greets guests who prefer a quieter atmosphere. The menu offers some interesting surprises such as mushroom *risotto* with strips of duck.

Yamato *($$$; 18 Belair St., ☎927-0077)* features Japanese cuisine with a twist – the chef prepares your meal right before your eyes! The menu includes classics, such as teriyaki steak and vegetable tempura, always fresh and tasty.

Boba *($$$-$$$$; 90 Avenue Rd., ☎961-2622)* is an inviting and charming little restaurant which has acquired a solid reputation thanks to its fine cuisine and courteous service. In-house specialties include beef, duck, and lamb, and desserts are particularly delicious.

Bistro 990 *($$$$; 990 Bay St., ☎921-9990)* is quite simply one of the best eating spots in Toronto. Delicious *nouvelle cuisine* items are offered in a Mediterranean setting, with outstanding preparations of lamb, salmon and duck.

Truffles *($$$$; Four Seasons Hotel, 21 Avenue Rd., ☎964-0411)* is not within the reach of every budget, but if you have the resources you will be absolutely delighted. This restaurant has truly earned its reputation as one of the most esteemed dining establishments in town.

 TOUR I: CABBAGETOWN

Rashnaa *($; 307 Wellesley St. E., ☎929-2099)*, a modest Tamil/Sri Lankan joint in Cabbagetown, is a great place to linger over a meal with friends, especially if your budget is getting tight. Rashnaa's interior is fairly standard for Indian restaurants, with tacky dinette sets and paintings of Hindu gods on the walls, but it's a warm place, always filled with the scent of floral incense and the sound of sitar music. Most of Rashnaa's dishes are fairly mild, but the chutneys are deliciously piquant, and they do an excellent rendition of Sri Lankan specialties including *masala dosa*, *kottu roti* and *string hoppers*. It's simple Sri Lankan fare but the prices and the chutneys make it worth going back for.

Just down the road, another inexpensive Sri Lankan eatery is **Radhika** *($; 587 Parliament St., ☎924-2111)*, a no-frills take-out and catering place with *biryanis*, *masala dosa*, chicken and vegetable curries.

RESTAURANTS

A few steps down from street level, just south of Carlton on Parliament, **Fatgirl** *($$; 460 Parliament St.,* ☎*923-0063)* is barely noticeable from the outside. Inside it's all sleek minimalist vogue in industrial shades of grey and silver. The cement walls are decorated only with round, convex mirrors, the ceilings made of metal sheeting. It's an intimate den with savoury aromas from the open kitchen flavouring the air, but the music, which morphs from R&B to more trancey tracks, can be too loud for comfortable dinner conversation. The menu is an ambitious fusion of Japanese (sushi, miso soup), Chinese (veggie spring rolls, roasted duck on mandarin pancakes), Thai (jackfruit coconut curry, honey garlic spareribs) and Jamaican (jerk chicken wings) which is great when it hits the mark, but can be a disappointment on some nights.

Timothy's Chicken *($$; 556 Parliament St. at Wellesley,* ☎*964-7583)* prepares tandoori, vindaloo and jalfrezi-style chicken. The flavours of India are at their best in the melt-in-your-mouth naan bread and savoury mulligatawny soup.

Walking into **Tapas Restaurant and Bar** *($$-$$$; 226 Carlton St.,* ☎*323-9651)* is like stepping into a Spanish *taverna*. Guitar music fills the room, and sides of cured meat hang over the bar, which is covered by a faux awning of red terra-cotta bricks. The waiter pulls up a chair at your table, with its red-and-white checkered tablecloth, to take the order. It's tapas, so the menu offers dozens of choices for little dishes of seafood, meat and vegetarian this and that. Favourites include cod croquettes, stewed baby octopus, saffron rice and home-made sausages sauteed in white wine. There are a few main course dishes, including the standard Spanish *paella*, which takes awhile to arrive but is worth the wait.

The Keg Mansion *($$-$$$; 515 Jarvis St.,* ☎*964-6609)* has a wonderful location in an old mansion on Jarvis Street. Traditional North American-style cuisine, with an emphasis on steak and roast beef, is served in a charming atmosphere.

TOUR J: THE ANNEX

Future Bakery *($; ☎922-5875)* see p 220.

Kilgour's *($-$$; 509 Bloor St. W., ☎923-7680)* is a comfy café-style walk-up restaurant with couch seating as well as stools at the bar. Aside from the New York sirloin, most of the chicken and vegetable dishes (including burgers, wings, nachos and sandwiches) are under $10. This is also a popular brunch spot, although it can be smoky on the weekends.

Dang de Lion Vietnamese Restaurant *($$; 549 Bloor St. W., ☎538-0190)* serves up simple Vietnamese fare, most of it fried, with rice or vermicelli, but there are lots of vegetarian options. The owner greets the constant flow of customers personally and brings the menus to each table.

Nataraj *($$; 394 Bloor St. W., ☎928-2925)* is a typical Indian restaurant with sparse, clean decor and too-bright lighting. The cuisine, all from northern India, is very good, but the service is a bit slow. Breads from the tandoori oven are almost flawless.

With its ground-to-ceiling front window and stark minimalist aesthetic, **Goldfish** *($$$; 372 Bloor St. W., ☎513-0077)* is the latest Annex hot-spot. Luckily, there's substance to go with the style, and the pricey food is fabulous. The top-notch chef deftly prepares appetizers such as duck prosciutto with potato rosti and caper-studded salmon tartare, and entrees which include beet ravioli with cranberries and curried cream and grilled ostrich tenderloin. It's advisable to make reservations in advance.

There are a number of Korean restaurants and supermarkets clustered along Bloor west of Bathurst. **Korea House** *($$$; 666 Bloor St. W., ☎536-8666)* has a pleasant wood and stucco decor. Complete dinners, including rice or noodles with mixed meat or seafood and an array of vegetable and pickle dishes, are $25.

Le Paradis *($$$; 166 Bedford Rd., ☎921-0995)* serves authentic French bistro cuisine at authentic bistro prices. The

RESTAURANTS

decor is simple and the service reserved, but a devoted following and the delicious cooking make it a must.

At the **Kensington Kitchen** *($$$; 124 Harbord St., ☎961-3404)* you can enjoy Mediterranean dishes while seated comfortably in a pretty New Age dining room. This is a good spot to go on fine summer days, when you can enjoy the same specialties on the rooftop terrace.

TOUR K: ROSEDALE, FOREST HILL AND NORTH YORK

On a small street off Yonge, just above the Summerhill train tracks, the bright red exterior of **Nothing in Common** *($$$; 8 Birch Ave., ☎975-9150)* makes it glaringly apparent that this restaurant has nothing in common with staid, upper-class Rosedale. Inside, it's as warm and cozy as a living room — with just three four-seater booths and three booths for two, making reservations a necessity most nights. The seats are covered in faux-leopard prints and the brick-red walls provide a showcase for '70s and '80s kitsch. Even the music is retro, with tunes from the Supremes to ABBA. The mandarin almond salad is a favourite, and the menu includes items such as gourmet pasta and blackened swordfish.

Fillppo's *($$$$; 744 St. Clair Ave. W., ☎658-0568)* serves savoury gourmet pizzas and pastas with a Mediterranean accent. A cozy and chic atmosphere for the trend-setter in everyone.

Five Doors North *($$$; 2088 Yonge St., ☎480-6234)*, on Yonge south of Eglinton, is a challenge to find, but the reward is worthwhile. It doesn't have a sign, but lies beneath a banner for "Future Furniture" (the shop above it). Inside, a narrow hallway opens out into a large, lively backroom. There are no windows and the restaurant is heady with smells from the open kitchen. The menu is based on a four-course meal (sort of like Italian tapas), with a selection of antipasto, pasta, meat or fish, and vegetables, but you need quite an appetite to finish off all four courses. Both the food and the service are excellent.

Gios's *($$-$$$; 2070 Yonge St., ☎932-2306)* is the original restaurant by the same owners as Five Doors North, and is located, well, five doors south of its sister-establishment. It is identifiable only by the huge pink nose which looms above the doorway. Inside is a long narrow room which feels like the inside of a train coach. The walls are covered with markered graffiti from customers. If Five Doors North is the sophisticated, modern child, Gio's is the traditional Italian parent. With meals based on the same four-course structure, the atmosphere is more casual and the matriarch Mama Rosa serves up basic, hearty southern Italian meals from an impossibly small kitchen.

At the **Pyramid Cakery** *($; 2519 Yonge St., ☎489-2246)*, you may feel you have been invited into the living room of a stylish house for a delectable dessert. If you listen to your heart, you may show a little daring and accompany your wonderful sweet dish with this establishment's famous hot chocolate.

 North 44 *($$$-$$$$; 2537 Yonge St., ☎487-4897)* is one of the *in* restaurants with the hip Toronto crowd. This is not just a place to see and be seen, however, since its food is also exquisite. The chef culls from several culinary traditions to create a decidedly innovative menu.

 For a memorable evening, the **Auberge du Pommier** *($$$$; 4150 Yonge St., ☎222-2220)* is the place to go, with its quiet, elegant atmosphere and refined French cuisine, including specialties such as caviar and *foie gras*. Meals here can be accompanied by fine wines from a very elaborate list.

✖ TOUR L: EASTERN TORONTO

The two main eating corridors in the eastern part of the city are the Beaches, (that's "the Beach" to locals) with its lively pedestrian-filled sidewalks, and the Danforth (known as Greektown), although its plethora of eating establishments has expanded over the years to include a variety of cuisines. Finally, Little India, just north of the Beaches on Gerrard Street between Coxwell and Greenwood, is a unique neighbourhood with all the character of New Delhi and a number of restaurants serving authentic Indian cuisine.

RESTAURANTS

The Beaches

A copious traditional breakfast just like on the farm. Eggs, bacon, sausages and home fries are cooked up all day long at the **Sunset Grill** *($; 2006 Queen St. E., ☎690-9985)*. The French toast and omelettes are also done to perfection. Burgers and sandwiches complete the packages. Expect a line-up for the famous Sunday brunch.

Whitlock's *($$; 1961 Queen St. E. ☎691-8784)* is a longstanding tradition in the Beach. Located in a lovely old building, the atmosphere is simple, casual and unpretentious. The menu is varied and down-to-earth. It typifies the real "Beach", as compared to the glitz and trendiness of what some like to call the "Beaches".

Just a hop, skip and a jump from the beach, the **Café Juniper** *($$$; 2305 Queen St. E., ☎694-7514)* boasts a laid-back ambiance. Diners are invited to settle in for a friendly evening and a good meal. Chicken and fish dishes figure prominently on the menu, while the choice of wines is laid out right in front of you.

El Perro *($$$; 2282 Queen St. E., ☎690-9030)* is a comfortable, informal spot in the Beach where you can sample an array of Mediterranean fare, from a selection of tapas starters to fabulous Spanish main dishes including seafood *paella*, veggie lasagna and smoked salmon cheesecake. It even has a children's menu.

For Indian fare with a bit of flare, **Jadoo** *($$$; 2222A Queen St. E., ☎686-7684)* is a casual little place with an ambitious chef. Dishes like eggplant bharta puree with chickpeas and artichoke hearts or corn-studded potato tikki with almond-coriander chutney and tomato and red onion salsa add pizzazz to the usual Indian standards.

From the outside, **Quigley's** *($$$; 2232 Queen St. E., ☎699-9998)* looks like it could just be a pub, but beyond the bar and the beer on tap there is a comfortable dining area at the back. Serving upscale pub food from pasta to Pad Thai, this is a casual place to eat, just east of the hustle and bustle of the Beach's main drag.

The Beach is a wonderful place to watch the world go by from a sidewalk café, and **Spiaggia Trattoria** *($$$; 2318 Queen St. E., ☎699-4656)* is just the place. A wonderful mix of people frequent this spot, all the better to people-watch. All the exotic ingredients we've come to expect from a trendy trattoria figure on the menu here, from fresh herbs to asiago and sun-dried tomatoes.

The Danforth

🛵 The owner of the **Bibiche Bistro** *($$; 1352 Danforth St., ☎463-9494)* is so friendly that will you soon overlook the very ordinary decor. In fact, you'll soon forget all about the surroundings as you enjoy your meal, especially the fabulous desserts.

A bright yellow sign framed with flashing lights hangs above the door of **La Carreta** *($$-$$$; 469 Danforth Ave., ☎461-7718)*, making it look more like a karioke joint than a Cuban tapas bar. Inside, it's polished and modern, with mint-green textured walls, a long bar of glass and mahogany and blue glass lamps. A unique selection of tapas, with the emphasis on seafood, offers abundant choice for the undecided.

Christina's Ristorante *($$-$$$; 492 Danforth Ave., ☎463-4418)* is probably the most famous of the trendy Danforth Greek eateries. The restaurant is known for its vibrantly coloured interior and its Wall of Fame which features dozens of framed pictures paying homage to famous customers from Tom Hanks to Alanis Morissette. They serve a full Greek menu until 4am on the weekends and have live Greek music and belly-dancing shows.

Fancy Shoes *($$$; 507 Danforth Ave., ☎463-4166)* serves very good traditional Italian fare, with a few innovative pasta and seafood dishes, but rings in at a considerable price. The chef's specials include gemelli pasta with anchovies, capers, smoked tomatoes and mini-croutons, and seared peppercorn-crusted tuna.

One of the Danforth's typical eateries, **Ouzeri** *($$$; 500-A Danforth Ave., ☎778-0500)* is often noisy and crowded, but what a great menu. The freshest ingredients come together in a fine selection of Greek dishes, including some 14 vegetarian meals.

Stop in at **Silk Road** *($$$; 341 Danforth Ave., ☎463-8660)* and you'll think you've really embarked on this historic route, though this is a culinary journey. Savour the cuisines of Tibet, India and China in an exotic ambiance.

Little India

The New Sidhartha Restaurant *($$; 1423 Gerrard St. E., ☎466-2222)* is typical of restaurants in the area — a long, bright room with a buffet table (serving a $7.99 all-you-can-eat buffet) in the centre. Although the waiter fails to bring the requisite complementary basket of pappadams, the food (mainly from southern India) is decent, with prices to match.

Gujurat Durbar *($$; 1386 Gerrard St. E., ☎406-1085)* specializes in food from Gujarat, a state in western India which is strictly vegetarian. Gujurati food differs noticeably from most other Indian menus, with no naan bread or tandoori. Here, the pappadams just keep on coming and the food is a unique blend of interesting specialties.

 TOUR M: NIAGARA FALLS

Niagara-on-the-Lake

The pretty terrace of the **Buttery** *($; Queen St.)*, located in the heart of all the downtown action, is sure to catch your eye. You can enjoy a good meal here while watching the activity on the street.

You can also stop by for a sandwich or a salad at **The Epicurean** *($; Queen St.)*, a simply decorated place with flowered tablecloths.

The elegant **Prince of Wales** *(6 Picton St., ☎905-468-3246)* has two dining rooms. The first *($$$$)* and more ritzy of the two has a refined menu and is harmoniously decorated with antiques. The second *($$)* has a more relaxed atmosphere, a pub-style decor and a simple menu that's perfect for lunch, with selections like chicken fingers and salads.

At the **Ristorante Giardino** *($$$$; 142 Queen St., ☎905-468-3263)* you can enjoy a delicious Italian meal while comfortably seated in a magnificent room with big picture windows looking out onto the street.

🦞 The dining rooms of **The Oban** *(160 Front St., ☎905-468-2165)* occupy a good part of the ground floor of a magnificent house. Some of the tables are set on a long veranda with big picture windows, and it is in this section of the restaurant *($$$-$$$$)* that you can sample some of the succulent dishes that have conquered both the hearts and the palates of so many people. Another room inside *($$)* is more of a pub, with pictures covering the walls, antique furniture, all sorts of knick-knacks, a piano and a fireplace. Seated in a captain's chair or on a love seat, your plate on your knees or on a coffee table, you'll feel a bit like you're in your own living room. The menu lists simple dishes, such as chicken cacciatore and fried shrimp.

Niagara Falls

Clifton Hill is lined with fast-food restaurants, which are devoid of charm, but will suit your needs if you're simply looking for a quick bite.

For ribs or roast chicken, visit **Tony's Place** *($; 5467 Victoria Ave.)*.

The nearby **Casa D'Oro** *($$$; 5875 Victoria Ave.)* serves a decent selection of Italian specialties.

RESTAURANTS

For a refined meal, try the restaurant at the **Old Stone Inn**
(*$$-$$$; 5425 Robinson St., ☎905-357-1234)*, where you'll
find a lovely dining room in a building dating back to the turn
of the century. The menu lists an excellent selection of
specialties from a number of different countries.

Finally, if your top priority is a view of the falls, your best bet
is the restaurant in the **Skylon Tower** *($$$-$$$$;
5200 Robinson St., ☎905-356-2651)*. The menu features fish
and meat dishes. Of course, you pay for the view, but what a
view it is!

ENTERTAINMENT

Toronto's club scene has burgeoned in recent years, partly bolstered by a change in the law to allow bars to stay open until 2am instead of 1am. In fact, there is a whole section of town, dubbed locally as "Clubland", devoted to discos and massive, sleekly-decorated dance clubs. Rave culture and after-hours, all-night dance clubs (mainly catering to a very young crowd) ensure that parts of the town at least are going all night. Toronto also has a vibrant underground live music scene that has only become stronger in recent years. On any night of the week there are numerous bands, from big names to local acts, playing live at one or another of the city's many watering holes. Along lively strips such as Queen Street West, College Street in Little Italy and the Annex's Bloor Street, there is always something going on, and even just strolling along the sidewalks to soak up the atmosphere can be entertaining.

The flourishing of the city's theatre industry has also had an enormous impact on Toronto's entertainment scene. Toronto is now the third-largest theatre city in the English-speaking world, surpassed only by New York and London. Summertime brings festivals celebrating everything from jazz to the music of the Caribbean. Whether it be cultural activities, major festivals, professional hockey, baseball or basketball games or Formula

One car racing, Toronto has something for everyone, any time of the year.

 ## BARS AND NIGHTCLUBS

Clubland

Clubland is squeezed into the area between University Avenue and Peter Street, Richmond Street West and Wellington. This is where most of the city's dance clubs are concentrated. While there are a few that have survived over the years, the names and faces of many of the area's clubs tend to change rapidly. As fast as one closes down, another sleekly designed venue springs up in its place, trying hard to attract the growing weekend crowds that flock to the area from both the city and the suburbs. Many of the places in this area have a dress code and won't allow jeans or sneakers, so check before you go, or better yet, throw on your best clubbing outfit!

Beat Junkie *(306 Richmond St. W., ☎599-7055)* is smaller than some of the mega-clubs nearby and hosts both live music and DJs. The sounds change each night from Thursday to Saturday, from drum 'n' bass to hip hop to old school.

Crocodile Rock *(240 Adelaide St. W., ☎599-9751)* is a large joint with garage-type doors opening out onto the street in the summer. It's got pool tables and dance floors, and DJs play classic rock and retro '80s.

You can dance at **Dirk Gently's** *(244 Adelaide St. W., ☎599-9030)*, where DJs play on two floors.

Fluid Lounge *(217 Richmond St. W., ☎593-6116)* is a swanky-looking basement nightclub with chill-out areas filled with animal-print '70s couches and DJs spinning eclectic grooves from disco to R&B to old school. Their hip hop nights are always very packed, and very steamy.

G-Spot Nightclub *(296 Richmond St. W., ☎351-7768)* has rotating DJs spinning unique sounds from Thursday to Saturday.

Joe Rockhead's *(212 King St. W., ☎977-8448)* doubles as a restaurant and bar where DJs play Top 40 music.

Joker *(318 Richmond St. W., ☎598-1313)* is one of Clubland's most popular four-floor emporiums, with pool tables in the basement, prominent local DJs rotating on the next two levels, spinning everything from R&B to old school to progressive house, and a rooftop patio that seats 200 and provides an aerial view through the skylight to the third-floor dance floor.

Limelight *(250 Adelaide St. W., ☎593-6126)* not only has two bars, but two hot tubs as well! With different DJs on different floors on different nights, their repertoire is incredibly diverse, spanning dance and progressive underground house, retro, electronica and classic alternative sounds.

The Living Room *(330 Adelaide St. W., ☎979-3168)* has different sounds on different nights, with DJs spinning R&B, classic house and dance every weekend.

My Apartment *(81 Peter St., ☎348-9884)* is an office worker's pick-up joint, with dancing and DJs playing classic rock and retro '80s.

Montana's *(145 John St., ☎595-5949)* appeals to the after-work office crowd, with a mediocre "Americana" menu and a dance floor where DJs play "urban contemporary" music.

Plush Lounge *(287 King St. W., ☎351-8494)* is one of the area's posh nightclubs catering to people who go out to be seen. There is a dress code and the music is house and R&B.

Tonic *(117 Peter, entrance on Richmond, ☎204-9200)* is the newest nightclub on the strip, with a dress code and the requisite bouncers outside.

Whisky Saigon *(250 Richmond St. W., ☎593-7707)* is one of the area's original massive multi-storey dance emporiums. The three floors are different, with a 250-seat rooftop patio, and DJs playing music that spans the decades.

ENTERTAINMENT

The Entertainment District/Downtown

The entertainment and theatre district covers roughly the same area as Clubland (extending a bit further west), but in order to differentiate night spots that are not mega dance clubs, the rest of the area's bars are listed here separately.

A hip crowd of journalists, actors and film people gathers at **The 606** *(606 King St. W., ☎504-8740)*, a combined restaurant, bar and lounge, to sip martinis while DJs spin acid jazz, R&B and funk.

Churchill's Cigar and Wine Bar *(257 Adelaide St. W., upstairs from Houston's, ☎351-1601)* is an elegant place to have a drink with friends. It has entertainment and dancing on some nights and even has a special ventilation lounge to disperse cigar fumes.

It's not hard to surmise what the drink of choice is at **The Devil's Martini** *(136 Simcoe, ☎591-7541)*, which has a patio and three pool tables.

Fez Batik *(129 Peter St., ☎204-9660)* is a Moroccan-themed restaurant and lounge, with a fabulous outdoor patio in the heart of Clubland. The upper level is a lounge where couches are littered with colourful Moroccan cushions, and later at night DJs spin soul, deep sounds and drum 'n' bass.

In front of Roy Thompson Hall, the **Elephant & Castle Pub** *(212 King St. W., ☎598-4455)* offers all the cozy charm typical of an authentic English pub.

The Garage Paradise *(175 Richmond St. W., ☎351-8101)* is a casual drinking spot with DJs and not so much attitude.

The Hard Rock Café SkyDome *(1 Blue Jays Way, ☎341-2388)* resembles Hard Rocks the world over, with rock and roll music and memorabilia, except this one overlooks the Blue Jays baseball field in the SkyDome.

Horizons Bar, located at the top of the CN Tower, offers a breathtaking view of Toronto's skyline, which, at night, is a blaze of light. A must-see spectacle.

N'Awlins *(299 King St. W., ☎595-1958)* is an elegant jazz restaurant with a bar at the back and excellent live jazz and R&B nightly.

Pearl's Duelling Pianos *(180 Pearl St., ☎596-1132)* showcases cabaret-style shows, with high-energy performances on twin grand pianos throughout the evening.

Peel Pub *(276 King St. W., ☎977-0003)* is Toronto's incarnation of the infamous university hangout on Montreal's Peel Street. Basically a pub-like watering hole, it attracts big crowds on the weekends.

If you have not had the chance to stay at the **Royal York** (see p 189) but want to admire its timeless elegance, you can enjoy a drink in one of its bars. Both the **Lobby Bar** and the **Library Bar** will give you a taste of this turn-of-the-century hotel. An excellent place to sit and relax before catching a train at the Union Station located directly in front of the hotel.

Taking its name from the notorious movie about the L.A. scene, **Swingers** *(57 Duncan St., ☎587-0202)* is an upstairs nightclub, bar and cigar lounge playing retro and Top 40 dance music. There is a dress code.

Xango and Mambo Lounge *(106 John St., ☎593-4407)* is a restaurant that serves Nuevo Latino cuisine, but also has a bar and lounge area with DJs and Latin American-style music on the weekends.

Old Town of York

C'est What? *(67 Front St. E., ☎867-9499)*, located in the basement of an older building, is a charming pub with regular live blues, jazz, funk and rock performances. Great selection of beer and scotch.

ENTERTAINMENT

Local and international celebrities give shows at the **Montreal Bistro-Jazz Club** *(65 Sherbourne St., ☎363-0179)*, considered one of the city's finest jazz clubs.

Top O'the Senator *(253 Victoria St., ☎364-7517)*, a jazz bar that dates from the 1920s, is a real Toronto institution. International jazz stars perform here regularly. The **Victory Lounge**, a cigar lounge with a quieter ambiance, is located in the same building.

Queen West

Starting just around the corner from Clubland, Queen West is ground zero for Toronto's alternative music scene. Most of the bars are casual and grungy, with hipster patrons decked out in black. Many of these places have live music and/or pool tables.

The Rivoli *(332 Queen St. W., ☎977-5082)* is one of the trendiest spots on the strip, with a cozy bar, a small, crowded outdoor patio in the heart of Queen West's alterna-scene, an Asian-fusion restaurant and a back room showcasing live alternative music or comedy every night of the week. Upstairs at the "Riv" is a large pool hall with live jazz on Sundays.

The Horseshoe Tavern *(368 Queen St. W., ☎598-4753)* is a long-standing Queen West tradition, with a front room tavern and live rock, country and indie bands in the back.

The 360 *(326 Queen St. W., ☎593-0840)*, just up from the Rivoli, is an old legion hall, with beer on tap and live music in the back room. Its bare-bones patio lacks glamour but has a prime Queen West people-watching location.

The Bamboo *(312 Queen St. W., ☎593-5771)* can't be missed with its exterior painted in colourful Caribbean themes. The Bamboo is a cornerstone of the Queen Street scene, playing worldbeat, reggae, jazz and hip hop nightly.

The **Beverly Tavern** *(240 Queen St. W., ☎598-2434)* is a long-standing casual drinking spot with pool and darts.

The **Black Bull Tavern** *(298 Queen St. W., ☎593-2766)* has the best patio on Queen, a huge space that sprawls along the side of the building near Soho Street. Once frequented mainly by bikers who lined their Harleys up on the sidewalk, the "Bull" is now a meeting place for all sorts of people looking for a summertime beer in the sun.

The Rex Hotel Jazz Bar and Grill *(194 Queen St. W., ☎598-2475)* has a casual pub-like atmosphere with live jazz and blues acts nightly.

At **Carboneight** *(271 Queen St. W., ☎599-2121)*, you can hear old school, R&B, techno, trance, jungle, classic house or current rock, depending on what night you go.

The Bishop and the Belcher *(361 Queen St. W., ☎591-2352)* is a traditional English-style pub with 16 beers on tap and a rec-room-style basement with pool and darts.

The Cameron House *(408 Queen St. W., ☎703-0811)* has been transformed over the years from a grungy drinking pub to an eccentric cocktail lounge. DJs liven up the front room, while some of the city's well-known local talent plays live in the back.

Savage Garden *(540 Queen St. W., ☎504-2178)* is all Goth, every night, with industrial, retro, Goth and electronic music.

At **Velvet Underground** *(510 Queen St. W., ☎504-6688)* the black-clad clientele — from Goths to the glamourous — gathers for alternative music and dancing.

Zoo Bar West *(526 Queen St. W., ☎703-WILD)* plays new rock and alternative with live DJs on Friday and Saturday nights.

Exit 609 Lounge and Café *(609 Queen St. W., ☎504-8356)* has live jazz and stand-up comedy nights. Imported drafts, single malts and 20 specialty martinis are served.

The name alone might be enough to keep some people away from **The Bovine Sex Club** *(542 Queen St. W., ☎504-4239)* — and to attract others. There is no sign on the door, but it's hard to miss the tangle of recycled bicycle wheels and twisted steel adorning its façade. The crowd is alternative and there is live music the last week of every month.

Left Bank *(567 Queen St. W., ☎504-1626)* is a restaurant that doubles as a place to dance to music from disco to classic rock. It attracts the singles office crowd on weekends.

Reverb/Big Bop/Holy Joe's *(651 Queen St. W., ☎504-6699)* is a live music venue with different acts playing on all three floors most nights of the week.

MFN *(473 Adelaide St. W., ☎603-9300)* is one of Toronto's newest slick nightclubs, with a 10,000-square-foot warehouse/dance floor setting. DJs spin a commercial dance mix.

Gypsy Co-Op *(817 Queen St. W., ☎703-5069)* has funky DJs every night in its lounge/bar at the back. Its "General Store" is stocked full of nostalgic candy.

Raq n Waq *(739 Queen St. W., ☎504-9120)* plays commercial rock, alternative and hip hop music and is mainly an upscale pool hall, with 13 Brunswick tables.

Needless to say, **Sanctuary Vampire Sex Bar** *(732 Queen St. W., ☎504-1917)* will not appeal to everyone, but is where the city's Goths, dressed all in black (right down to their lipstick and nail polish — and that's just the guys) hang out. There's no patio (Goths shun the sun).

Industry *(901 King St. W., ☎260-2660)* is down on King Street and far from Clubland, but is a notorious late-night and after-hours progressive and underground nightclub with techno, house and hip hop nights and some of the best live acts in these genres.

College Street/Little Italy

The stretch of College Street west of Bathurst still has all the Mediterranean flavour of Little Italy, with sidewalk cafés galore serving *gelato* and cappuccino, and *trattorias* open well into the night. But the area has also been annexed by a young, trendy crowd of students and musicians, who while away the evenings in the area's many bars.

Since the Rolling Stones played here in the 1960s, the **El Mocambo** *(464 Spadina Ave., ☎968-2001)* has been one of Toronto's most legendary live music venues. Indie bands play here every night of the week. It's a real musicians' tavern, with cheap drinks and a few beat-up pool tables.

Barcode *(549 College St., ☎928-5021)* has no sign out, but has a multi-coloured bar code running along its exterior. This is a casual bar where you can go for a drink, with an eclectic range of live rock music and events.

Upstairs from the Barcode, **Ted's Wrecking Yard** *(549 College St., ☎928-5012)* is a tavern where live bands — from alterna-rock to folk to country — play nightly.

The Clearspot *(489 College St., ☎921-7998)* is a pool hall with a bit of panache. With windows all around, it's not as dismal as some pool places, and with plenty of seating it attracts the local College Street crowd, even when they're not racking up the balls.

Next door to the Clearspot, **Ciao Edie** *(489 College St., ☎927-7774)* is so '70s it could be right out of *Austin Powers*. This groovy little martini lounge is all satellite lamp shades and leopard prints with DJs spinning lots of soul and '70s tunes.

Bar Italia *(582 College St., ☎535-3621)* is an Italian eatery that doubles as a chic night spot, with DJs throughout the week and live bands on Saturdays.

Bistro 422 *(422 College St, ☎963-9416)* is a bit of a dive, attracting local punks and musicians looking for cheap vegetarian food and a cool pint.

Caoba *(571 College St., ☎533-6195)* has a Latin feel, with DJs, live bands and a Latin guest band on weekends.

Corso Italia *(584 College St., ☎532-3635)* is a large, casual warm restaurant and bar with two pool tables.

ENTERTAINMENT

El Covento Rico *(750 College St., ☎588-7800)* is a sizzling Latin dance bar playing dance, disco and Latin music, with free Latin dance lessons.

Free Times Café *(320 College St., ☎967-1078)* is a cozy spot with live acoustic and folk music nightly in the back room.

Souz Dal *(636 College St., ☎537-1883)* is all acid jazz and worldbeat, with candles and martinis.

Lava Restaurant and Club *(507 College St., ☎966-LAVA)* has a suave '70s look and attracts a trendy set who combine lounging and dancing to a mixture of live music and DJs.

The Midtown *(552 College St., ☎920-4533)* is a College Street student hot spot for sharing a drink with friends, with draft beer, single malts and three pool tables.

The Midtown West *(558 College St., ☎966-6952)* is three doors west of its counterpart (see above). A similar crowd can choose from 35 wines by the glass.

Oasis *(294 College St., ☎975-0845)* is an earthy, no-frills tapas bar with live bands, DJs and stand up comedy.

The **Orbit Room** *(580A College St., ☎535-0613)* has live music Wednesday to Sunday, featuring some of the city's best R&B bands.

Sneaky Dee's *(431 College St., ☎603-3090)* is a smoky Tex-Mex joint where the local grungy student crowd hangs out to drink beer on tap and play pinball and pool to a background of alternative music. Upstairs there are dance DJs every night.

The Waterfront

The **Atlantis/Deluge Nightclub** (The Atlantis Pavilions) *(955 Lakeshore W. in Ontario Place, ☎260-8000)*, situated right on Lake Ontario in Ontario Place, is a large nightspot with high-tech laser lights and the largest rooftop patio in Toronto. It's a mainstream dance club attracting mainly visitors to Toronto and people from the suburbs.

The Guvernment/The Warehouse *(132 Queen's Quay E., ☎869-1462)* is a massive warehouse that was retrofitted in the '80s (it was formerly called RPM) and has been one of the city's coolest clubs ever since. From Thursday to Saturday, hot live DJs spin house and dance music. If you can get into the VIP lounge upstairs (a model of hip chic, with pink vinyl couches and fun fur walls) you'll be rubbing shoulders with the city's beautiful people. The "Guv" is also a part-time concert venue for major international artists. The Warehouse, which has a separate entrance at the side of the building, is just that — a high-ceilinged, cement-floored warehouse space which hosts live bands and raves.

The Docks *(11 Polson, ☎461-DOCKS)* is a newly-renovated entertainment complex located east of downtown near Cherry Beach. The patio, which is over 40,000 square feet and extends out over the waters of Lake Ontario, has outdoor pool tables and boat docking facilities. Live DJs play on weekends and for special events in three different nightclubs.

The Annex

Just east of the Annex's main drag, **Panorama** *(55 Bloor St. W., 51st floor, ☎967-5225)* sits atop the Manulife Centre. The drinks and cocktails are pricey, but then again the view is spectacular. Proper dress is required. The patio is open all summer long.

Roof Restaurant and Lounge *(4 Avenue Rd., ☎924-5471)* is on the 18th floor of the Park Plaza Hotel, overlooking the city. It is the place to go for a real cocktail experience.

Toronto's most popular student hangout is the **Brunswick House** *(481 Bloor St. W., ☎964-2242)*. Large-screen televisions, shuffle board, billiard tables, lots of cheap beer and a local character named Rockin' Irene are the mainstays here.

525 West *(525 Bloor St. W., ☎537-3044)* is a New York-style jazz lounge with R&B and funk.

ENTERTAINMENT

James Joyce Irish Pub *(386 Bloor St. W., ☎324-9400)* is fairly self-explanatory: imported beer on tap, traditional live Irish music in a lively atmosphere, and pool tables.

Lee's Palace *(529 Bloor St. W., ☎532-7383)* stands out with its colourful façade, adorned with cartoon characters. Live rock and alternative bands play in the large space downstairs. Upstairs is the Dance Cave.

Pauper's Pub *(539 Bloor St. W., ☎530-1331)* is, well, a pub. It also has a large rooftop patio and a side patio.

Gay Bars

Woody's *(465-467 Church St., ☎972-0887)*, set in the heart of the gay village, is a popular meeting place for gay men, with a casual and friendly pub-like atmosphere. Special events include drag performances and men's "best chest" contests.

Boots Complex *(592 Sherbourne, ☎921-0665)* is a popular, sprawling dance bar frequented by a gay and straight clientele. DJs spin different tunes on the large dance floor, in loungy chill-out rooms and on the decadent outdoor patio in summertime. Theme nights include fetish nights.

Wilde Oscars (518 Church St., ☎921-8142) is a restaurant and bar with a large patio right on Church Street, subscribing whole-heartedly to the "see and be seen" credo of patio season. It's a prime spot to take in the Village sights. Inside, it's pub-like with a comfy lounge bar upstairs.

The Orange Room *(132 Queen's Quay E., in the Guvernment, ☎869-1462)* is a club within a club at the Guvernment that is packed on Friday nights with gay men and women, dancing to progressive house and techno spun live by DJs.

Ciao Edie *(489 College St., ☎927-7774)* is a '70s cocktail lounge in the trendy College Street area, and has a lesbian night on Sundays with excellent soul and drum 'n' bass DJs spinning. Men and straight clientele are welcome. Different from the Church Street scene, Ciao Edie's Sunday nights draw the city's funky, arty, tattooed lesbians out of the woodwork.

The martinis are fabulous but the music is deafening after 11pm.

Just east of the Village, in Cabbagetown, **Pope Joan** *(547 Parliament St., ☎925-6662)* is a casual women's meeting place and bar with a large outdoor patio. The music is rock and retro '80s.

The **Black Eagle** *(457 Church St., ☎413-1219)* is a men's leather cruising bar, with a pool table, videos playing and dungeon equipment.

Crews/Tango *(508-510 Church St., ☎972-1662)* are located in a grand old Victorian house which has been converted into two bars with everything from karaoke to pool to live comedy shows and drag performances. Tango, a cozy bar with bay-window seating, is primarily a lesbian bar but men are welcome.

Slack Alice Bar and Grill *(562 Church St., ☎969-8742)* is artfully decorated with wrought iron and a modern, industrial-style decor. There is a decent restaurant in the back, but the front half, which spills ever-so-slightly onto the Church Street sidewalk, is a funky, lively cocktail bar and meeting place for both men and women.

Bar 501 *(501 Church St., ☎944-3272)* is known for its view of the neighbourhood and for entertainment including music, art and drag shows.

Byzantium *(499 Church St., ☎922-3859)* is a swanky martini bar and neighbourhood lounge, with one of the city's most extensive martini lists.

Pegasus Billiard Lounge *(491 Church St., 2nd floor, ☎927-8832)* is an alternative to the dance clubs. With professional-sized pool tables and dart boards, it's a good place to sit and relax. The clientele is both gay and straight, men and women.

The Stables/The Barn *(418 Church St., ☎977-4702)* is a three-storey dance club where men are more into jeans than leather. There is, however, a leather shop inside that sells pants, vests

ENTERTAINMENT

and fetish items. Thursday and Friday there are charity bingo
games, with the proceeds going to a local AIDS organization.

The Web *(619 Yonge St.,* ☎*922-3068)* is a gay dance club with
light snacks and two pool tables.

Niagara Falls

The Oban *(160 Front St.,* ☎*905-468-2165)* is *the* place in town
for a drink with friends, or even alone, ensconced in a
comfortable armchair by the fireplace.

 CULTURAL ACTIVITIES

Theatre, Dance and Opera

Toronto is the third-largest theatre centre in the English-
speaking world, after New York and London. More than
200 professional theatre and dance companies comprise the
season's lineup. The offerings are astounding, and a night at
the theatre, the opera or the symphony is fast becoming a must
for any visit to Toronto.

Roy Thompson Hall
60 Simcoe St.
☎593-4828
The **Toronto Symphony Orchestra** and **Toronto Mendelssohn
Choir** both make their home in this hall, which boasts
outstanding acoustics.

Massey Hall
178 Victoria St.
☎593-4828
Excellent acoustics enhance all types of spectacles, from rock
and roll to theatre.

Hummingbird Centre (O'Keefe Centre)
1 Front St. E.
☎872-2262
For presentations by the **Canadian Opera Company** and the **National Ballet of Canada**, as well as hit broadway shows and big-name concerts.

St. Lawrence Centre for the Arts
27 Front St. E.
☎366-7723
The **Canadian Stage Company** performs here; classical music concerts round out the bill.

North York Performing Arts Centre
5040 Yonge St.
☎870-8000
A brand new complex to host the best in broadway shows.

Premiere Dance Theatre
Queen's Quay Terminal
☎973-4000
Contemporary dance companies from Toronto and abroad perform in this theatre designed specially for dance. Home of the **Toronto Dance Theatre**.

Tafelmusik Baroque Orchestra
St. Paul Centre at Trinity Church
427 Bloor St. W.
☎964-6337
An intimate opportunity to enjoy "table music" played on period instruments.

Royal Alexandra Theatre
260 King St. W.
☎872-3333
Opened in 1907, this venerable Beaux-Arts theatre is a joy to behold. Broadway-style musicals and the like are showcased here. Tickets $35-$91.

ENTERTAINMENT

Princess of Wales Theatre
300 King St. W.
☎872-1212
Built for the production of the musical *Miss Saigon*, this brand new theatre (1994) still presents this show, and many others. Tickets $25-$91.

Pantages Theatre
263 Yonge St.
☎872-2222
This vaudeville theatre was refurbished and is the home of the lavish production of *The Phantom of the Opera* until September, 1999. Tickets $56-$91; discounted a few hours before showtime.

Elgin and Wintergarden Theatres
189 Yonge St.
☎872-5555
Spectacular stacked theatres that play host to classic theatre, musicals, opera, jazz, etc. Guided tours offered (see p 118).

Théâtre Français de Toronto
26 Berkeley St.
☎534-6604
Established in 1967 as the Théâtre du P'tit Bonheur, this is the only French-language theatre in Toronto.

Young People's Theatre
165 Front St. E.
☎862-2222
A terrific option for younger visitors. All of the productions are entirely devoted to children.

Théâtre Passe Muraille
16 Ryerson Ave.
☎504-7529
Innovative productions of Canadian theatre.

Buddies in Bad Times Theatre
12 Alexander St.
☎975-8555
One of the biggest gay and lesbian theatre companies in the world, Buddies in Bad Times produces radical, controversial and influential Canadian stage works. **Tallulah's Cabaret** is Buddies'

cabaret bar for smaller performances, art shows, book launches and screenings.

Dream in High Park
High Park at Bloor and Keele Streets
☎368-3110
Summertime productions of Shakespeare in a magical setting, in a tree-lined hollow in High Park.

Factory Theatre
125 Bathurst St.
☎504-9971
The latest in English-Canadian theatre.

Cabaret/Dinner Theatre

Famous People Players Dinner Theatre
110 Sudbury St.
☎532-1137
This Canadian performing troupe showcases a uniquely dazzling performance with exciting music.

Legends in Concert
123 Queen St. W., in the Sheraton Centre Hotel
☎603-0005
Direct from its 15-year run in Las Vegas, *Legends in Concert* features live re-creations of the greatest superstars of yesterday and today.

Medieval Times Dinner and Tournament
Exhibition Place
☎260-1234 or 800-563-1190
Guests will be regaled with an evening of sorcery, pageantry, horsemanship and excitement in this medieval theatre show. Knights on horseback re-enact an authentic 11th-century Spanish tournament while dinner guests feast on a four-course banquet.

ENTERTAINMENT

Mysteriously Yours...Mystery Dinner Theatre
Various locations
☎486-7469 or 800-NOT-DEAD
Participate in solving an interactive "whodunit" with dinner and
a show, or come just for the show.

Yuk Yuk's Comedy Cabaret
1280 Bay St.
☎967-6425
Toronto's hottest showcase stand-up comedy club, with alumni
including Jim Carrey, Norm McDonald and Howie Mandel.

Ticket Agencies

Tickets for these and other shows are available through:

Ticketmaster
☎870-8000

Ticket King
☎872-1212

T.O. Tix
corner of Yonge and Dundas streets, in the Eaton Centre
☎536-6468, ext. 1
Reduced-price tickets for same-day musical and theatrical
events. In-person sales only, Tuesday to Saturday noon to
7:30pm, Sunday 11am to 3pm.

Cinemas

Toronto has many movie houses. Check local listings in
newspapers for schedules and times of first-run movies in the
city. Special rates are offered on Tuesdays and for matinees.
The regular price is $8.50 (except at repertory theatres).

Carlton Cinemas
20 Carlton St. (at College Subway stop)
☎598-2309
Plays a lot of art-house and independent festival-type films.

National Film Board
150 John St. (St. Andrew Subway stop)
☎973-3012

IMAX Theatres
There is an IMAX theatre at Ontario Place *(☎314-9900)* and in
the new Paramount complex *(downtown at Richmond and John
streets, ☎925-4629)*.

Repertory Theatres

Toronto has six repertory cinemas, called **Festival Cinemas:**

The Fox *(2236 Queen St. E., in the Beaches, ☎691-7330)*
Kingsway Theatre *(3030 Bloor St. W., ☎236-1411)*
The Music Hall *(147 Danforth Ave., on the Danforth,
☎778-8272)*
Paradise Cinema *(1006 Bloor St. W., ☎537-7040)*
Revue Cinema *(400 Roncesvalles Ave., ☎531-9959)*
The Royal Cinema *(608 College St., in Little Italy, ☎516-4845)*

Many of the Festival cinemas are in beautiful, ornate old
theatres. Admission is $6.50, or $3.50 with a membership
card, which can be purchased at the box office for $6. A free
Festival Cinemas Movie Guide has reviews and listings for all of
the theatres and is available in cafés and bars around the city.
You can also call the Festival Hotline at ☎690-2600.

 SPORTING EVENTS

ENTERTAINMENT

The Air Canada Centre
40 Bay St.
☎815-5500
In 1999, the Air Canada Centre replaced Maple Leaf Gardens
as the arena where The National Hockey League's Toronto
Maple Leafs play from November to April. The play-offs follow
the regular season and can last right into June. It is also home
to Toronto's basketball team, the Raptors.

SkyDome
1 Blue Jay Way
☎341-3663
The Toronto Blue Jays of the American Baseball League, the Toronto Argonauts of Canadian Football League (CFL) and the Toronto Raptors of the National Basketball Association (NBA) all play their matches at the Skydome.

The **Woodbine Race Track** is the largest racing property in North America and home of the Queen's Plate thoroughbred races in August, the longest-running uninterrupted event in North America. It is located north of Highway 401, on Highway 27 at Rexdale. For information call ☎675-RACE (7223). Thoroughbred Racing post times: Mar to Dec, Wed 6pm, Thu to Sun 1pm. Harness Racing post times: Jan to Mar and Jun to Sep, Mon, Tue, Thu to Sat 7:30pm.

Lake Ontario hosts the historic **Toronto International Dragon Boat Race Festival** *(☎364-0046)* in early June.

The **Molson Indy** *(☎872-4639)* races through the streets of Toronto in mid-July.

The **Canadian International Marathon** *(☎972-1062)* takes place along Toronto's avenues and streets at end of October.

The biggest names in tennis are matched in the **Du Maurier Intenational Canadian Tennis Open** *(☎665-9777)* which is held at the National Tennis Centre, north of downtown on the campus of York University. The men's and women's competitions alternate every other year.

The **Royal Agricultural Winter Fair** *(☎393-6400)* is held every year in November on the grounds of the Canadian National Exhibition. This premier event includes the Royal Horse Show.

FESTIVALS AND SPECIAL EVENTS

Harbourfront Centre
231-235 Queen's Quay W.
Information: ☎973-3000, Tickets: ☎973-4000
In a breezy, picturesque waterfront setting, the Harbourfront Centre offers arts, culture and recreation all year round. Annual events include free and ticketed concerts and musical performances (showcasing folk, jazz, worldbeat and pop artists), dance, theatre, art exhibitions, craft activities and festive celebrations.

Toronto Winterfest
mid-February
☎395-7350
Toronto hosts a party to celebrate the season of snow. Three family-friendly sites feature everything from skating shows and midway rides to pancake breakfasts.

Canada Blooms, The Flower and Garden Show
mid-March
☎593-0223
Canada's largest annual indoor flower and garden show, with six acres of gardens, arrangements and a gardening marketplace.

North by Northeast
mid-June
☎469-0986
More than 300 folk, rock, blues and funk groups gather in the bars and venues of Toronto for this music festival.

Toronto International Caravan Festival
mid-June
☎977-0466
This festival celebrates the city's many ethnic communities as well as cultures from around the world with dancing, international cuisine, films, theatre and music.

ENTERTAINMENT

Benson & Hedges International Fireworks Festival, the Symphony of Fire
mid-June through July at Ontario Place, by the lake.
☎870-8000 or 314-9900

Du Maurier Downtown Jazz
end of June
Jazz, gospel and blues performers are booked into venues big and small all over the city. The festival includes a parade and free shows.
www.tojazz.com

Lesbian and Gay Pride Week
last week in June
☎927-7433
One of the summer's most colourful events is the parade that caps off a week of festivities and one of the largest gay and lesbian pride celebrations in North America.

The Fringe — Toronto's Theatre Festival
beginning of July
☎534-5919
More than 90 theatre companies participate, staging shows that can only be described as unique, diverse, unexpected.

Toronto Outdoor Art Exhibition
mid-July
☎408-2754
Canadian and international artists display their work in Nathan Phillips Square.

Caribana
mid-July to beginning of August
☎465-4884
The premier festival of Caribbean music and culture, culminating in the famous parade, which is the largest in Canada and lasts 12 hours!

Beaches International Jazz Festival
third week of July
☎698-2152
More than 100 bands perform free on indoor and outdoor stages at this five-day festival, held in Toronto's most summery

spot. Thousands of people picnic in the Beaches' main park, where beer gardens and vendors add to the atmosphere.

Fringe Festival of Independent Dance Artists
August
☎975-8555 or 410-4291
More than 90 dance artists stage performances at various venues around the city.

Canadian National Exhibition
mid-August to beginning of September
☎393-6000
Midway rides and games in a carnival atmosphere, plus pavilions with various exhibits, music and a wide diversity of entertainment.

Krinos Taste of the Danforth
first week in August, in Greektown
☎469-5634
Greektown is transformed into a massive street festival during this weekend event, with outdoor stalls featuring food from the area's many restaurants. There is also live entertainment on special stages.

International Film Festival
beginning of September
☎967-7371
Toronto's own film festival is fast becoming a truly star-studded event. *Variety* magazine calls it the best film festival in North America.

International Festival of Authors
third week of October
☎973-4000
Now in its 20th year, this event continues to dazzle literary buffs by bringing in the most popular writers of the moment to read from their latest works.

Kensington Festival of Lights
third week of December
☎598-2829
This festival celebrates the winter solstice, Hanukkah and Christmas with a costumed, lantern-lit procession through the Kensington Market neighbourhood.

ENTERTAINMENT

Toronto International Pow Wow
end of November to the beginning of December,
at the SkyDome
☎519-751-0040
This festival celebrates native dancing and culture.

The "One of a Kind" Canadian Craft Show & Sale
December and end of March, at Exhibition Place
☎960-3680

Niagara-on-the-Lake

The internationally renowned **Shaw Festival** *($35 to $70, reservations ☎905-468-2172 or 800-511-7429, ⇒468-3804, http://shawfest.sympatico.ca)* has been held every year since 1962. From April to October, visitors can take in various plays by George Bernard Shaw at one of the three theatres in town; the **Festival Theatre**, the **Court House Theatre** and the **Royal George Theatre**.

SHOPPING

Downtown Toronto is a shopper's paradise. From big designers to discount bonanzas, there is certain to be a store that sells what you are looking for.

Toronto's shopping areas are quite distinct from one another, so a few of the major ones are listed here, along with their individual atmospheres and styles.

 TOUR A: THE WATERFRONT

Shopping Malls

Harbourfront Antique Market
390 Queen's Quay W., ☎260-2626

Queen's Quay Terminal
207 Queen's Quay W.
Located at Harbourfront near Lake Ontario, this mall has upscale shopping and many artsy boutiques.

Crafts

Bounty
Queen's Quay Terminal

| TOUR C: THE THEATRE AND
FINANCIAL DISTRICTS

Sports Equipment and Clothing

Europe Bound
383 King St. W., ☎205-9992
A traveller's one-stop shop, with tents, backpacks, sleeping bags, camping and climbing gear as well as travel books. The Front Street location has a Travel Cuts student travel agency at the back.

Mountain Equipment Co-Op
400 King St. W., ☎340-2667
This massive camping store has clothing, backpacks, camping equipment, climbing gear and more, and even has an indoor climbing wall.

Crafts

The Guild Gallery (Ontario Crafts Council)
120 Adelaide St. W., ☎367-0349
Arts and crafts.

| TOUR D: OLD TOWN OF YORK

Public Markets

St. Lawrence Market
Front Street between Market and Jarvis Streets

Second Hand Stores

There is a whole block of pawn shops selling everything from jewellery to coins to camera equipment on Church Street between Richmond and Shuter streets.

Sports Equipment and Clothing

Europe Bound
49 Front St. E., ☎601-0854
A traveller's one-stop shop, with tents, backpacks, sleeping bags, camping and climbing gear as well as travel books. The Front Street location has a Travel Cuts student travel agency at the back.

Europe Bound Travel Outfitters
65 Front St. E., ☎601-1990
Outdoor hiking and travel clothing.

Hiker's Haven
41 Front St. E., ☎365-0033
A hiking, camping and travelling store.

Out There by Athlete's World
35 Front St. E., ☎363-8801
In-line skates, shoes and clothing for running and hiking.

Trailhead
61 Front St. E., ☎862-0881
Clothing and equipment for outdoor adventures.

Camera Equipment and Accessories

Alt Camera Exchange
69 Queen St. E., ☎362-6400
Used and new camera equipment and accessories.

Broadway Camera
121 Church St., ☎363-4117
Used and new camera equipment and accessories.

SHOPPING

Downtown Camera
55 Queen St. E., ☎363-1749
Used and new camera equipment and accessories.

Henry's
119 Church St., ☎868-0872
Superstore of new and used camera equipment and
accessories.

Bookstores

Nicholas Hoare Books
45 Front St. E., ☎777-2665
Specializes in large-format, coffee table and art books. With
hardwood floors and a spacious high ceiling, it's a great place
to linger and browse.

Open Air Books and Maps
25 Toronto St., ☎363-0719
Travel literature.

Crafts

Arts on King
169 King St. E., ☎777-9617
Canadian art.

Flatirons
51 Front St. E., ☎365-1506
Unique gifts from around the world, greeting cards, some joke
gifts.

Frida Craft Store
39 Front St. E., ☎366-3169

 TOUR E: QUEEN WEST

Queen Street West is the centre of the city's young, artsy
scene and the shops here reflect that. Toronto's young
independent street fashion designers have become some of the

best in North America, holding their own even when compared with those from New York. Most of the streetwear and rave shops are along Queen West. In addition to a few big-name retailers such as the Gap and Roots, there are bookstores, funky shoe stores and lots of independent clothing shops with unique fashions. There are also vendors selling jewellery and other items year-round on the sidewalk just west of Soho Street.

Shopping Malls

Eaton Centre
Yonge Street, between Queen and Dundas streets
The Eaton Centre is Toronto's largest mall and one of its biggest tourist attractions. Beneath its towering glass ceiling are a fountain and a number of restaurants and shops spanning a range of budgets.

Clothing

Alkatraz Vintage Clothing
475 Queen St. W., ☎504-3609

Brava Vintage Clothing
483 Queen St. W., ☎504-8742

Chateau Works
336 Queen St. W., ☎971-9314
This industrial-looking mega-store is part of the Le Chateau chain, but also has a children's wear section and a hair salon inside and sells accessories such as bags, fun-fur-covered address books and greeting cards.

Get Out Side
437 Queen St. W., ☎593-5598
Wild shoes and rave wear.

Groovy
393 Queen St. W., ☎595-1059
New and used clothing and shoes.

SHOPPING

ModRobes
329 Queen St. W., ☎340-1222
Skater fashion by a Toronto designer that is much more reasonably priced than that in many of Queen West's other streetwear shops.

Noise
275, Queen St. W., ☎971-6459
Designer streetwear and skater fashion.

So Hip it Hurts
323 Queen St. W., ☎971-6901
This second-floor shop has three rooms filled with surfer fashions and accessories.

Uncle Otis
383 Queen St. W., ☎597-6847
Designer street fashion.

Footwear

Aldo Shoes
393 Queen St. W., ☎340-9882
Casual shoes – from funky to conservative.

Australian Boot Company
791 Queen St. W., ☎504-2411

John Fluevog
242 Queen St. W., ☎581-1420
Funky British styles with lots of platforms and some absolutely outrageous footwear.

Pegabo
349 Queen St. W., ☎977-3401

The Showroom
278 Queen St. W., ☎340-8880
Funky shoes and running shoes.

Twinkle Toes
320 Queen St. W., ☎977-6435
Funky styles and platforms.

Body Care and Makeup

Lush
312 Queen St. W., ☎599-5874
Intoxicating aromas envelop you in this store full of home-made, all-natural soaps, shampoos, bath oils and skin care products. Gift packages are available.

The Body Shop
286 Queen St. W., ☎599-4385
Natural bath and body products.

Gift Shops

Friendly Stranger
226 Queen St. W., ☎591-1570
Hemp products.

Used Records, CDs and Tapes

CD Cat
539 Queen St. W., ☎703-4797
Used CDs – there really is a cat that lives in the shop!

KOPS and Vortex Records
229 Queen St. W., ☎598-4039
Used CDs and vinyl.

Penguin Music
2 McCaul, ☎597-1687
Used CDs.

Record Peddler
619 Queen St. W., ☎504-3828
Used CDs and vinyl. Alternative music.

SHOPPING

Rotate This
620 Queen St. W., ☎504-8447
Used CDs and vinyl. Alternative music.

Musical Instruments

Songbird Music
801 Queen St. W., ☎504-7664
Used musical instruments.

Steve's Music Store
415 Queen St. W., ☎593-8888
New musical instruments and equipment.

Bookstores and Magazine Shops

Pages Books and Magazines
256 Queen St. W., ☎598-1447
Specializes in large-format photography books, alternative and obscure authors, and has a wide selection of both common and obscure magazines.

Silver Snail
367 Queen St. W., ☎593-0889
Comic books.

Crafts

Shattered
880 Queen St. W., ☎537-9103
Very unique and funky hand-crafted items all made by local artists.

Galleries

Stephen Bulger Gallery
700 Queen St. W., ☎504-0575
Photographic gallery.

The Thompson Gallery at the Bay
176 Yonge St., at the corner of Queen St., 9th floor,
☎861-4571.

Jane Corking Gallery
179 John St., ☎979-1980.

Fine Food

Sugar Mountain
320 Richmond St. W., ☎595-8294
Every kind of candy, local and imported, you can think of.

Miscellaneous

Condom Shack
231 Queen St. W., ☎596-7515

Solar Waves
316 Queen St. W., ☎599-5921
Sunglasses and hats.

 ## TOUR F: CHINATOWN AND KENSINGTON

Kensington Market

The "Market" is one of Toronto's most interesting neighbourhoods. Located on the edge of Chinatown, it has long been home to kids from the local punk scene. On the weekend, it is a lively place to walk, soak up the atmosphere or shop for some second-hand clothes. Reggae music from the local cafés fills the street and the overall ambiance is very laid-back. All along Kensington, the main street, there are old Victorian houses transformed into shops selling second-hand clothing. The Market is also a food market and has Asian, Caribbean, Middle Eastern and Indian shops selling dry goods, fruit and vegetables and take-away food.

SHOPPING

TOUR G: QUEEN'S PARK AND
THE UNIVERSITY OF TORONTO

Gift Shops

The Royal Ontario Museum Shops
100 Queen's Park, Royal Ontario Museum, ☎586-5551

Crafts

WORK
655 College St., ☎533-4103
Unique and funky hand-crafted items and jewellery made by
local artists.

Fine Food

Ten Ren Tea Co. Ltd.
454 Dundas St. W., ☎598-7872

TOUR H: BLOOR AND YORKVILLE

Bloor Street, between University Avenue and Yonge Street, is
Toronto's centre for *haute couture* and designer fashion. These
few blocks boast some of the world's finest labels and most
prestigious jewellery sellers.

Meanwhile, Yorkville is a pleasant area to stroll through, with
lots of upscale boutiques and galleries. It also has the highest
concentration of hair salons and aesthetics studios in the city.
The two main streets, Yorkville and Cumberland, are joined by
pedestrian walkways in a number of places and their upscale
restaurants are frequented by stars and socialites from the
nearby hotels.

Shopping Malls

Hazelton Lanes Shopping Centre
55 Hazelton (in Yorkville), ☎968-6130
In the fashionable shopping district of Yorkville, Hazelton Lanes is a quiet mall with designer shops selling *haute couture* fashions.

Manulife Centre
At the corner of Bloor and Bay streets.

Hudson's Bay Centre
At the corner of Bloor and Yonge streets.

Clothing

Chanel
131 Bloor St. W., ☎925-2577

Dolce Boutique
86 Yorkville Ave., ☎961-8107
Women's fashion.

Gianni Versace
83 Bloor St. W., ☎920-8300

Hermès
131 Bloor St. W., ☎968-8628

Holt Renfrew
50 Bloor St. W., ☎922-2333

Marc Laurent
151 Bloor St. W., ☎928-9124
Designer men's and women's suits, from Armani to Nino Danieli.

Marina Rinaldi
131 Bloor St., W., ☎969-6977
Designer clothing for larger sized women.

SHOPPING

Max Mara
131 Bloor St. W., ☎928-1884

Rainbow Jeans
101 Yorkville Ave., ☎967-7448
Designer jeans and casual fashions.

Swimsuit Essentials
116 Yorkville Ave., ☎921-7946

United Colors of Benetton
102 Bloor St., W., ☎968-1611

Footwear

Corbo Boutique
131 Bloor St. W., ☎928-0954
Designer and dress shoes.

Nike Toronto
110 Bloor St. W., ☎921-6453

Nine West Shoes
93 Bloor St. W., ☎920-3519

Pegabo
91 Bloor St. W., ☎323-3722

Town Shoes
131 Bloor St. W., ☎928-0562

Jewellery

Henry Birks & Sons
55 Bloor St. W., ☎922-2266

Les Must de Cartier
101 Bloor St. W., ☎967-1785
Cartier jewellery.

Tiffany & Co.
85 Bloor St. W., ☎921-3900

Leather

Betty Hemmings Leathergoods
131 Bloor St. W., ☎921-4321

Dessa
87 Yorkville Ave., ☎924-4240
Leather and silver goods.

Taschen!
162 Cumberland St., Renaissance Court, ☎961-3185

Body Care and Makeup

Aveda Spa
95 Bloor St. W., ☎413-1333
Aveda products and massage and aesthetics studio.

MAC Makeup
89 Bloor St. W., ☎929-7555

The Body Shop
86 Bloor St. W., ☎928-1180
Natural bath and body products.

Music

Remenyi House of Music
210 Bloor St. W., ☎961-3111
Harps, grand pianos and prestige instruments.

SHOPPING

Bookstores and Magazine Shops

Chapters Books
110 Bloor St. W., ☎920-9299
A bookish department store with fiction, non-fiction, magazines, computer software, audio tapes and more.

Indigo Books, Music and Café
55 Bloor St. W., ☎925-3536
A massive, sprawling store with books, CDs, magazines and a café.

Lichtman's News & Books
Yonge and Bloor, ☎924-4186
Foreign magazines and newspapers.

Maison de la Presse Internationale
124-126 Yorkville Ave., ☎928-2328
Newspapers and magazines.

The Cookbook Store
850 Yonge St., ☎920-26650

Home Decoration

Muti
88 Yorkville Ave., ☎969-0253

Primitives & Co.
87 Yorkville Ave., ☎967-6357
Home furnishings and accessories.

Antiques

Antiques — Michel Taschereau
176 Cumberland St., ☎923-3020

Glorious Gallery
1256 Bay St., ☎944-8564

Gift Shops

Berson's Gifts and Antiques
132 Cumberland Ave., ☎964-1362

Nocean
97 Yorkville Ave., ☎923-6886
Fine pens, Cuban cigars, household gift items, silver.

Paper Things
99 Yorkville Ave., ☎922-3500
Cards and decorative paper products supporting the National Ballet of Canada.

The Papery
124 Cumberland Ave., ☎962-3916
Fancy paper, gift items and wrapping.

Galleries

Hollander York Gallery
130 Yorkville Ave., ☎932-9275

Meier-Naef Gallery
104 Yorkville Ave., ☎925-6681

Mira Godard Gallery
22 Hazelton Ave., ☎964-8197

Native Art

Feheley Fine Arts
14 Hazelton Ave., 1st floor, ☎323-1373

The Arctic Bear
125 Yorkville, ☎967-7885

The Guild Shop
118 Cumberland St., ☎921-1721

SHOPPING

The Isaacs/Innuit Gallery
9 Prince Arthur Ave., ☎921-9985.

Toys

Kidding Awound
91 Cumberland Ave., ☎926-8996
A dizzying display of unique hand-made children's toys.

The Toy Shop
62 Cumberland Ave., ☎961-4870

Fine Food

Dinah's Cupboard
50 Cumberland St., ☎921-8112
Fine grocer's.

Godiva Chocolatier
131 Bloor St. W., ☎922-4438
Chocolates.

Photo Developing

Black's Photography
2 Bloor St. W., ☎928-1520

Miscellaneous

Karir
2 Bloor St. W., ☎975-0536
Designer sunglasses.

Mont Blanc
151 Bloor St. W., ☎925-4810
Designer pens, watches and sunglasses.

World Eyewear Sunglasses Boutique
126 Cumberland Ave., ☎975-0977

 YONGE STREET

The longest street in the world, Yonge Street changes dramatically from one section to the next. However, it is the downtown portion of Yonge Street from the Eaton Centre up to Bloor Street, that visitors to Toronto will experience. This area is the real "downtown" of Toronto, with discount clothing and shoe stores, electronics stores, record, poster and comic shops, strip clubs, video arcades and army surplus outlets. Strolling up Yonge Street will give you a real feel for Toronto's inner-city energy, and there are definitely bargains and interesting fashions to be found if you're persistent!

Footwear

Aldo Shoes
723 Yonge St., ☎922-7398
Casual shoes – from funky to conservative.

Bootmaster Cowboy Boots
609 Yonge St., ☎927-1054

Western Boot Shop
277A Yonge St., ☎368-2668

Music

HMV Superstore
333 Yonge St., ☎596-0333
New CDs and tapes.

Sam the Record Man
347 Yonge St., ☎977-4650
New CDs and tapes.

SHOPPING

Traxx Tapes and CDs
427 Yonge St., ☎977-4884
A DJ's record shop — vinyl, dance, hip hop, techno and more.

Bookstores

Glad Day Bookshop
598A Yonge St., ☎961-4161
Gay and lesbian books.

Lichtman's News & Books
Yonge and Richmond, ☎368-7390
Foreign magazines and newspapers.

This Ain't the Rosedale Library
483 Church St., ☎929-9912
Gay, lesbian and sexual politics books.

World's Biggest Bookstore
20 Edward St., ☎977-7009
You'd be hard pressed to come up with a title that can't be found at this massive shop near the Eaton Centre.

Fine Food

Noah's Natural Foods
667 Yonge St., ☎969-0220
Health food and vitamins.

Camera Equipment and Accessories

Aden Camera
348 Yonge St., ☎598-1964
Camera equipment and photo developing.

Camera Place
338 Yonge St., ☎591-9222
Camera equipment and accessories.

TOUR J: THE ANNEX

Formerly an enclave for Eastern European immigrants, the Annex has grown over the years into a lively area of restaurants and shops, populated by students, people from the neighbourhood and weekend browsers. Bloor Street from Bathurst to Spadina is peppered with bookstores selling both new and used books, health food shops, second-hand CD and record stores and earthy gift shops.

Discount Stores

Honest Ed's *(581 Bloor St. W. at the corner of Bathurst St., ☎537-1574)* stands out like a neon light — literally. This discount bargain store takes up a whole block and is covered in flashing lights and garish yellow and red signs. It contains not only discount clothing, shoes and housewares, but also a hair dresser, an optician and an immigration lawyer! It is something to see — a real Toronto landmark that adds a particular flavour to the neighbourhood.

Music

Second Spin Used CDs
386 Bloor St. W., ☎961-7746

Bookstores

David Mirvish Books on Art
596 Markham St., ☎531-9975

Fine Food

Harbord Bakery Ltd.
115 Harbord St., ☎922-5767

SHOPPING

Noah's Natural Foods
322 Bloor St. W., ☎968-7930
Health food and vitamins.

Taste of Nature
380 Bloor St. W., ☎925-8102
Health food and vitamins.

 TOUR K: ROSEDALE, FOREST HILL AND NORTH OF TORONTO

Sports Equipment and Clothing

Sporting Life
2665 Yonge St., ☎485-1611
Specializing in sporting goods, equipment, shoes and clothing.

Bookstores

Writer's & Co.
2005 Yonge St., ☎481-8432

The Children's French Store
By appointment only, ☎486-1131

 TOUR L: EASTERN TORONTO

The Beach (as it's known to locals) is full of artsy boutiques and cute shops selling everything from designer children's clothes to Indonesian handicrafts. A stroll along Queen Street East, just minutes from the lakeside, is bound to be a lively experience, although the street and sidewalks are often packed on the weekends. All shops listed in this section are located in the Beaches.

Clothing

Posh
1936 Queen St. E., ☎690-5533
Handcrafted clothing and accessories.

Footwear

Nature's Footwear
1971A Queen St. E., ☎691-6706
Casual shoes, sandals, Birkenstocks.

Body Care and Makeup

Lush
2014 Queen St. E., ☎691-8822
Intoxicating aromas envelop you in this store full of home-made, all-natural soaps, shampoos, bath oils and skin care products. Gift packages are available.

Music and Books

Media Encore
1939 Queen St. E., ☎699-5511
Half-price books and music.

Galleries

Incurable Collector
1945 Queen St. E., ☎694-9485
Commercial art gallery.

Home Decoration

Posh Décor
1889 Queen St. E., ☎686-7727

SHOPPING

Fine Food

Sugar Mountain
1920 Queen St. E., ☎690-7998
Every kind of candy, local and imported, you can think of.

The Big Carrot Natural Food Market
348 Danforth Ave., ☎466-2129

Miscellaneous

Christmas on the Beach
1891 Queen St. E., ☎698-0682
Sells Christmas decorations and paraphernalia year-round.

 TOUR M: NIAGARA FALLS

Niagara-on-the-Lake

Downtown Niagara-on-the-Lake is home to all sorts of shops, each more enticing than the last, and a visit here wouldn't be complete without a little browsing.

Body Care and Makeup

Crabtree & Evelyn
Queen St.
Bath and beauty products.

Crafts

From Japan
Victoria St.
A magnificent assortment of Japanese crafts.

Souvenir Shop

J.W. Outfitters *(Queen St.)* looks like a simple souvenir shop, but inside you'll find terrific T-shirts and lovely posters of native art.

Toys

The irresistible teddy bears, dolls and other toys at **The Owl & the Pussycat** *(Queen St.)* are sure to be a hit with the kids.

Fine Food

Greaves *(Queen St.)* specializes in jellies, jams and marmalades, all delicious.

For an unforgettable treat for the tastebuds, stop by **Maple Leaf Fudge** *(Queen St.).*

Niagara Falls

There aren't any charming little shops or attractive store windows here in the land of factory outlets, where you can find surplus inventory at bargain prices. Mondi, Benetton, Levi's and Nautica merchandise can be found at the **Niagara Factory Outlets** *(1900 Military Rd.)*, but be prepared to search through the racks, since not all of the stock is that interesting.

SHOPPING

INDEX

INDEX

INDEX

TRAVEL
BETTER...
TRAVEL
THE NET

Visit our web site
to travel better...
to discover, to explore
and to enjoy more

www.ulysses.ca

Catalogue

Talk to us   Order   Distributors   History   Internet Travel

OTHER ULYSSES GUIDES

ULYSSES TRAVEL GUIDES

ATLANTIC CANADA, 2nd edition
This guide covers Newfoundland and Labrador, as well as New
Brunswick, Nova Scotia and Prince Edward Island. Picturesque fishing
villages, the famous Cabot Trail, national parks, beaches, the brand
new Confederation Bridge; it's all here!
Benoit Prieur
272 pages, 23 maps, 8 pages of colour photos
$24.95 CAN $17.95 US   £12.99   2-89464-113-3

BED & BREAKFASTS IN QUÉBEC 1999-2000
Four types of accommodations to help you discover the intimate side
of Québec: rooms in private homes with breakfast included, small
country inns, farm-stays, and country houses which can be rented for
a longer stay.
Fédération des Agricotours
300 pages, 19 maps, 14 pages of colour photos
$13.95 CAN $10.95 US   £6.50   2-89464-199-0

CALGARY
Calgary is one of the fastest growing cities in North America. This
guide reveals the best of this dynamic Western city: museums, parks,
gardens, Olympic installations and the famous Stampede.
Jennifer McMorran, François Brodeur
192 pages, 12 mpas, 4⅛ x 7" (10 x 18cm)
$16.95 CAN $12.95 US   £8.99   289464-168-0

CANADA 1999-2000
Every province and territory has been covered in depth in order to
produce the most complete travel guide. Major cities, small hamlets
and exhilarating outdoor adventures from coast to coast!
Collective
656 pages, 85 maps, 8 pages of colour photos
$29.95 CAN $21.95 US   £14.99   2-89464-198-2

MONTRÉAL 1999-2000
This guide reveals more than 300 sights in this Québec metropolis
along 20 walking, bicycling and driving tours. There are detailed maps
for each tour, plans of the galleries of the Museum of Fine Arts and
maps of the underground city. Practical addresses for every budget. A
comprehensive revision by real Montrealers ensures that the latest hip
spots are included.
François Rémillard et al.
4⅛ x 7, 416 pages, 26 maps, 8 pages of colour photos, French-
English glossary
$19.95 CAN $14.95   £9.99   2-89464-190-7

ONTARIO, 3rd edition
This guide covers Canada's richest and most populous province in depth, with sections on Niagara Falls, the Thousand Islands, Ottawa, Toronto, and even Northern Ontario.
Pascale Couture
384 pages, 40 maps, 8 pages of colour photos
$29.95 CAN $19.95 US   £11.50   2-89464-111-1

OTTAWA
The first complete practical and cultural guide to the Canadian capital. The fine museums, Parliament Hill, the best restaurants, and the festivals that enliven the streets in the summer and the Rideau Canal in the winter.
Pascale Couture
160 pages, 13 maps
$16.95 CAN $12.95 US   £8.99   2-89464-170-2

QUÉBEC 1999-2000
More sights and thousands of practical addresses for every region. Travellers will also find an expanded outdoor activities section, more maps, brilliant colour photos and illustrations.
François Rémillard et al.
576 pages, 81 mpas, 22 pages of colour photos
$29.95 CAN $21.95 US   £14.99   2-89464-202-4

WESTERN CANADA, 2nd edition
The only travel guide to cover both Alberta and British Columbia. The Rocky Mountains, with their ski resorts and national parks, as well as the metropolis of Vancouver, the burgeoning city of Calgary and stop in Victoria, for a cup of tea!
Collective
496 pages, 45 maps, 8 pages of colour photos
$29.95 CAN $21.95 US   £14.99   2-89464-086-2

ULYSSES GREEN ESCAPES

CYCLING IN ONTARIO
This unique guidebook provides all the information required to plan worry-free cycling holidays in the different regions of Ontario. It includes 35 tours, a multitude of safety-tips, plus details on accommodations, ground conditions, access to interesting trails, and more.
John Lynes
256 pages, 45 maps
$22.95 CAN $16.95 US   £9.99   2-89464-191-5

HIKING IN QUÉBEC, 2nd edition
The only hiking guide devoted exclusively to the regions of Québec!
Yves Séguin
368 pages, 22 maps
$22.95 CAN $16.95 US   £11.50   2-89464-013-7

ULYSSES CONVERSATION

FRENCH FOR BETTER TRAVEL
Thousands of words and expressions to make your next trip *à la française* a success. Colour illustrations, phonetic pronunciation and a two-way index help you get your message across.
Collective
192 pages, 6 double-pages in colour

$9.95 CAN	$6.95 US	£4.50	2-89464-181-8

ULYSSES TRAVEL JOURNALS

ULYSSES TRAVEL JOURNAL 80 DAYS
Here is the newest arrival in the Ulysses' Travel Journal series. In a larger format with more pages (224), it is ideal for Phileas Fogg-type travellers who take long trips and detailed notes about their adventures.
paperback, spiral bound, 5¼ x 8¼, 224 pages

$14.95 CAN	$9.95 US	2-89464-247-4

ULYSSES TRAVEL JOURNAL
These log books are the ideal travel companions and confidantes.
Sextant 2-89464-162-1

Blue	2-89464-163-X
Green	2-89464-164-8
Yellow	2-89464-165-6

paperback, spiral bound, 4½ x 7¼, 80 pages
$9.95 CAN $7.95 US   £4.99